A fascinating account of the development of the steam passenger locomotive on the Southern Railway from the grouping until Nationalization in 1948. The story evolves from the amalgamation of the three major constituent companies through the emergence of Ashford under Maunsell's leadership as the predominant design influence, development of the 'Arthurs', 'Nelsons', 'Schools' and finally the impact of Bulleid and his Pacifics.

'The inside story has been told with feeling and accuracy, and brought alive by a combination of design problems, policy changes and records of locomotive performance which explain so many of the somewhat contradictory moves that have been made over the twenty-five years covered.'

Railway Magazine

'Told in loving detail . . . Mr Nock is a locomotive engineer who knows what it is like to go full tilt down Seaton Bank on the footplate of an engine in urgent need of workshop attention, and he brings a practical man's interest into his history.'

Model Railway News

$6\frac{5}{8} \times 16\frac{1}{8}$

CONDITIONS OF SALE

The David & Charles Series

———

SOUTHERN STEAM

———

O. S. NOCK, B Sc, C Eng, FICE, FI Mech E

UNABRIDGED

PAN BOOKS LTD : LONDON

First published 1966 by David & Charles (Publishers) Ltd.
This edition published 1972 by Pan Books Ltd,
33 Tothill Street, London, SW1.

ISBN 0 330 02681 X

Printed in Great Britain by
Richard Clay (The Chaucer Press), Ltd, Bungay, Suffolk

CONTENTS

ILLUSTRATIONS IN PHOTOGRAVURE

(between pages 36 and 37)

On the Brighton main line near Purley: a down express, hauled by a 'B2X' 4–4–0 No 203, overtaking a goods hauled by one of the 'Vulcan' o–6–os
(*Real Photographs Ltd*)

An SE & CR Reading train via Redhill on the Brighton main line near Purley, hauled by a rebuilt Stirling 4–4–0 No 94
(*the late C. Laundy Esq*)

LB & SCR up morning business express leaving Bognor, hauled by 'B2X' class 4–4–0 No 321
(*Real Photographs Ltd*)

SE & CR through morning express for Cannon Street leaving Bexhill with 'L' class 4–4–0 No 776
(*British Railways SR*)

L & SWR. One of the Drummond 'T14' class 4-cylinder 4–6–os (paddleboats) in original condition on up Bournemouth express
(*F. E. Mackay Esq*)

Continental boat express in Folkestone Warren, hauled by 'King Arthur' class 4–6–0 No 771, *Sir Sagramore*
(*the late W. J. Reynolds Esq*)

One of the original Urie 'S15' class engines (ex-LSWR) as BR No 30506
(*author's collection*)

A Maunsell 'S15' class mixed traffic 4–6–0 No 833
(*author's collection*)

L & SWR Urie 4–6–2 tank engine No 519
(*the late W. J. Reynolds Esq*)

The celebrated Brighton war memorial 4–6–4 tank engine No 333 *Remembrance* in Southern livery, outside Victoria
(*author's collection*)

The 3-cylinder member of the Maunsell 'K' class of 2–6–4 tank No 890 *River Frome*, classified 'K1'
(*the late W. J. Reynolds Esq*)

O. S. Nock was born in 1905 and educated at Giggleswick School and the City and Guilds (Engineering) College. His entire professional career as an engineer was spent with the Westinghouse Brake and Signal Co Ltd where he became Chief Mechanical Engineer of the Signal and Mining Division. His work was mainly concerned with signalling and in 1969 he was elected President of the Institution of Railway Signal Engineers. A lifelong railway enthusiast, he has studied railways in all their aspects and travelled widely in the process. He has written more than sixty books, as well as contributing hundreds of articles to the technical and enthusiast press. His first-hand knowledge of locomotive working has been supplemented by many thousands of miles riding on the footplate with steam, and more recently, on diesels and electric trains: in addition to a wealth of British and Continental experience of this kind, he has ridden extensively in Australia, Southern Africa and Canada.

PREFACE

The steam locomotive history of the Southern Railway is primarily that of the work of two men, R. E. L. Maunsell, and O. V. S. Bulleid; and two men less alike in personality would be hard to imagine. Yet the whole story is not entirely of their products. The Southern Railway was formed of three highly individualistic concerns, each with strong traditions of its own; and Maunsell, partly from his own natural outlook, and partly from the mandate for economy that he assumed on taking office, made the most of each of those traditions – whether in adapting them to new construction, or using the inherent robustness and longevity of the designs to fulfil a useful function in traffic operation.

Some years ago I had occasion to write in detail of Maunsell's new constructional work, and the central chapters of this new book contain much that appeared in *The Locomotives of R. E. L. Maunsell*; but to this core I have added an extensive prelude, dealing particularly with the Brighton, the South Western, and with the South Eastern & Chatham positions before grouping. In the entire Southern story, however, Maunsell's work is only one side of the picture, and the swift transition from Maunsell to Bulleid was one of the phenomena of the British railway scene in the last years of private ownership.

Many friends have helped on numerous occasions towards the making of this book. Towards the earlier chapters I have had valuable assistance from Mr R. H. N. Hardy, A. B. Macleod and S. C. Townroe; Mr Holcroft made available to me his private records kept in the momentous years when he was an assistant to Maunsell, while T. E. Chrimes, when locomotive-running superintendent, gave me many opportunities for riding on the footplate. From Mr Bulleid I have had many kindnesses, including the vetting of some of my earlier writings on Southern locomotives. His observations have been invaluable towards the presentation of a true picture.

Silver Cedars,   O. S. NOCK
High Bannerdown
Batheaston,
Bath.
March, 1966

CHAPTER ONE

THE DIVERSE HERITAGE

At the time of the formation of the Southern Railway on January 1st, 1923, the locomotive departments of the three major constituents of the new company all had a strong individuality, with long-established traditions, and marked divergencies in practice and outlook. The choice of a chief mechanical engineer for the new group was made relatively easy for the management because R. W. Urie on the London & South Western, and Colonel L. Billinton on the Brighton were both almost due for retirement, whereas on the South Eastern & Chatham, R. E. L. Maunsell was still a relatively young man. Furthermore, in the ten difficult years during which he had been at Ashford, Maunsell had dealt with a diversity of problems in both engineering and administration with outstanding success and, unless someone from outside the three constituent companies were to be appointed, he was the obvious choice. The amalgamation of the locomotive departments of three such companies can never be an entirely smooth process, nor one in which everyone concerned is satisfied with the way things go; but Maunsell had already shown himself to be an administrator who could combine tact, discretion and firmness to the degree that each is required when dealing with a difficult situation. It can be said that under his leadership the staffs of the three former companies settled down much more quickly than might otherwise have been the case.

When he was appointed chief mechanical engineer of the South Eastern & Chatham Railway in 1913, Maunsell had virtually to build up an entirely new team of engineers at Ashford. As will be told in more detail later, the works there had been a rather inefficient mixture of the traditions of the South Eastern and the London, Chatham & Dover railways, and the period that had elapsed since the working union of those two one-time rivals in Kent had not been used to plan adequately for the future, either in workshop equipment or in the progressive training of men to take up senior posts as and when they fell vacant. Maunsell had, therefore, recruited his team almost entirely from outside, with the majority coming from the Great Western Railway at Swindon. From the viewpoint of personnel it was perhaps no more than natural that the men he had so carefully chosen and groomed during the period that had followed his appointment in 1913 should have been chosen to continue his work on a broader scale, covering the locomotive requirements of the entire Southern Railway. Naturally, the way in which Ashford men thus gained complete ascendency over those of the former Brighton, and South Western railways, did not go down too well at Brighton itself, nor at Eastleigh. But, as with the difficulties that arose during his re-organization of Ashford Works from 1914 onwards, Maunsell dealt tactfully and firmly with the human aspects of the big amalgamation.

The way in which the new organization was developed after 1923 will be told stage by stage in later chapters of this book, but in this introduction something of the diversities and origins of the various locomotives that were brought together in the Southern Railway at the time of grouping needs more than a passing mention. Each of the former railway dynasties had a contribution to make to the ultimate developments of a standard Southern Railway locomotive practice, though the influences were not always either obvious or direct. Until the end of 1922, the locomotive development of the London Brighton & South Coast Railway had perhaps been the most consistent and continuous of any. Brighton practice settled into a steady form during the time of William Stroudley, who superseded J. C. Craven as locomotive superintendent in 1865. It was Stroudley who established the very high standards of workmanship and codes of engineering practice for which the Brighton Works were famous, and which continued as a process of evolution rather than of violent change throughout the careers of the three successive holders of the office after Stroudley.

The Brighton school of locomotive engineering had a proud record of achievement, particularly in the period under Douglas Earle-Marsh and his exceedingly able chief draughtsman, B. K. Field. It was during this period that some of the pioneer work in the use of superheated steam took place, and this had an extremely wide and lasting influence on the railways of Great Britain as a whole. Men trained at Brighton fulfilled high office in the locomotive departments of railways in many parts of the world, and although the Brighton traditions and practices tended to recede into eclipse during the earliest years of the Southern Railway, they certainly came very prominently into the picture in later years, after O. V. S. Bulleid had succeeded Maunsell as chief mechanical engineer.

On the London & South Western Railway there was continuity only in certain aspects of locomotive practice. From the year 1877 onwards, William Adams carried out a thorough modernization of the locomotive stud of the company and succeeded in producing at Nine Elms Works some of the largest, most powerful, and most efficient locomotives running in Great Britain at the time. But in matters of design and in many details of constructional practice, locomotive work on the London & South Western Railway underwent a profound change in 1895 when Adams retired and was succeeded by Dugald Drummond. It was then that the Scottish influence came very prominently into the picture. Drummond had the reputation of being a very hard task-master, a martinet, and sometimes a very bad-tempered one at that; but many recognized in him a leader of rare qualities, and the number of Scotsmen who followed him from Glasgow to Nine Elms, whether as draughtsmen, workshop technicians, or footplate men, was quite remarkable. The Glasgow school of locomotive design, which could be broadly described as a blend of Caledonian and North British practice, embodying the world-wide experience of private locomotive-building firms such as Neilson Reid, and Dübs, settled upon the London & South Western Railway in perpetuity. Its influence remained at Eastleigh Works

long after the LSWR had ceased to exist, and came into some
prominence when that works was engaged in building the
modern Maunsell-designed locomotives for the Southern
Railway.

But to revert for a moment to Drummond: he began his
career on the LSWR by building locomotives of what could be
termed the standard family pattern which had originated on
the North British Railway and been developed with great
success on the Caledonian. His brother, Peter, also introduced the same general type on to the Highland Railway.
But having established excellent standards with smaller
power units Drummond then began to experiment, and to
participate in what appeared to be a race to produce the
largest, heaviest and most powerful locomotives running in
Great Britain at the time. In so doing he departed from the
traditional simplicity that had marked all his earlier work,
and became addicted to the use of gadgets and complexities
that were not entirely satisfactory. Although in the '330'
class of four-cylinder 4-6-0s, built at Nine Elms in 1905,
Drummond had certainly produced something that eclipsed
everything else running in Great Britain for sheer size and
weight, and was a very impressive engine to look at, it was
not successful and his later 4-6-0s, in which mere size was
second in importance to functional reliability, were considerably better. Throughout his time on the LSWR his best
locomotives were still of the 4-4-0 type, increasing in size to
the handsome '463' class of 1912, the first of which was
completed only a short time before his death.

As a locomotive engineer, Dugald Drummond will be
remembered best by other stages in his career rather than by
his largest locomotives. He will be remembered – and his
precepts were continued long after his death – for the
massive construction of his locomotives; for the generous
bearing surfaces incorporated in them and their consequent
reliability in traffic. He will also be remembered as a first-
class workshop man. It was under his direction that the
locomotive department of the LSWR was moved from the
original and rather cramped works at Nine Elms to the

entirely new works at Eastleigh. Eastleigh Works, indeed, is possibly the most enduring monument to his memory. His latest engines were all built there, and the removal of the works from Nine Elms to Eastleigh was a masterpiece of industrial organization. Robert Urie succeeded Drummond and, although he made changes in the basic design of loco-motives, he continued in its entirety the traditions of massive reliability which paid such handsome dividends in the way of freedom from trouble on the road in the heaviest and fastest of passenger traffic.

Robert Urie was another engineer of what might be termed 'The Glasgow School of Locomotive Engineers'; but, unlike Drummond in his later days, he was an apostle of the utmost simplicity in design; on the LSWR he originated the practice that became a watchword on the Southern Railway in Maunsell's day, 'make everything get-at-able'. There was no more building of four-cylinder locomotives with a multiplicity of working parts between the frames; all new engines build under Urie's superintendency had two cylinders only, outside and operated by outside Walschaert's valve gear. Not only this, but in maintaining the stud of locomotives left behind by Dugald Drummond he simplified the workings of them very considerably by removing some of the gadgets which cost more in maintenance than the saving in fuel they effected by increasing thermal efficiency. Firebox water-tubes were removed from all engines in due course and the Drummond steam drier which was the nearest approach that the South Western had yet made towards superheating was replaced by superheaters of the orthodox type.

Although much of Urie's work was done while the LSWR was in the throes of intense wartime traffic, a very com-mendable amount of new development work was done at Eastleigh during the war years, and it resulted in the pro-duction, in 1918, of the celebrated 'N15' class of 4-6-0 express passenger locomotive which was destined to be the forerunner of the Southern 'King Arthur' class. Variations upon this basic design made up the total of Urie's new

construction on the South Western. There were small-
wheeled varieties of the 4-6-0 for mixed traffic and goods
working, and there were very heavy tank engines of the
4-6-2 and 4-8-0 type for working in conjunction with the
new hump marshalling yard at Feltham. All these locomotives yielded a high degree of reliability in working and
earned dividends by their low repair and running costs; and
if the 'N15' class, as built by Urie, were not in the top flight
of British express locomotive practice at that time, they had
certainly most of the ingredients of outstanding success.
How that success was achieved in later years is described in
subsequent chapters of this book.

The locomotive position on the South Eastern & Chatham
Railway had changed profoundly in the last ten years before
grouping took place. Until 1913, Ashford had not entirely
cast off the reputation for inefficiency and sloth that had
stigmatized much of the proceedings of the two constituent
companies. Although the standards of engineering developed
at Ashford under James Stirling were very good, the permanent way of the South Eastern Railway had been such as
to make necessary the imposition of an overall speed limit of
60 mph. This had certainly been lifted in the first decade of
the twentieth century, but timekeeping left a good deal to
be desired. On the Chatham side, there had not been any
inhibitions about maximum speeds, and the way in which
the boat trains were run on favourable stretches of the line
was inclined to be hair-raising, having regard to the
standards of rolling stock often to be found on quite fast
trains. The locomotive practice of Longhedge Works had
been the exact opposite of Ashford. While the latter maintained traditions of very fine workmanship and close toler-
ances in manufacture, the Chatham line over the years had
been forced to use less accurate measures that required
greater working clearances. Consequently, while South
Eastern engines worked with the precision and quietness of
a sewing machine, albeit not a very rapid one, the Chatham
engines went like the wind and earned the nickname of
'clatterbangs' from the nature of their going.

The management of the South Eastern & Chatham Railway found in R. E. L. Maunsell an ideal man to consolidate the best features of both the constituent companies. Moreover, he was given a mandate that extended far beyond the mere tidying up of the existing organization. The management of the railway were set upon a most ambitious course of development that required a very considerable degree of re-equipment of the works, and expansion in order to deal with an extended sphere of activity. Very few of the existing senior staff who had grown up either on the South Eastern or on the London Chatham & Dover Railway measured up to the required standards of capability, and Maunsell was given a free hand to recruit an entirely new top-line staff. While the foresight and business acumen of Sir Herbert Walker, as general manager of the London & South Western Railway, laid the foundations of future Southern Railway development in electric traction and traffic operating during the years 1913 to 1922, so equally did Maunsell in his re-organization work at Ashford lay the foundations of Southern Railway steam locomotive practice.

The staff he built up on the South Eastern & Chatham Railway in 1913–14 and the standards of design that were developed in the ensuing years carried the Southern Railway through almost to the time of the Second World War. Maunsell was fortunate in being able to carry on his existing organization with very little alteration after grouping took place. The situation might not have been so easy, nor so favourable, if the locomotive engineers of the London & South Western and of the Brighton Railway had not been near retiring age at the time of the grouping, and the Southern might then have experienced those uncertainties and reversals of policy that bedevilled the locomotive practice of the London Midland & Scottish Railway for so many years after grouping. As it was, there was a straight continuity of South Eastern & Chatham personnel into the Southern Railway and, so far as Eastleigh was concerned, a skilful blend of South Western and South Eastern practice that was to prove of great advantage in the grouping era.

As previously mentioned, it was the Brighton Railway whose practice largely faded out.

Such, in broad outline, was the situation that existed in the three constituent companies of the Southern Railway on the eve of grouping. The number of different classes of locomotive was great and anyone attempting to carry out a process of standardization between one and the other would have been faced with an almost impossible task. In post-grouping years, Maunsell adopted very largely the policy of 'live and let live'. The merits of existing engine designs were recognized, and so long as they successfully carried out their appointed duties they were allowed to continue. The Southern locomotive policy stood completely aside from the popular practice of the northern lines in running competitive trials between one pre-grouping type of locomotive and another. The London Midland & Scottish ran many of these trials from 1923 onwards, and some equally interesting ones were carried out on the London & North Eastern Railway.

On the Southern, nobody seems to have conceived the idea of running comparative trials, largely because the locomotives of the constituent companies were eminently suited to their own lines. This suitability was not a question of thermodynamic performances, nor of differences in basic dimensions; it was rather a matter of engineering restrictions and water supply. One could not, for example, expect a Brighton 4–6–4 tank to undertake the duties regularly worked by the London & South Western 'N15' class, the water capacity of the tanks made it impracticable. Similarly, at the time of grouping, there was a severe limitation in maximum axle load over much of the principal boat-train route to Dover and Folkestone, and the large engines of the Brighton and of the London & South Western Railway would have been prohibited. As things turned out, the early stages of Southern Railway locomotive development resolved themselves into a refinement of London & South Western practice by introducing the precepts of Churchward, as adapted to SE & CR needs at Ashford.

CHAPTER TWO

THE BRIGHTON LOCOMOTIVES

In boyhood, before the First World War, my home was at
Reading. During holidaying expeditions to seaside resorts in
Kent and Hampshire I saw a good deal of the South Western
and of the South Eastern & Chatham railways and was able
to absorb something of their atmosphere. One saw the
chocolate engines and trains of the Brighton at Redhill, or
Fratton, but that was about all. Then, when the war was
over, my first southward expedition was to Eastbourne, in
1919, and at once I became an ardent fan of the Brighton
Railway. There was fascination in the tremendous variety of
locomotives to be seen, whether on main line, country
branch or suburban duties in the London area. All were alike
in the smartness of their turn-out, and in their chocolate-
brown livery. Wartime austerity had not robbed them of
their lining-out, nor diminished the standards to which they
were kept. We did not see the big 4-6-2 and 4-6-4 tanks at
Eastbourne, but examples of almost every other class
worked in; and I returned north with snaps of 'Atlantics',
'B4's, 'B2X's, 'Gladstones', and many varieties of tank
engine.

Many a railway enthusiast would find it hard to put into
precise phraseology his reasons for being attracted to one
particular railway or another; but I certainly came under the
spell of Brighton, and in recalling my early days at the City
and Guilds College, when I was living at South Kensington,
I am sure that I spent more time photographing at the lineside of the Brighton Railway around Purley, Coulsdon and
Merstham Tunnel than anywhere else in the London area.
Perhaps it was because the Brighton authorities were
particularly friendly so far as lineside photographic permits
were concerned. But from one cause or another, I must say
I enjoyed those days as much for the interest of the railway

working as for the very pleasant country in which my expeditions were made. The steep-sided cuttings in the chalk south of Coulsdon made a most attractive setting for photographs. There was also the added interest that one never knew for certain what type of locomotive would be working a particular train. On the principal Brighton expresses at that time one would find 4–6–4 and 4–6–2 tanks, 'Atlantics' and not infrequently the 'B4' 4–4–0s.

In my first photographic days on the line, in 1921 and 1922, there were only two engines of the 4–6–4 tank class and two engines of the 4–6–2 tank class, and these four locomotives were very much sought after by photographers. In 1922, the express passenger locomotive stud of the Brighton Railway was as follows:

4-6-4 tanks, class 'L'	2
4-6-2 tanks, class 'J'	2
4-4-2 non-superheated 'Atlantics', class 'H1'	5
4-4-2 non-superheated 'Atlantics', class 'H2'	6
4-4-2 tank engines, class 'I3'	27
4-4-0 class 'B4'	33
4-4-0 class 'B2X'	25

In addition to these, there were the survivors of the famous 'Gladstone' class, though these were rapidly being scrapped and were rarely seen on anything but secondary passenger work. In the last months before grouping took place, a start had been made in rebuilding some of the 'B4' class engines with larger boilers, superheater equipped. Engines 55 and 60, so rebuilt, went into traffic early in 1923 and began taking turns with the largest of the existing passenger engines, thereby adding to the variety that could be expected on almost all important duties. In the summer of 1922, five new engines of the 4–6–4 tank class 'L' were put into traffic and from that time, with seven of them available, this class was regularly used on the heavier of the Brighton expresses, including the 'Southern Belle'.

One can only remark upon the rather lavish variety of different classes all engaged in first-class work on so relatively small a railway. It seemed as though the twentieth century had seen a rapid breakaway from the policies of standardization which had been practised so assiduously by Stroudley. Whereas in his day there were virtually only two classes of express passenger locomotive engaged in first-class duty on the line, namely, the 2–2–2s of the 'G' class and the 0–4–2s of the 'Gladstone' class, his successors had produced a large number of different designs, of which the super-heater 'I3' tanks were the most numerous. Of the smaller engines still engaged in fast passenger work, those of the 'B2' class, introduced by R. J. Billinton, were not far removed from failures in their original condition, and al-though in their rebuilt state as 'B2X' they were reliable power units they could never be regarded as anything but fit for the lightest of trains. The 'B4's, first introduced in 1899, were excellent engines up to a point, but in the year 1922 they would be considered as definitely obsolescent.

Although the six most recent passenger classes, 'B4X' 4–4–0, 'H1' 4–4–2, 'H2' 4–4–2, 'I3' 4–4–2 tank, 'J4' 4–6–2 tank and 'L' 4–6–4 tank were all excellent engines in them-selves – steady and reliable runners and moderate consumers of coal – there were not really enough of them to warrant their consideration for future Southern Railway standards. The tank engines had their limitations because of their restricted length of non-stop run; the 'Atlantic' tender engines belonged to a type which, in 1922, was definitely becoming obsolescent. Phenomenal though the work of 'Atlantic' engines had been on some railways – and as it continued to be for many years on the Great Northern Section of the LNER where the type was well known and widely appreciated – it was not likely that the 'Atlantic' type would appeal as a future Southern Railway standard. Especially when the haulage of 500-ton trains at average speeds of 55 mph was being contemplated over the main lines from Waterloo, and considerable acceleration of the Continental boat expresses was in prospect on the Eastern group of lines. From this it is easy to see why the Brighton stud of locomotives came to be passed over when future standards were being considered. They were left to work on their own routes until such time as electrification of the main lines to the South Coast was in hand, and it was only in one isolated case – that of the 'L' class 4–6–4 tanks – that any steps were subsequently taken to adapt them for use other than on their native system.

Although the Brighton stud as a whole exerted little or no influence on future Southern Railway locomotive practice, the engines themselves have a definite place in locomotive history, and from the time of grouping in January 1923 they were to render many years of excellent service to their new owners. Many of them were still doing excellent work in the years after the Second World War and I have vivid memories of footplate journeys on 'I3' and 'J' class tank engines in 1947 and 1948, which shows that the engines were still in excellent condition and had obviously been maintained with care and skill during the difficult years of the war. So far, I have spoken only of passenger engines, but the Brighton had one of the earliest British examples of a genuine mixed-traffic engine of modern design in the 'K' class 2–6–0s, first introduced in September 1913. Further engines of this class were under consideration at the time of grouping.

Also at that time, the London suburban electrification had not been extended beyond the original circuit on the South London line, and the great majority of the outer suburban train services were worked by steam. The Brighton was admirably served by a positive swarm of small but highly efficient tank engines, of which some of the best were the celebrated 'D1' 0–4–2s designed by William Stroudley. At the time of grouping there were no fewer than 111 of these engines in service – more than one-sixth of the entire locomotive stock of the London, Brighton & South Coast Railway! Other passenger tank engines were the Billinton class of 0–4–4 tanks of which there were thirty-four, and the various 'E' class six-coupled side tanks 0–6–2 type. The thirty engines of the 'E5' class with radial trailing axles did many years of excellent work on the line. The least successful of the passenger tank engines were, strangely enough, those of the 4-4-2 type designed by Earle-Marsh for suburban work and classified 'I1' and 'I2'. Both types suffered from inadequate boiler capacity and were generally inferior, not only to the Billinton radial 0-6-2s but also to the Stroudley 'D1's. In 1921 the Brighton, out of a total locomotive stock of 606, had no fewer than 434 tank engines. In addition to the passenger engines just mentioned, there was a large stud of 0-6-0 goods tanks, and the survivors of the famous Stroudley 'Terriers' of the 'A' class.

So far as the duties performed by the various classes of engine were concerned, priority was always given to the express trains between London and Brighton making the journey non-stop in the even hour. Naturally, special attention was always given to the working of the 'Southern Belle', which made the journey between Victoria and Brighton, four times a day. At the time of grouping, the departure times were 11 AM and 3.10 PM from Victoria, and 12.20 PM and 5.55 PM up from Brighton. After the restoration of this fine service following the end of the First World War, the train was for a time available to ordinary non-Pullman passengers and it loaded very heavily in consequence. I should explain also that right up to the time of grouping, the Brighton had no corridor carriages at all, and those who required meals or refreshment of any kind had to travel in the Pullman cars. By the time of grouping, however, practically all the principal express trains to Brighton, Eastbourne, Hastings and Portsmouth had Pullman cars, though, of course, their accommodation was limited.

In the years before the First World War the 'Southern Belle' was an all-Pullman train; but in the last year before grouping, when the passenger accommodation was once again all-Pullman, the traffic was such that an additional passenger luggage-van of ordinary stock was necessary. From the appearance point of view, this rather spoilt the look of the all-Pullman rake, but was evidence of the excellent business that was being done. There were also evening expresses for City workers, leaving Victoria in the evening and running non-stop to Brighton in an hour. But apart from the 'Southern Belle', one of the heaviest and most popular trains on the Brighton service was the 'City Limited' which ran non-stop between Brighton and London Bridge, also in an hour. This was popularly known among the railway staff as 'The Stockbrokers' Express' and arrived at London Bridge at 9.45 AM.

The largest express locomotives on the lines were stationed mostly at Brighton or Battersea. These two sheds did the bulk of the express working between them and included in their rosters some triangular workings, such as the Brighton to Victoria; Victoria to Portsmouth, and Portsmouth back to Brighton along the coast. Similarly, workings were arranged to cover certain of the Eastbourne trains. The morning and evening 'Stockbrokers' express to and from London Bridge had no immediate balancing turns from that station, and the usual practice was for the engine of the up morning express to work light engine from London Bridge to Victoria by the South London line and then return to Brighton from Victoria. Similar working was in force for the down evening departure from London Bridge.

The Portsmouth service of the Brighton, which was in friendly competition with that worked by the London & South Western Railway, was always one to which careful attention was given both by the traffic and the locomotive departments. The best trains on this service made the longest non-stop runs to be found on the Brighton system, namely, from Clapham Junction to Fratton. This run of 81¾ miles over a very hilly route was an exacting test of locomotive efficiency and skilful driving and firing; for while the loads of the non-stop trains were not heavy by comparison with the most popular of the Brighton expresses, the duty was normally performed by engines of the superheater 'I3' class. The tank capacity of these engines was 2,110 gallons. This would have been ample if the run had been a straightforward one but, quite apart from the awkward gradients, there were many points on the route where speed had to be reduced because of curves, and, as so frequently happens, these speed restrictions were immediately followed by stiff

rising gradients. This was particularly the case on the down
run at Mitcham with the steep climb to Sutton to follow;
at Dorking, immediately before the hard climb over the
North Downs, and again at Horsham. While the working of
the 'Southern Belle' between London and Brighton did, of
course, constitute the 'Blue Riband' of all Brighton locomotive workings, the Fratton non-stops definitely demanded
the greater artistry in running. Very heavy loads were also
conveyed at times on the Newhaven boat-train expresses,
and just before the grouping these trains were usually
worked by the 'Atlantic' tender engines.

To illustrate the everyday work of the Brighton engines in
the years just before and after the grouping, I have prepared
two tables of non-stop runs from London to Brighton, the
first from Victoria and the second on the famous 'City
Limited' from London Bridge. The run from Victoria, as
well as being slightly longer was the more difficult of the two,
so far as the start out of London was concerned. First of all,
there was the steep half-mile from the immediate start, at
1 in 64 up to Grosvenor Road bridge, and then after a sharp
descent to Clapham Junction another awkward pitch 1 in
166–94 – 1¾ miles of it – to Balham Junction. The going is
then easier, though still adverse in the aggregate, until the
two lines converge at East Croydon. To this point the line
from London Bridge is virtually level, except for the 2½-mile
bank at 1 in 100 from New Cross Gate to Forest Hill. From
East Croydon, the fine grading of the original Brighton
Railway prevails, with a ruling inclination of 1 in 264 uphill
and down, except on the deviation line through Merstham
New Tunnel, to which south-bound trains have to climb
1½ miles at 1 in 165.

The first run tabulated among the Victoria–Brighton non-
stops was made with an 'I3' superheated 4–4–2 tank. The
start from Victoria right out to Merstham Tunnel was so fast
that the train was nearly two minutes ahead of time at
Quarry Box, just at the south end of the tunnel; and despite
a signal check at Earlswood time was still in hand and
relatively easy running followed. One of the 4–6–2 tanks,

TABLE I

VICTORIA–BRIGHTON: 60-MINUTE TRAINS

			1		2		3		4	
Run No			1		2		3		4	
Engine No			24		326		333		422	
Engine Class			4-4-2T		4-6-2T		4-6-4T		4-4-2	
Load (tons gross)			245		290		310		405	
Miles		Sch. min	min	sec	min	sec	min	sec	min	sec
0·0	VICTORIA	0	0	00	0	00	0	00	0	00
0·6	Grosvenor Road		2	18	2	00	2	35	2	12
2·7	CLAPHAM JUNCTION	5	5	28	5	10	5	35	5	54
4·7	Balham		7	57	7	38	8	05	8	45
7·5	Norbury		11	03	10	53	11	24	12	39
10·5	EAST CROYDON	15	14	29	14	14	14	41	16	46
13·5	Purley		18	00	17	31	18	00	20	46
15·0	Coulsdon		19	44	19	05	19	39	22	39
			—		p.w.s.		—		—	
18·8	Quarry Box	26	24	22	24	50	23	57	28	00
			sigs		—		—		—	
21·9	Earlswood	29	27	39	28	44	26	45	31	01
26·0	Horley		31	52	32	44	30	11	34	38
29·5	THREE BRIDGES	37	35	30	36	02	33	16	37	59
32·0	Milepost 31¾		38	17	38	50	35	43	40	54
34·1	Balcombe		40	22	40	57	37	42	43	09
			—		—		sigs		—	
38·0	HAYWARDS HEATH		43	54	44	32	42	07	46	40
41·1	Keymer Junction	49	46	41	47	18	45	05	49	20
			sigs		sigs		sigs		—	
49·6	Preston Park		56	50	sigs		55	54	57	38
50·9	BRIGHTON	60	59	28	59	32	58	41	59	57
Net times		60	56½		55½		54½		60	
Speeds (mph):										
Streatham			56½		57		58		49	
Quarry			46		48		50		41	
Horley			65		69		77		72½	
Milepost 31¾			51		52½		60		50	
Keymer Junction			68		70½		68		74	
Clayton Tunnel			—		53		—		55	

No 326, *Bessborough*, made an even faster start, and did not fall below 48 mph at Merstham Tunnel. The driver was getting time in hand to offset the effects of a permanent way slowing through the tunnel itself, and with some brisk subsequent work Keymer Junction was passed 1¾ minutes early. A series of signal checks in the approach to Brighton did not prevent a punctual arrival.

The third run in the table is the last steam-hauled trip of the 'Southern Belle' on December 31st, 1932, after which it became an electric multiple-unit train. With some regard for the historical significance of the occasion, the Southern

TABLE 2
LONDON BRIDGE– BRIGHTON:
'THE CITY LIMITED'

			1	2	3
	Run No		1	2	3
	Engine No		67	41	333
	Engine Class		4–4–0	4–4–2	4–6–4T
	Load (tons full)		280	325	385
Miles		Sch. min	min sec	min sec	min sec
0·0	LONDON BRIDGE	0	0 00	0 00	0 00
2·8	New Cross Gate		4 44	4 42	5 05
5·5	Forest Hill		8 15	8 16	9 25
8·6	Norwood Junction		12 35	12 12	13 45
			—		sigs
10·3	EAST CROYDON	15	14 32	14 06	15 45
13·3	Purley		18 08	17 50	20 05
14·8	Coulsdon		19 47	19 43	22 05
18·6	Quarry Box	26	24 22	24 56	27 10
			sig stop		—
21·7	Earlswood	29	31 06	27 53	30 10
25·8	Horley		35 04	31 35	33 50
29·3	THREE BRIDGES	37	38 15	35 06	37 20
31·8	*Milepost* 31¾		40 45	38 03	40 20
33·9	Balcombe		42 41	40 18	43 00
37·8	HAYWARDS HEATH		45 48	43 52	46 45
40·9	*Keymer Junction*	49	48 17	46 41	49 25
			—	sigs	—
49·4	Preston Park		55 37	56 14	58 00
50·7	BRIGHTON	60	58 20	58 46	60 10
	Net times (min)	60	54½	58	58½
Speeds (mph):					
	New Cross Gate		—	54	49
	Forest Hill		39	40	31
	Norwood Junction		—	56½	56
	Quarry		48½	41	41½
	Horley		—	69	70½
	Milepost 31¾		58	50	50
	Keymer Junction		79	69	71½
	Clayton Tunnel		64½	46½	52

Railway authorities put on the Brighton memorial engine, 4-6-4 tank No 333, *Remembrance*, whereas for some years previously the train had been almost invariably worked by a 'King Arthur' class 4-6-0. The load was not unduly heavy and a very fast run was made, as a grand finale with steam. All concerned were anxious to make a spectacularly early arrival; and when the train was nearly four minutes ahead of time as early in the run as Three Bridges hopes ran high. But, unfortunately, that crowded route could not be kept clear so far ahead of the scheduled path of the train, and adverse signals were encountered after Balcombe.

The Marsh 'Atlantics', like their counterparts on the Great Northern, were capable of extremely fine work, but what was perhaps more surprising was their remarkable capacity for sturdy hill-climbing. Thus, in the fourth run in the table, we find engine No 422 making the fastest but one of all climbs up the 1 in 64 to Grosvenor Road bridge, even though she was hauling nearly 100 tons more than the 4-6-4 tank on the 'Southern Belle' farewell trip. The 'Atlantic' engine was not pressed up to Merstham Tunnel; but excellent work followed with no checks and the train clocked into Brighton in almost exactly the even hour. This run was made by one of the superheater 'Atlantics', and the second run in the London Bridge table shows the work of one of the original non-superheated batch. Although these engines were so clearly derived from the Ivatt '251' class on the GNR, Marsh used much larger cylinders, namely, 19 ins by 26 ins against 18¾ ins by 24 ins. Engine No 41 made a good steady run without any spectacular features. There was, of course, no need for any particular hurry after the excellent start, the fast climb of Forest Hill bank and the smart running out to Croydon.

One of the most interesting runs in this collection is that made by 4-4-0 No 67, one of the 'B4' class, rebuilt and superheated, albeit with no more than a moderate load. To Coulsdon, this engine was making closely similar times to the non-superheated 'Atlantic' No 41; but she was driven much harder up to Merstham Tunnel. Then came a dead stand for signals at Earlswood. One would not imagine that the relatively short run from London to Brighton would give much chance of recovery from a delay of this kind; but engine No 67 was driven with tremendous vim, recording such excellent speeds as 58 mph minimum at Balcombe Tunnel, 79 mph at Keymer Junction, and $64\frac{1}{2}$ mph entering Clayton Tunnel. Thus the train was $1\frac{3}{4}$ minutes early on arrival, having made a net time of $54\frac{1}{4}$ minutes. Even allowing for the much greater weight of the train, the run of the 4–6–4 tank No 333 in column 3 was commonplace by comparison. It was a good steady run with just enough in hand to offset the effect of the two slight checks. My chief recollection of it was the noise the engine made climbing Forest Hill bank, where the work was nevertheless inferior to that of engines Nos 67 and 41, even allowing for the difference in load. The 4–6–4 tank was clearly being thrashed, and such phenomena were becoming rare on the Southern in the year of grace 1931!

CHAPTER THREE

THE SOUTH WESTERN LOCOMOTIVES

The London & South Western Railway, with its fine locomotive works at Eastleigh and its stud of efficient, modern
locomotives, was to form the backbone of the modern locomotive stock of the Southern Railway. It is true that at least
one South Eastern & Chatham type was adopted as a future
standard, and that the design practice of Ashford became
the standard practice for the new group. But it was the
locomotives of the former London & South Western Railway
that provided the core to which finer points of design were
afterwards added. As briefly described in Chapter One of
this book, South Western practice had passed through a
stage of evolution in the years following the death of Dugald
Drummond in 1912 and the formation of the Southern Railway at the end of 1922. Robert Urie had taken in hand the
more recent of the Drummond locomotives and greatly increased their usefulness by substituting an orthodox form
of superheater for the Drummond steam drier; and although
none of the Urie designs, nor the Urie rebuilds of Drummond's designs, were accepted in their entirety, all these
engines were good enough to be worked in main-line service
for the whole period between the formation of the Southern
Railway and the outbreak of the Second World War.

This longevity was characteristic of locomotives from all
three main constituents of the Southern Railway, and it
arose partly as a result of the motive-power policy of the top
management of the new company, but no less through the
inherent soundness of design of the locomotives themselves.
None of the three constituents of the Southern Railway had,
in their last years, produced any locomotives of outstanding
thermal efficiency; but their sound construction, massive
proportions, and the good maintenance which they enjoyed
gave them all a reliability on the road that was worth more

than a few decimal points in the overall figures of coal consumption per DBHP hr. Because of the managerial policy of extending the electrified system of the Southern Railway, first to Brighton, and then to other South Coast resorts, the amount of money available for investment in new steam power was limited, and Maunsell had to do the best he could with the locomotives of the constituent companies. It was fortunate that these older locomotives were all such tough, reliable machines.

On the London & South Western Railway, the locomotive stud that came into the ownership of the Southern Railway can be grouped into three broad categories:

1. The Drummond 4-4-0 locomotives that had been rebuilt and superheated by Urie.
2. The Drummond 4–6–0 locomotives, some of which had been drastically rebuilt, but others like the 'T14' class, which were good enough in themselves to require merely the addition of superheating to keep them abreast of current requirements.
3. The locomotives of Robert Urie, including four different classes of 4–6–0 and the special tank engines of the 4–6–2 and 4–8–0 types built for work in connexion with Feltham Hump marshalling yard. The latter engines were designed and built in quite small numbers for a specific duty on which they remained for the whole of their working lives; but it was the Urie 4–6–0s, particularly those of the 'H15' and 'N15' classes, that formed the basis of an important Southern Railway development.

Turning now to a more detailed consideration of the various engine classes, the Urie superheated rebuilds of the Drummond 4–4–0 designs were all extremely successful. At the time of grouping, no more than the first examples of the rebuilt 'T9' class were at work; but these were showing very great promise, and under Southern Railway management all the surviving members of the class were subsequently altered. By the time of grouping, all ten of the 'D15' class had been modified, and most of the 'L12' class. At this time, the London & South Western Railway was relying almost entirely upon 4–4–0 locomotives for the working of the

express passenger train service between Waterloo, Bournemouth and Weymouth. In 1921, a standardized timetable
had been introduced for this service giving even-hour
departures from Waterloo. The fastest trains were allowed
an overall time of $2\frac{1}{4}$ hours between Waterloo and Bournemouth Central, 108 miles, but non-stop running as practised
with some of the principal Bournemouth expresses before
the war was not at that time restored.

All the fastest trains on the Bournemouth service made an
intermediate stop at Southampton. The standard time
allowances were 92 minutes in each direction between Waterloo and Southampton West, 79·3 miles, and 36 minutes for
the 28·7 miles from Southampton to Bournemouth Central.
The gross trailing loads worked on these services were rarely
less than 300 tons and sometimes, even in normal working,
the maximum trailing loads exceeded 400 tons. The
standard engines for these duties were the 'D15' class
4–4–0s stationed at Bournemouth Central; but the 'L12'
engines were frequently called upon to deputize for the large
class and, generally speaking, they deputized extremely well.
Superheating had made a very useful improvement in the
performance of the 'D15' class, but in the case of the 'L12',
the rebuilding had virtually transformed them. Though so
handsomely proportioned in their original form, the
Drummond 'L12's were, in general, disappointing engines
and rarely showed any marked superiority over the considerably smaller 'T9' class, which will always be regarded
as Dugald Drummond's greatest success.

One or two examples of individual running with the
Bournemouth expresses, in the years dating from the time
of the reintroduction of the accelerated service to Bournemouth in 1921, will give a good idea of the kind of running
one expected at that time with these locomotives. The three
runs tabulated (Table 3) were all made on the $2\frac{1}{4}$-hour trains,
allowed 92 minutes for the non-stop run of 79·2 miles from
Waterloo to Southampton West, and include examples of
the work of all three classes of Drummond 4–4–0, each rebuilt and superheated by Urie. The first of the three, with

TABLE 3
LSWR WATERLOO–SOUTHAMPTON WEST

		1	2	3
Run No		1	2	3
Engine 4–4–0 No		417	468	336
Engine Class		'L12'	'D15'	'T9'
Load (tons gross)		310	375	380
Miles	Sch. min	min sec	min sec	min sec
0·0 WATERLOO	0	0 00	0 00	0 00
		—	sigs	—
3·9 CLAPHAM JUNCTION	7	7 20	9 00	7 10
		—	sigs	—
7·3 Wimbledon		11 15	13 25	11 18
12·0 Surbiton		16 05	19 05	16 38
19·1 Weybridge		22 50	26 40	23 59
24·4 WOKING	29	27 50	32 30	29 38
		sigs	—	
31·0 *Milepost* 31		36 55	40 30	37 31
		sigs	—	
33·2 Farnborough		39 55	43 10	40 03
36·5 Fleet		44 45	46 35	43 24
42·2 Hook		50 50	52 40	49 22
47·8 BASINGSTOKE	56	56 20	58 30	55 04
50·3 *Worting Junction*	59	59 10	61 45	58 05
56·3 *Litchfield*		66 00	69 45	65 31
66·7 WINCHESTER		75 45	79 05	75 25
73·6 EASTLEIGH	83	82 40	85 35	82 24
78·1 Northam Junction	88½	—	90 35	87 33
79·2 SOUTHAMPTON	92	91 10	93 10	90 23
Net times (minutes)	92	88	90½	90¼
Speeds (mph):				
After Weybridge		65	60	60½
At Milepost 31		checked	46	48
Before Basingstoke		61	58½	—
After Worting		45½	41	44½
Max to Eastleigh		66	73½	70

an 'L12' engine, was logged from the footplate by Mr Cecil
J. Allen but, unfortunately, in describing the run many
years ago, he gave no details of the engine working other
than that it was not necessary to take water at Southampton.
It was a smart run, though with a relatively light train for
that period. It was the excellent start from Waterloo that

put the engine completely on top of the job, despite signal checks at Brookwood and Farnborough to cross over to the slow lines, and then back to the fast after the diversion. With this hindrance, the speed at Milepost 31 was of no significance, but the climb from Basingstoke on 1 in 249 was good.

The second and third runs were with heavier trains typical of regular loading on the 6.30 PM down. My own trip, with No 468, was on a Friday evening and we lost some three minutes by signal checks at the start. Then the big engine did reasonably well, particularly in the climb from Weybridge to Milepost 31 with its minimum speed of 46 mph. But the work along the level from Farnborough, and uphill from Basingstoke, was no more than moderate, and No 468 dropped 1½ minutes on the times of No 417 between Basingstoke and Litchfield. Fast down-hill running regained most of the lost time. Most of the honours go to the little 'T9', rebuilt and superheated, for an excellent run characterized by strenuous uphill work, as shown by the minimum speeds of 48 mph at Milepost 31 and of 44½ mph beyond Worting.

The first of the 'T9'-class 4–4–0s to be rebuilt and superheated was put on to the Bournemouth service and some excellent runs were recorded. In general, however, these splendid little engines were drafted to other duties and later came to be used on many other sections of the Southern Railway. It was certainly a tribute to this London & South Western design that the locomotive running superintendent of the Southern Railway, himself a South Eastern & Chatham man, should have drafted them to South Eastern and to Brighton duties. The post-grouping history of locomotive working on the Southern Railway is indeed a very pleasant example of an appreciation of good locomotive design. While the absence of any ruthless policy of 'scrap and build' made it necessary for the running superintendent to make the best use of the locomotives that were available, there seemed to be a happy absence of partisanship on the part of authority towards the locomotives of one constituent or another; and Brighton, South Eastern and South Western engines of the

medium-power classes were drafted in a rational manner to
the duties they could do best.

Mention should also be made of the small-wheeled
Drummond 4–4–0s, of both small- and large-boilered varieties. The latter were rebuilt and superheated in a similar way
to the 'L12' express passenger engines, and a number were
drafted to work the Portsmouth express passenger service
over the South Western route. Because of their smaller-
diameter driving wheels, they were very suitable for climbing the heavy gradients experienced in the crossing of both
the North and the South Downs; nor did their small wheels
prevent them from running freely on the downhill sections
of the line, and they did excellent work until larger engines
were available. In 1925, however, when the new 'King
Arthurs' were introduced and a batch sent new to Bournemouth Central shed, the 'D15' class was drafted, almost in
its entirety, to the Portsmouth route and continued to do
very good work there.

The stud of 4–6–0 locomotives with two outside cylinders,
built up by Robert Urie between 1913 and 1922, came to
form an integral part of the Southern Railway locomotive
stock. There were four individual classes, as set out in
Table 4 overleaf; the first of these, the 'H15', was put
on to the road very shortly after Urie had succeeded Dugald
Drummond, and so far as boiler maintenance and general
appearance were concerned, they followed very much in the
Drummond tradition. An immediate change, however, was
to the use of tenders with outside bearings for the bogie
wheels, and of a high-raised running plate which gave ready
access to the motion. The later engines, built at Eastleigh
from 1918 onwards, included those touches of austerity that
characterized the latter part of the Urie régime on the
London & South Western Railway, notably in the use of
stove pipe chimneys. The small-wheeled 4–6–0s of class
'F15' were used exclusively on goods work, and in this
respect they shared some duties with the rebuilt Drummond
4–6–0s of the '330' class. The 'H15's, both of the original
series of 1913 and also the later ones built shortly after the

grouping, were frequently used on passenger services; in fact, a group of the latter were drafted new to Bournemouth Central shed in 1924.

The 'H15' class of 1913 had the reputation of being very free-running engines, and speeds up to 80 mph were registered with them. In this, they followed in the tradition of the

TABLE 4

URIE 4-6-0s: London & South Western Railway

Class Date	'H15' 1913	'N15' 1918	'S15' 1920	'H15' 1924
Cylinders Dia. stroke in	21 × 28	22 × 28	21 × 28	21 × 28
Coupled wheel dia. ft in	6 - 0	6 - 7	5 - 7	6 - 0
Heating surfaces sq ft				
Tubes	1,716	1,716	1,716	1,716
Firebox	162	162	162	162
Superheater sq ft	308	308	308	337*
Combined total sq ft	2,186	2,186	2,186	2,215
Grate Area sq ft	31·5	30	28	30
Boiler pressure psi	180	180	180	180
Nom. TE at 85% BP lb	26,200	26,200	29,860	26,200

* Maunsell superheater.

smaller-wheeled Drummond 4-6-0s of the 'G14' class, which also had an excellent turn of speed. But for some reason the later 'H15's seemed to have very little 'go' in them, and their advent on the Bournemouth service was not to the advantage of the timekeeping. To the outward observer, logging the run from inside the carriage, they seemed little better than the 'D15' class 4-4-0s in climbing the banks; and they were nothing like so fast downhill. Their stay on the Bournemouth expresses was, however, relatively short and in the autumn of 1925 they were replaced by the 'King Arthurs'.

The 'N15' class, of which twenty were built by the London & South Western Railway, have a special place in ocomotive history. There is no doubt that Robert Urie was very proud of these engines and put a great deal of care and thought into their design. They were the outcome of the long process of engineering development on the London & South Western Railway that had commenced when Drummond and the Scottish contingent took over at Nine Elms. Urie had been responsible for the construction of the Drummond engines and had had to live with them during their many vicissitudes. He could not have been other than conscious of their undoubted weak points, and equally conscious of their many admirable features. He took the tradition of massive frame construction and first-class boiler making, and combined it with an 'engine' that was simple to the last degree. The result was a very sturdy free-running machine: a shedmaster's dream so far as reliability and low maintenance cost were concerned, yet one that could be ordinary to mediocre in its thermodynamic performance on the road.

Many records exist of the working performance of these locomotives in their original condition, and one could say that the results at best were respectable, and at their worst, very poor. The trouble with them lay almost entirely in the steaming. The draughting arrangements do not appear to have been very effective, so that with anything but the most expert firing and careful nursing, engines were inclined to run short of steam on the long and very gradual climb out to Oakley on the West of England road. One could often witness runs on which drivers ran for many miles completely without steam on the favourable gradients towards Andover, while attempts were being made to rally the boiler. At their best, the 'N15's could rarely rise to the heights of performance normally put up by the Drummond 'T14' class which Urie had fitted with superheaters. These latter engines, when capably handled, were the fastest and most effective express passenger engines on the London & South Western Railway in the last years of its existence. Naturally, however, they were relegated to second place in favour of Urie's own 'N15' class, even though the performance of the latter was often unsatisfactory.

CHAPTER FOUR

ASHFORD AND THE NEW PROTOTYPES

From the South Eastern & Chatham Railway, the Southern inherited four thoroughly reliable types of locomotive that had been produced in the period between the working union of the South Eastern and the London Chatham & Dover Railway and the time when R. E. L. Maunsell was appointed chief mechanical engineer of the SE & CR. These types were as follows:

Class of Service	Wheel Arrangement	Classification	No of engine in class
Express passenger	4–4–0	D	50
Goods and mixed traffic	0–6–0	C	108
Suburban and Branch passenger	0–4–4T	H	64
Express passenger	4–4–0	E	26

All these locomotives were built to the massive standards developed at Ashford under James Stirling, but incorporated the artistry in design that came from Robert Surtees, who had been chief draughtsman at Longhedge and had brought a pleasing blend of Chatham tradition to Ashford. None of these classes was outstanding in its thermodynamic efficiency. They were adequate for the job; but because of their excellence in detailed mechanical design and the robustness of their working parts they were light in maintenance costs and gave little trouble in service. All four classes could, when required, stand up to hard and continuous thrashing without sustaining any harm or trouble from overheated bearings.

During the First World War the locomotives in all these classes had been stripped of their original finery, whereas, when first produced, they were among the most brilliantly ornate locomotives running in Great Britain. Their turn-out had included a profusion of colour, intermingled with much polished brass and copper work; in striking contrast to their wartime guise when they were painted a dull greenish-grey, without any lining, and all their polished parts were suppressed. While austerity of turn-out had been adopted by many British railways during the war of 1914–18, most of them were reintroducing their old lining and colours by 1920 or soon after. This brightening-up did not, however, take place on the South Eastern & Chatham and, at the time of grouping, this once-decorative stud of locomotives was probably the most dowdy in all Britain.

The locomotive, carriage and wagon superintendent who had served the managing committee of the SE & CR from the time of the union until 1913 was Harry S. Wainwright, an engineer who had previously been entirely a carriage man. It was he, undoubtedly, who brought the artistry into the external design of the new locomotives, while their mechanical excellence could be attributed jointly to Surtees and the Ashford Works staff. Wainwright, however, was not a strong personality, and affairs within the locomotive department at Ashford had drifted into a rather unsatisfactory state. No one of sufficient ability or strength of character was coming forward in the department, and the directors were more or less forced to look outside for a successor to Wainwright when his retirement drew near. The choice fell upon R. E. L. Maunsell, who was then locomotive, carriage and wagon superintendent of the Great Southern & Western Railway in Ireland. An Irishman by birth, and a graduate of Dublin University, Maunsell had, in the course of his early career, spent a valuable period in the services of the Lancashire & Yorkshire Railway before returning to Ireland as works manager at Inchicore on the GS & WR, and then as locomotive superintendent. He had already shown himself a man of great drive and ability, a strict disciplinarian and a very shrewd judge of men. This latter quality was to prove of the greatest importance to the South Eastern & Chatham Railway, and eventually to the Southern.

On taking up his new appointment at Ashford in 1913, he found designs prepared for a superheater 4–4–0 locomotive, in which the proportions were generally larger than anything then running on the South Eastern & Chatham Railway. This design was the work of Surtees; but although it did represent a considerable enlargement, it was still nothing like so large as the locomotive department would have desired. During Wainwright's time, two proposals had been put forward for a design of a 4–6–0 passenger engine, and both had been vetoed on account of weight by the civil engineer. Some experiments had been made towards enhanced express passenger motive power by fitting two of the 'E' class 4–4–0s with superheaters. These two engines, Nos 36 and 275, were extremely successful, and the new design that Maunsell found on the drawing-boards at Ashford in 1913 was largely a development of the superheater 'E', with a somewhat larger boiler.

Subject to certain small modifications to the valve gear, over which Maunsell consulted his former chief draughtsman at Inchicore, the design was accepted and consideration given to getting a number of the engines constructed quickly. The need was urgent, because important developments in the holiday train services were planned for the summer of 1914. At the time, however, the British locomotive-building industry was exceptionally busy; and the work could not be undertaken at Ashford because Maunsell had already begun the re-organization of manufacturing facilities there. So the unprecedented step was taken by the directors of the SE & CR of placing an order for ten of these locomotives with the German firm of A. Borsig, of Berlin. An order for a further batch was placed with Beyer, Peacock & Co. The Borsig engines were delivered in parts and erected at Ashford only a very short time before the outbreak of war; and to within a few weeks of the momentous August Bank Holiday weekend of 1914, Borsig's men were at work in the Ashford shops, putting the finishing touches to these locomotives. Ironically, it transpired that some of their earliest work was in hauling troop-trains and other specials in connexion with the war against Germany. The 'L' class, as they were known, were very good engines by all the well-established standards of the SE & CR: but, equally, they lacked those finer points in performance that can yield a really high standard of thermodynamic efficiency.

At the time of Maunsell's appointment as chief mechanical engineer, the directors of the South Eastern & Chatham Railway made an important change in organization which relieved the locomotive department of some of its previous authority. Following to some extent the Midland example, they created an independent locomotive running department: A. D. Jones from the Lancashire & Yorkshire Railway was appointed as superintendent and the headquarters of the new department was made at London Bridge. Thus Maunsell's title of 'chief mechanical engineer', as distinct from that of Wainwright his predecessor, 'locomotive, carriage and wagon superintendent', was a logical one. The position of the locomotive running superintendent on the South Eastern & Chatham Railway – and indeed throughout Maunsell's chieftainship on the Southern – differed from that of his counterpart on the Midland, and later from those on the LMSR, in that it was partly an independent command, responsible only to the general manager for administration, though to the chief mechanical engineer for locomotive maintenance and to the traffic manager for operation.

In 1913 and for a few years subsequently, Maunsell certainly had enough to absorb his energies, quite apart from the responsibility of running. Within six months of his arrival at Ashford he had made an exceedingly clean sweep, and had gathered around him a new team of young and able engineers, who served not merely the South Eastern & Chatham, but became the backbone of the enlarged CME's department when amalgamation took place in 1923. Almost the whole success of Southern Railway locomotive practice up to 1937 can be traced back to this momentous re-organization at Ashford in the early months of 1914. In the British locomotive world, the altogether outstanding event of the previous ten or twelve years had been the establishment

of the famous eight, new, standard designs on the Great
Western Railway, accompanied by advances in principle
and detail which set and maintained that company in the
forefront of British practice for more than thirty years. By
1911 the last of the new standard designs was completed
and, with a slackening of pressure on the 'new work' side
at Swindon, some of those who had been closely concerned
with important developments were looking for fresh
opportunities of a 'new work' character elsewhere.

Maunsell seems to have realized earlier than most other
British engineers the extreme importance of Churchward's
work, and there was a strong Great Western flavour about
the new team he recruited. First and foremost came G. H.
Pearson, carriage works manager at Swindon and formerly
assistant locomotive works manager, to be assistant chief
mechanical engineer, and works manager at Ashford; as
assistant to him, C. J. Hicks from Inchicore was appointed.
Surtees was due for retirement, and James Clayton was
selected to succeed him as chief locomotive draughtsman;
an appointment of particular interest and importance. After
serving his time with Beyer, Peacock & Co, Ltd, Clayton,
when a young man of twenty, had joined the SE & CR as
a draughtsman under Surtees, but had left in 1903, in search
of experience and advancement. Soon afterwards he became
privately associated with Sir Cecil Paget in connexion with
the design of the celebrated experimental 2–6–2 locomotive,
No 2299. He joined the Midland Railway in 1905, and from
1907–14 was chief assistant in the locomotive drawing-
office at Derby.

Thus under Maunsell's leadership there were brought
together two locomotive engineers, not merely able in themselves but who had severally been associated with the two
greatest railway engineering figures of the day: Pearson,
from his pioneer work under Churchward, and Clayton from
his intimate association with the dynamic, brilliant personality of Paget. To reinforce this distinguished opening
pair, Maunsell recruited the rest of his team almost exclusively from Swindon. L. Lynes was appointed chief

draughtsman of the carriage and wagon section: H. Holcroft, who caught the eye of Churchward early in his career and had taken part in the design of GWR locomotives, was appointed as an assistant, with the particular task of reorganizing and extending the entire works layout at Ashford. Finally, there was H. J. Tonkin, who was appointed cost accountant, and though his post may not seem particularly relevant to the present theme, under Maunsell's direction it became an important, integral unit of the team. All new schemes were carefully estimated in their early stages, and the design-costing and actual production of all items were always closely coordinated.

The new staff had, however, scarcely been gathered at Ashford before war was declared in August 1914, and all schemes for new locomotives and new works had soon to be shelved. The South Eastern & Chatham, together with all other British railways, was taken over by the Government, and the Railway Executive Committee was brought into being to coordinate the work of the numerous independent companies. Maunsell was appointed chief mechanical engineer to the REC, and one of his first tasks was, strange to say, the rehabilitation of Belgian rolling-stock which had been evacuated in the face of the German advance; by that time it was ensconced behind the Allied line in France, but immobilized by lack of stores and spare parts. Ashford was made the depot for manufacturing parts for these Belgian locomotives, and as no drawings were available they had to be made from actual samples. The work, being of extreme urgency, was given priority over any new developments Maunsell and his staff had in mind.

Provision of spare parts for the Belgian engines was only a part of the war work at Ashford, and Maunsell, as CME to the Railway Executive Committee, had the task of supplying the Railway Operating Division, and the military railways in France and other theatres of war, with a multiplicity of stores. All this involved sending out inquiries, placing orders, inspection and so on, the responsibility for which at first fell mostly upon Clayton. Later, as the prospects of extending Ashford Works receded, Holcroft was brought in to relieve Clayton, and when the work became thoroughly organized it was possible to devote some time to new locomotive designs. So, despite the stress of wartime conditions, an excellent prototype was gradually evolved.

There is a striking parallel here between Maunsell's early work at Ashford and Gresley's at Doncaster. It was during the same years of national effort and anxiety that the 'N' class 2–6–0 took shape at Ashford, while the first three-cylinder locomotive with conjugated valve gear was under construction for the Great Northern. Although both designs underwent changes, and in the Doncaster case the changes were far-reaching and significant, the underlying ideas remained and provided the Southern and London & North Eastern Railways with the fundamental bases of their standard practice for many years to come.

The first really new designs for which Maunsell was responsible on the South Eastern & Chatham Railway were the 'N' class 2–6–0 goods and the 'K' class 2–6–4 passenger tank. During the 1914–18 War, occupation of the line became as important as we have known it in more recent times, and the demands of that period served to accentuate a need which had been growing on the SE & CR for some time. Freight traffic tended to be concentrated at Ashford on the one hand, and Hither Green on the other, and heavy 'block' loads were worked between these two points. Intermediately, remarshalling took place only at Paddock Wood. The relative severity of the gradients between Hither Green and Tonbridge called for some reduction in the maximum rostered load below the tonnage that could be worked over the easy line through the Weald of Kent, but in order to reduce occupation of the line as much as possible it was desirable to operate heavy trains, and to run them non-stop over the 21·3 miles from Paddock Wood to Ashford.

The 'N' class 2–6–0 engine was designed primarily to meet this demand; but with the 'general utility' attributes of the 2–6–0 type in mind, and its success in this respect on the Great Western, London Brighton & South Coast and

Great Northern railways already evident, the 'N' class was designed to be suitable for working passenger trains, heavy seaside excursions, Tattenham Corner race specials, and so on. The broad principles of the design – taper boiler, high working pressure, top feed, long-lap valves – were almost pure Great Western; but in Clayton's working out of the detailed design many features of Midland practice were incorporated, such as the large diameter smokebox, the shape of the chimney, and of the cab and tender. The arrangement of the top feed differed, however, from that of the Great Western. What appeared to be a dome on the boiler was actually a casing for the trays of the top-feed system; the trays were helical in form, and the whole affair rapidly became known at Ashford as the 'helter-skelter lighthouse'. After its incorporation on the first of the 2–6–0s, this arrangement was tried out on one of the 'B' class Stirling 4–4–0s, No 13.

In view of the Great Western flavour in the 'N' class engine, due to Pearon's influence, it is interesting to compare the leading dimensions of the class with those of Churchward's '43XX' class 2–6–0s. The Belpaire firebox had the top and sides slanting downwards and inwards towards the back plate; the regulator was in the smokebox, though an important difference lay in the adoption of Walshaerts gear arranged outside. At the time the prototype engine No 810 was completed at Ashford, in the summer of 1917, details were published of the motion, but little significance was then attached to the length of the valve travel, $6\frac{7}{16}$ ins. In actual fact, No 810 and the companion 2–6–4 tank engine, No 790, proved to be the most outstanding locomotives built for service in this country since the pioneer work of Churchward in 1903–7. Their rather gaunt lines and austere finish were, however, unlikely to appeal to those whose minds dwelt upon the ornate creations of the pre-1914 era.

The Maunsell superheater was first introduced on No 810, wherein the regulator was incorporated in the superheater header. The layout of the elements was a clever piece of designing in which any element could be detached from the header and withdrawn without interference with any other element. This facility is, of course, provided for in the standard Swindon superheater, but only with two tiers of elements. On the SE & CR engine, No 810, there were three tiers. At first, the heating surface of the superheater was kept small in conformity with Great Western practice, but in later engines of the class the elements were extended to almost the full length of the flues and the heating surface was increased from 203 to 285 sq ft.

No 810 was very thoroughly tested on the road. Numerous indicator diagrams were taken, and on SE & CR freight duties these showed excellent characteristics. Optimum power output was attained at a little over 50 mph, when working at 25 per cent cut-off; then the indicated horsepower was approximately 1,000. At this stage it should be mentioned that fifteen engines of the class were constructed at Ashford by the SE & CR between 1920 and 1922, and bore the running numbers 811 to 825; of these, No 822 was built with three cylinders and conjugated valve gear. More detailed reference to this latter engine will be made in a later chapter.

The period following the armistice of November 1918, was one of uncertainty, both in the railway world and in the country at large. The Government of the day, to avoid large-scale unemployment at Woolwich Arsenal, decided to build locomotives for the home railways, on which serious shortages had developed during the war. Even then, the prospect of nationalization was in the air and the Association of Railway Locomotive Engineers had been asked to see what could be done towards the production of new standard designs. Nothing tangible in the way of finished designs came from their deliberations though, as will be told later, this phase was an important one for Maunsell and his assistants. But to enable the Government building programme to be started, Maunsell's 'N' class was selected as a standard, and a first order for 100 placed. When the outcome of long negotiation came to be grouping and not nationalization, no one of the four groups made any bid to purchase the

Upper: On the Brighton main line near Purley: a down express, hauled by a 'B2X' 4-4-0 No 203, overtaking a goods hauled by one of the 'Vulcan' 0-6-0s

Lower: An SE and CR Reading train via Redhill on the Brighton main line near Purley, hauled by a rebuilt Stirling 4-4-0 No 94

Upper: LB and SCR up morning business express leaving Bognor, hauled by 'B2X' class 4-4-0 No 321

Lower: SE and CR through morning express for Cannon Street leaving Bexhill with 'L' class 4-4-0 No 776

Upper: L and SWR. One of the Drummond 'T14' class 4-cylinder 4-6-0s (paddleboats) in original condition on up Bournemouth express

Lower: Continental boat express in Folkestone Warren, hauled by 'King Arthur' class 4-6-0 No 771, *Sir Sagramore*

Top: An original Urie 'S15' class engine (ex-LSWR) as BR No 30506
Centre: A Maunsell 'S15' class mixed traffic 4-6-0 No 833
Bottom: L and SWR Urie 4-6-2 tank engine No 519

The celebrated Brighton war memorial 4-6-4 tank engine No 333 *Remembrance* in Southern livery, outside Victoria

The 3-cylinder member of the Maunsell 'K' class of 2-6-4 tank No 890 *River Frome*, classified 'K1'

Upper: Hastings–Ashford stopping train leaving Rye: engine 'D' class 4-4-0 No 1738

Lower: Brighton express near Coulsdon, hauled by Marsh Atlantic locomotive No 41

Upper: A rebuilt Stirling 'B' class 4-4-0, No 1443, and a 'T9' 4-4-0 No 30708 alongside at Reading sheds, shortly after nationalization

Lower: A 'Schools' class 4-4-0 No 934 *St Lawrence*

Upper: London Bridge–Tunbridge Wells (via Oxted) train near Woldingham. Engine ex-LBSC 4-4-2 tank No 2078, class '13'

Lower: Lewes–Victoria stopping train near Woldingham. Engine: ex-LBSC 4-6-2 tank No 2325 (formerly *Abergavenny*)

Government-built engines, and work came to a standstill after fifty had been erected. Eventually, these were purchased at a reduced price by the Southern Railway.

Never before had locomotives been built at Woolwich Arsenal, and it was only natural that lack of experience landed the engines in trouble when they first took the road. Furthermore, these fifty engines were drafted, not to the SE & C section, where the design was well known, but to the West of England, for working over such heavily-graded lines as that from Exeter to Plymouth, and from Barnstaple to Ilfracombe. These new engines were, however, maintained at Ashford, and after their first general repairs they partook of the characteristic performance common to the Ashford-built engines. The 'Woolworths', as they became known by the staff, were numbered 826–876. Although it is going somewhat beyond South Eastern & Chatham history, the account may now be concluded by reference to some of the excellent work done west of Salisbury by these engines, on both passenger and goods trains.

A diagram in my possession shows the working of one of the Woolwich engines, No 851, on an express passenger train, as between Salisbury and Yeovil Junction. The steaming of the engine, on Welsh coal, does not appear to have been so consistent as on SE & CR duties, but the unfamiliarity of the crew with the type must be taken into account. At about the same time some interesting trials were conducted with No 837 between Exeter and Ilfracombe, to enable the traffic and locomotive running departments to agree timings and loads, particularly over the exceptionally severe inclines between Braunton and Ilfracombe. Four runs in all were made, on each of which the load consisted of seven bogie coaches, a tare weight of 204 tons. On the first outward trip, the test train ran through Braunton without stopping, at about 50 mph, but then no less than 23 minutes were taken to climb the $5\frac{3}{4}$ miles to a stop at Mortehoe. The train very nearly stalled. On the following day, however, from a standing start at Braunton, the bank was climbed in $21\frac{3}{4}$ minutes, with speed steadily maintained at 12 mph on the 1 in 40, until reaching the final curved stretch, where some falling off nearly always occurs.

In the reverse direction, the $3\frac{1}{4}$ miles from Ilfracombe to Mortehoe were climbed in $16\frac{3}{4}$ minutes on the first trip; on the second the going was much better with a time of $14\frac{3}{4}$ minutes. To achieve it, however, the engine had to be driven practically all-out; the cut-off was 60 per cent at first, increased to 63 and finally to 66 per cent while on the 1 in 36, to counteract some falling off in the pressure. Approaching Mortehoe, water level was down by $4\frac{1}{2}$ inches, and both ejectors were put on for a brief spell. At Barnstaple Junction, the test load was made up of 292 tons tare, and it was intended to make a non-stop run to Exeter St David's, $39\cdot1$ miles. Actually, inclusive of a signal stop for one minute at South Molton Road, the $37\cdot8$ miles to Cowley Bridge Junction were covered in $58\frac{1}{4}$ minutes, but the train had to wait some little time outside St David's Station. From the grading point of view the route from Barnstaple is not difficult; but the section of single line, from Umberleigh to Copplestone, $18\cdot6$ miles, with severe slacks for tablet exchanging at seven stations, precludes anything in the way of fast overall times.

With the production of the 'K' class 2–6–4 tank engine, No 790, the SE & CR had the prototype for a potentially successful fast passenger type with a tractive effort considerably higher than that of the 4–4–0 tender engines then working on the system; but due to a variety of circumstances no further engines of 'K' class were built until after grouping. The end of the war in 1918, and the desire to restore regular passenger services to the Continent via Dover and Folkestone, brought a locomotive problem of some urgency. With intensification of suburban services at Charing Cross and Cannon Street in view, together with electrification, it was decided that all Continental boat-train traffic should in future be worked from Victoria. The connexions between the former SER and LC & D lines at Chislehurst already provided a number of alternative routes to Dover, including those via Maidstone and Ashford, and via Chatham, Faversham and Canterbury, and these were available when, owing to late arrival of the steamers, the regular parths via Ashford and Tonbridge had been missed.

A study of a map shows clearly the elaborate system of routes that are available. The principal one passes through Herne Hill, Knockholt and Tonbridge, though the Catford loop line is often used for relief trains in the outward direction. For inward-bound trains, the alternative route via Maidstone is often followed, while at times of very heavy outward traffic I have known second and third portions of the regular trains to be worked via Chatham and Canterbury. The operating arrangements were very carefully worked out to avoid delay and congestion to ordinary traffic in the event of late arrivals of the cross-Channel steamers. An up boat train running no more than ten minutes late on the main line via Tonbridge might well cause a good deal of dislocation; and so for every scheduled departure time from Dover, or Folkestone, provisional paths were laid down covering every amount of late running. No special arrangements had to be made for each case; an up boat train takes the first provisional path available from the time it is ready to start. To fit in with other traffic, some of these bookings necessarily involve slower running, quite apart from that involved in any case over the heavy gradients of the Maidstone route, or in the ascent of Sole Street bank in case of a diversion via Canterbury and Chatham. From the viewpoint of locomotive performance, however, the main interest centres upon the working of the regular down boat expresses, and especially the popular 11 AM from Victoria – the service that eventually developed into the world-famous 'Golden Arrow'.

The exclusive use of Victoria as the boat-train terminus, however, meant that all such trains had to pass over the former LC & D line at some stage in their journey, and from this line the most powerful passenger engines, the 'L' class 4–4–0s, were prohibited on account of their weight. The heaviest engines permitted over any of the Chatham lines were the Wainwright 'E' class 4–4–0s. The normal formation of the post-war boat trains was to be 300 tons tare, and this was definitely beyond the capacity of the class 'E' engines; 250 tons was about their limit on the timings laid down. The two superheated 'E's, 36 and 275, could have tackled 300-ton trains, but they also were too heavy, having a maximum axle load of 18 tons 10 cwt, against the 17 tons 12 cwt of the non-superheater 'E' class. The civil engineer had already envisaged a comprehensive programme of bridge strengthening and track renewal which would permit the running of much heavier engines; but this work could not be completed for some years. In the meantime, the operating department was naturally averse to the regular double-heading which would have been necessary if reliance had been placed on existing types, and so Maunsell set about the difficult task of producing an engine of 'L' class capacity, but weighing no more than a non-superheated 'E'. He had to effect a weight reduction of at least 9 per cent on that of the 'L' class engines.

The problem was solved by an ingenious rebuilding of the 'E' class engine No 179. It was truly a rebuild. Some engines nowadays termed rebuilds retain little more than the frames and wheel centres of the original locomotives; but in No 179 the boiler barrel and dome were used, and most of the 'E' class motion. The new design was built up as a blend of 'N' class and 'E' class practice, with the eminently practical result that no additional stocks of spare parts were required at the running sheds, since everything was interchangeable either with 'E' or 'N' class standards. In planning the work, Clayton's earlier experience of the rebuilding of Midland 4-4-0s at Derby was of some importance, and certainly the work was quickly and cheaply done. The basic principles of the new design were very simple, namely, to provide a larger grate and greater capacity for burning coal, high-degree superheat, and to replace the original slide-valves by large diameter piston-valves having ample port openings and longer laps. This formula for a fast and successful engine sounds familiar enough today, but its significance was hardly appreciated, if at all, in 1919; that is, outside Swindon and Ashford.

The new cylinders had the same diameter and stroke as the old ones, 19 ins by 26 ins, and so the nominal tractive effort of the engine was unchanged; but with 10-in diameter piston-valves and the advantages of the modified motion those cylinders had such a capacity for taking steam, and using it effectively, that care had to be taken not to work beyond the capacity of the boiler. At 25 per cent cut-off the port opening to steam was no less than 0·5 ins against the 0·33 ins at the same cut-off on the Great Western two-cylinder 4–6–0s. The increased firegrate area, in combination with relatively short flue-tubes, made the boilers very free in steaming, however, and at the same time steam temperatures after passing through the superheater ranged between 650 and 700 degrees Fahrenheit. The superheater, smokebox regulator, collector pipes, boiler mountings and firebox stays were of the same type as used on the 'N' class, and the 'helter-skelter lighthouse' was accommodated in the original dome. The chassis was stripped of all superfluous weight; the coupled wheel splashers were narrowed to the minimum width; the heavy toolboxes in the cab were removed, and the cast-iron dragbox was replaced by a fabricated steel one. The engineman had been accustomed to use the wooden lids of the toolboxes as seats, and to compensate them for this loss Maunsell provided tip-up seats for both driver and fireman, as on the 'N' class 2–6–0s.

In external appearance the modified 179 had more than a passing likeness to the Midland Class '2' superheater rebuilds, not only in the cut-away running plate and the shape of the cab, but in many constructional details, where Clayton had followed Midland practice. The chimney, as on the 2–6–0 and 2–6–4 tank engines, looked like a shortened version of the later Derby pattern, and anticipated by some seven years the appearance of the true Midland short chimneys, which became so familiar on the later compounds and standard class '4' goods engines. No 179 was rebuilt at Ashford, and completed in April 1919. At first, she was painted black instead of the wartime grey but when, after successful trials, it was decided to convert more of the 'E' class and ten were sent to Beyer, Peacock & Co in 1920, the grey painting was retained. Comparative dimensions of the class 'E' engines before and after rebuilding are given in the accompanying Table 5.

TABLE 5

	Class 'E'	Class 'E1'
Cylinders:		
Diameter	19 ins	19 ins
Stroke	26 ins	26 ins
Valves	Slide	10-in dia. piston
Heating Surface:		
Tubes	1,396 sq ft	322·25 sq ft (large tubes) 827·6 sq ft (small tubes)
Firebox	136 sq ft	127·13 sq ft
Superheater	nil	228 sq ft
Total	1,532 sq ft	1,504·98 sq ft
Grate Area	21·15 sq ft	24 sq ft
Boiler Pressure:	180 lb per sq in	180 lb per sq in
Weights (in working order)		
On Bogie	17 tons 7 cwt	19 tons 0 cwt
On Drivers	17 tons 12 cwt	17 tons 10 cwt
On Trailing Coupled	17 tons 6 cwt	16 tons 0 cwt
Total Engine	52 tons 5 cwt	52 tons 10 cwt

At various times when locomotives having a long valve travel in full gear were introduced, many engineers feared that the increased travel would result in excessive wear. In service, however, such engines are run with the motions well linked up, and the actual valve travel at, say 60 mph, will be little if at all greater than that of an engine with the old conventional valve motion on which drivers often kept the cut-off at 35 per cent, or more, throughout the trip. The 'E1' class were usually run at about 25 per cent though they could be pulled up to about 18 per cent before they began to 'kick'. The valve travel in full gear was $6\frac{1}{2}$ ins; the steam lap was $1\frac{5}{8}$ ins and the exhaust clearance $\frac{1}{8}$ in. In working the 300-ton boat expresses they were an outstanding success,

once the men had got used to the long sloping firegrate.
They had to be fired just as one sees on large modern 4–6–0s
and 'Pacifics', with a thick fire in the back corners and under
the door, gradually tapering to a relatively thin layer under
the arch. They needed close attention throughout the run,
for the natural vibration of the engine tended to shake the
fire down, and care had to be taken to maintain the ideal
formation.

Coming to their work on the road, I have before me details
of thirty-six runs on down Continental boat expresses with
tare loads varying between 288 and 301 tons, in which every
one of the ten Beyer, Peacock rebuilds is represented. The
timing for the 78 miles from Victoria to Dover Marine was
at first 103, and then 100 minutes; the quickening was
effected entirely by the resumption of normal-speed running
through the Folkestone Warren when the line had fully
consolidated after re-alignment following the great landslip
of December 1915. These trains were allowed 46 minutes,
pass-to-pass, for the 41·4 miles from Tonbridge (passed at
20 mph) to Folkestone Junction, and on one occasion this
was cut to 41¾ minutes in recovering time lost by delays
earlier in the run. On the earlier journeys, in November and
December 1921, small amounts of time up to three minutes
were lost on the complete run from London to Dover through
steaming troubles developing, but after mid-December 1921
there is in this comprehensive series of recordings no instance of time lost due to engines. On two notable occasions
the 70-minute allowance for the 59·5 miles from Bickley
Junction to Folkestone Junction was cut to 65½ and 65
minutes by engines Nos 497 and 19 respectively, the latter
including a signal check at Knockholt which cost about 1½
minutes in running. Having regard to the severe nature of
the road between Bickley Junction and Knockholt, and to
the heavy slack through Tonbridge, these were remarkable
runs with trainloads of 300 tons. On another occasion No 511
took a similar load over the old Chatham route to Dover,
covering 78·4 very difficult miles in 107½ minutes. The work
throughout was extraordinarily good, especially that

between Faversham and Dover, over long adverse gradients of 1 in 100, with the severe speed restriction through Canterbury and the need for reduced speed on the final descent towards Dover.

TABLE 6

'E1' CLASS ENGINES ON DOWN BOAT TRAINS
VICTORIA–DOVER MARINE: 78 MILES

Date	Engine No.	Load Tons tare	Actual time min	Remarks
24/11/21	511	294	102¼	
29/11/21	19	294	105½	Engine not steaming well
30/11/21	67	294	105½	Brakes dragging
1/12/21	511	294	106	Engine not steaming well
5/12/21	511	294	100¼	
6/12/21	19	294	99¾	Signal check at Knockholt
9/12/21	19	294	102½	
16/12/21	507	294	102	Signal check at Sydenham
6/2/22	511	296	101	
9/2/22	163	294	102½	Signal check at Tonbridge
10/2/22	163	301	100½	
16/6/22	504	291	102	
30/8/22	507	291	106¼	P. W. Slack at Bickley. Engine not steaming well
16/4/23	506	300	101	Signal check at Beckenham. P. W. Slack at Paddock Wood
30/4/23	506	289	99¼	Signal checks at Knockholt, Dunton Green, and Tonbridge
10/8/23	497	289	99	Signal check at Brixton

In everyday running the 'E1' class engines were capable of sustaining continuously an output of 900 to 1,000 indicated horsepower at 60 mph and contemporary records suggest that they ran equally well with a partly-opened regulator and cut-off of 25 to 30 per cent as with full regulator and early cut-off. Summarized details of some boat-train runs of 1921–3 are given in the accompanying Table 6. These runs are selected as typical from the much larger collection previously referred to and, while they show generally close adherence to booked time, there was not a great deal of margin with the full 300-ton load. On the run of December 6th, 1921, engine No 19 was developing about 950 indicated horsepower for 42 minutes on end between Paddock Wood and Sandling Junction. Although this was probably an exceptional effort the power output demanded by the boat-train workings was really high in relation to the size and nominal tractive effort of the engines. Details of this fine effort by engine No 19 show that the cut-off was 30 per cent throughout, and that the regulator was half open.

The average speed during this spell was 59 mph. The boiler pressure had been steadily maintained at 175 lb per sq in until the summit point near Chart was passed; there, as the water level had dropped a little, the second injector was put on for a short time, and with the regulator closed for a brief period following an adverse distant signal, the water level was quickly raised. After Smeeth, matters were comfortably in hand, and the firing relaxed. This was an extremely fine piece of running. The log of this run, as compiled by Mr Holcroft, is tabulated overleaf, alongside another fine run on the same train with engine No 497 (Table 7).

The eleven engines of class 'E1' were all stationed at Battersea and worked mostly on the boat trains. Their success led to consideration of further rebuilding to improve the motive-power situation on the Kent Coast line. There were thirteen non-superheated engines remaining, but these were in excellent condition and doing good work with lighter trains, and it was felt that it would be more advantageous to rebuild some of the 'D' class engines, which were older than the 'E's, as a greater advantage in power could be obtained by converting 'D' class engines to 'D1', than by rebuilding 'E' to 'E1'. Accordingly, ten of the 'D' class were dispatched to Beyer, Peacock & Co in 1921 for rebuilding on the same lines as the 'E1' class. These engines differed from the 'E' class in having coupled wheels of 6 ft 8 in diameter against 6 ft 6 ins, and this made the tractive effort of the 'D1' class, as the rebuilds were known, slightly less than that of the 'E1's. Top feed was not used on the 'D1's

TABLE 7
SE & CR VICTORIA–DOVER MARINE
11 AM Continental Boat Express

	Date		*6/12/21*		*18/8/23*	
	Engine No		*19*		*497*	
	Load, tons tare		*294*		*289*	
Distance miles		*Sch. min*	*Actual Speeds* min*	*mph*	*Actual Speeds* min*	*mph*
0·0	VICTORIA	0	0		0	
—					p.w.s.	
3·2	Brixton	7½	7¾	24·7	7¾	24·7
—		—	sigs		sigs	
4·0	Herne Hill	8½	9	38·4	9½	27·4
—			sigs			
8·7	Beckenham Junction	16½	19¾	29·1	18½	31·3
12·6	Bickley Junction	22½	26	37·4	24	42·6
13·4	Orpington Junction	24½	27¼	38·4	25¼	38·4
14·9	Orpington	27½	29¾	38·4	27¾	38·4
—			sigs	—		—
17·8	Knockholt	31½	34½	35·5	32	39·5
23·2	Sevenoaks	38½	41½	47·2	38¼	52·8
30·6	TONBRIDGE	46½	49¼	58·1	46	58·1
35·9	Paddock Wood	53	55¼	53·0	52¼	50·9
46·3	Headcorn	63	64¾	65·7	61¾	65·7
57·2	ASHFORD	75	75½	60·3	72¾	58·9
66·5	Sandling Junction	86½	85¾	55·0	84	50·1
72·0	Folkestone Junction	92½	91	62·9	89½	60·0
78·0	DOVER MARINE	100	99¾	—	99	—

* Average speeds.

and the regulator was kept in the dome. In actual work on the road, there was little or nothing to distinguish the performance of the 'D' and 'E' engines, and eleven more were rebuilt at Ashford Works – two in 1923, one in 1926 and eight in 1927. This rebuilding provided a stud of efficient modern engines which could be used at will anywhere on the old SE & CR system, and which put up some very fine running with the seaside expresses from Victoria to Margate and Ramsgate.

Reference has already been made to the bridge-strengthening programme undertaken by the civil engineer. As this proceeded, successive relaxations on loading limits were made on certain routes though, generally speaking, these were of most immediate importance to the locomotive running superintendent. One such relaxation, however, led to a small though significant change on the 'D1' and 'E1' engines, and it came about in a rather roundabout way. One day in October 1923, the engine of the 11 AM down Continental boat express failed with a broken crank-axle at Westenhanger. When the engine was towed into Ashford it was found that she was not an 'E1', but one of the superheater 'E's, No 275. Interest was naturally aroused as to what 275 was doing on the boat train at all, and inquiries elicited the news that weight restrictions on the line between Bickley and Victoria had been relaxed sufficiently to permit 36 and 275 being used, and that the running superintendent had been quick to take the opportunity of increasing his stud of boat-train engines.

The 'E1' class was then reconsidered in the light of this relaxation and Maunsell put forward a proposal to increase the adhesion weight on the rear pair of coupled wheels by approximately one ton. This was accepted by the civil engineer and the change was made by reinstating the old cast-iron dragbox of the Wainwright 'E' class, instead of the fabricated one used as a weight-saving device on the 'E1's as originally built. The replacement was carried out on all engines of classes 'D1' and 'E1' as they passed through the shops for general repairs. While on the subject of weight relaxations, I may add that the civil engineer announced that he would be prepared to accept 'L' class 4-4-0s on certain sections of the Chatham line from July 1924, subject to some special speed limits being observed but, in view of the supreme competence of the 'E1's, 'L' class engines were

never used on the boat trains, and, in any case, by the
summer of 1925, 'King Arthurs' were permitted to run on
the principal boat-train route from Victoria to Dover, via
Tonbridge. It was, however, some little time before the
4–6–0 engines could be used on the alternative routes via
Maidstone or Faversham, and, in the summer particularly,
the 'E1's continued to do great work. These little engines
indeed rank among Maunsell's most brilliant successes.

CHAPTER FIVE

CONSOLIDATION INTO THE SOUTHERN

During the first fifteen years of the Southern Railway the locomotive policy followed a straightforward and efficient, if not a very exciting course. This policy was the natural outcome of the higher strategy of Southern Railway development, laid down by Sir Herbert Walker and carried out in a process of steady and continuous evolution. Walker's plan was for the electrification of the entire Southern Railway network east of Portsmouth, and within such an over-riding policy the opportunities for any spectacular development of steam power were slight, to say the least of it. As general manager of the London & South Western Railway, Walker had shown himself a master in the handling of great schemes of development, and the inauguration of the first stages of the London & South Western suburban electrified system during the First World War was an outstanding example of far-sighted planning. The 'Riverside Electric', as it was then called, could be considered no more than a pilot scheme to a broader plan of electrification; but it was essentially right from the very inception, and the principles involved formed the basis for all subsequent electrification work on the Southern Railway and later still on the Southern Region of British Railways.

Again, Walker, a past-master of management, enabled vast schemes to be put through in the most economic manner. When he took up his appointment on the London & South Western Railway in 1912, the great project for the complete rebuilding of Waterloo Station was well under way, and several of the new platforms were already in commission. But by a re-examination of that part of the work which remained to be done, and utilization of the structure of the former Windsor line station, Walker was able to effect a very considerable reduction in the cost of the work as a whole. When he became general manager of the Southern Railway, in January 1923, his mandate to the locomotive department was one of economy, so far as steam-locomotive running and maintenance were concerned. With electrification in view, no large-scale replacement of locomotive stock was contemplated and, with existing services being efficiently run, there was every inducement to continue with the locomotive power already in commission.

In R. E. L. Maunsell, Walker had an ideal officer for carrying out such a policy. Maunsell was no imaginative or restless inventor; he was a solid, down-to-earth, practical railwayman, with a very human side to his character. In the fifteen years following the grouping he built up, and brought to a very high degree of efficiency, a department that might easily have become frustrated and lacking in interest through the evident managerial policy of avoiding anything in the way of capital investment on behalf of the steam locomotive stud. Most of the capital allocated to motive power came to be lavished on the equipment of the electrified lines. Steam running sheds had little or nothing spent on their equipment – let alone anything in the way of modernization; but, Maunsell's leadership, and the reliability of his locomotives, bred a remarkably fine tradition of engineship in the working of the trains. The high morale of the locomotive department was reflected in another way. In the years 1930 to 1937, when elsewhere in Great Britain there was a gradual decline in the smartness of turn-out in steam locomotives, the Southern excelled not only in the cleanliness of the top-line express locomotives, but of every passenger locomotive at all depots from Ramsgate and Dover in the east, to the smaller sheds in Devon and Cornwall. The depots may have been starved of capital for their maintenance and improvement but, to judge from the results, there was no lack of 'elbow grease' put into the cleaning of the engines.

So far as personnel were concerned, it was not surprising that Maunsell built up his enlarged team for the Southern Railway largely upon the men he had gathered around him at Ashford, following his appointment as chief mechanical engineer of the South Eastern & Chatham Railway. G. H. Pearson remained at Ashford and became assistant chief mechanical engineer of the Southern; Clayton remained personal assistant to the chief mechanical engineer, and was responsible for most of the new design work on steam locomotives, while Holcroft was also appointed an assistant to the chief mechanical engineer. It was realized that most of the larger new construction work would have to be done at Eastleigh Works, and to introduce a blend of South Eastern & Chatham practice there, Maunsell transferred some younger draughtsmen to work under the former London & South Western Railway's chief draughtsman, T. S. Finlayson.

Maunsell set up his own headquarters at Waterloo, where he established a small but expert central design staff to work out preliminary schemes for new locomotives and other projects. There, broad principles could be settled before ideas were passed on to the Eastleigh or Ashford drawing-offices for working out details of the design. The leading draughtsman chosen for this important task was W. G. Hooley, a former Ashford man. One notes, with whatever significance one cares to attach to it, that men of the former London, Brighton & South Coast Railway were almost completely absent from the leading positions in the new organization. This was naturally a matter of disappointment to a works with such great traditions as Brighton; but it so happened that grouping came at one of those stages in the history of all locomotive establishments when there is a pause in the continuity. Several of the railways amalgamated into the London, Midland & Scottish systems were caught in exactly the same way at the time of grouping, and their traditions were similarly submerged for some time. Even the London & South Western Railway, whose locomotive department had flourished so strongly under Robert Urie, came to play very much of a secondary part to the South Eastern & Chatham Railway.

Viewing the new set-up in retrospect, more than forty years after the event, it does seem that the ascendancy of

Ashford was a perfectly natural consequence of what had happened on the three railways in the preceding twenty years. The South Eastern & Chatham was the only one of the three on which the locomotive department had been steadily built up with an eye to the future; the other two were carrying on largely in the old traditions.

The grouping of the railways tended very soon to simplify the overall picture of locomotive development in Great Britain. Instead of a considerable number of companies, some large, some small, pursuing their own particular ideas in a rather parochial way, one had, in 1923, four large groups, each charged with a policy of coordination of practice to achieve economies in both operating and maintenance costs. And it is certainly not without significance that the mechanical-engineering management of the four new groups was in the hands of men who had been very closely associated with each other during the war years. After the end of the First World War there was much talk of railway nationalization. The very difficult conditions that had existed in the latter part of the war had led to the establishment, on a national basis, of certain wage structures in the railway industry. These had reflected the gradual increase in cost of living at the time, so far as the larger English railways were concerned; but they involved very substantial increases in basic wages for the less prosperous companies and particularly those of Scotland. Had the railways been released from Government control to their previous private ownerships without any other adjustments, the financial structures of the Scottish companies, and of certain others, would not have been able to support the new wage scales that were already in force in 1919. It was felt, therefore, that nationalization of the entire network was the only answer.

So far as locomotive engineering was concerned, the question began to arise of standard locomotive types, and the locomotive engineers of the numerous independent companies were asked to consider the formulation of standard designs, particularly as there was need to maintain employment in the heavy industries following the end of munition

production. The question of standard designs had been discussed within the Association of Railway Locomotive
Engineers, that rather exclusive professional club to which
only the chief engineers of each of the companies and their
immediate assistants belonged. Within the Association, four
railways took a leading part in the discussion towards new
standard designs, namely the Great Western, the Midland,
the Lancashire & Yorkshire and the Great Northern; these
four were represented, respectively, by Churchward, Sir
Henry Fowler, George Hughes and H. N. Gresley. In his
wartime capacity as chief mechanical engineer to the Railway Executive Committee, Maunsell was also very much
concerned in these discussions and when the time came
for ideas to be sketched out, it was Maunsell's personal
assistant, James Clayton, upon whom this work devolved.

In passing, it is perhaps a little strange that two such
powerful concerns as the London & North Western, and the
North Eastern railways took no active part. Be that as it
may, when the eventual legislation for the future of the
railways took the form of the grouping scheme under private
ownership, instead of nationalization, the new 'Big Four'
companies all had between them, as chief mechanical
engineers, men who had been actively engaged in the discussions of the new British standard designs. It is true that
Churchward had retired before grouping took place, but his
successor on the Great Western continued his policy without
the slightest deviation. For the rest, Hughes became chief
mechanical engineer of the LMSR, with Fowler as his deputy.
Gresley filled the same appointment with the LNER and
Maunsell with the Southern.

Through his association with Churchward during work on
the proposed British standard locomotive designs, James
Clayton had developed a very deep appreciation of Churchward's work on the Great Western Railway, and for him it
became the yardstick for future Southern Railway designs.
Thus, from the early 1920s onwards, Clayton's admiration
for Churchward, backed up by Pearson's earlier experience
at Swindon, brought a strong flavour of Great Western

practice into the future work of Maunsell's department. At
the time of the grouping, however, yet another outside
influence happened to be very prominent, and it arose
through Holcroft's earlier work at Swindon. In his drawing-
office days, Holcroft had worked out a conjugated valve
gear for operating the valve of the central cylinder in a three-
cylinder locomotive by a means of mechanism derived from
the motion of the two outside valve gears. This had greatly
interested Churchward, and on his instruction it was
patented; but he was too far committed to the policy of
standard two-cylinder and four-cylinder locomotives on the
Great Western Railway for any practical use to be made of
this invention.

Then, in 1918, H. N. Gresley on the Great Northern Railway produced his first three-cylinder locomotive, also with a
conjugated valve gear. This was a 2–8–0 heavy mineral
engine and the gear was a very elaborate adaptation of a
three-cylinder valve-gear mechanism that had previously
been used on the Prussian State Railway. The Great
Northern valve-gear mechanism came in for a good deal of
hostile criticism in the technical Press of the day, and one
critic was Holcroft himself, who referred to the very much
simpler mechanism he himself had invented when he was in
the Swindon drawing-office. The correspondence in the
technical Press, and a paper which Holcroft was invited to
read to the Institution of Locomotive Engineers, stimulated
quite a wide interest in three-cylinder locomotives, and at
one stage Gresley approached Holcroft with a view to further
collaboration. The result of all this, however, was that
Maunsell decided to try a three-cylinder locomotive and
Holcroft had the task of designing the cylinder and valve-
gear layout for a three-cylinder variant of the standard
South Eastern & Chatham 'N' class 2–6–0.

This locomotive, No 822, was completed at Ashford less
than a month before grouping, so that apart from a few
preliminary trial runs, its history belongs almost entirely to
the Southern Railway and not to the South Eastern &
Chatham Railway. The Southern had acquired sufficient

experience of the running of this locomotive for Clayton to take a prominent part in the discussion that ensued when Gresley read a paper on three-cylinder locomotives at the summer meeting of the Institution of Mechanical Engineers held in the Railway Centenary Year of 1925, at Newcastle. This paper would, in other circumstances, have been rather like putting one's head into the lions' den; because the North Eastern Railway, up to the time of grouping, had been the largest user of three-cylinder locomotives in Great Britain, and none of its locomotives of this type used any form of modern conjugated gear, relying instead on three sets of the conventional Stephenson's link motion.

By 1925, however, Gresley had become well established as chief mechanical engineer of the London & North Eastern Railway and the practice of the former North Eastern Railway was being passed over in favour of that of the Great Northern. To some extent, therefore, Gresley's paper was, to the railwaymen of North Eastern England, a taste of what they were going to receive in future rather than any tribute to what they themselves had done in the past. Certainly, the layout of valve gear using derived motion for the inside cylinder was an extremely neat one from the drawing-office point of view, and apart from the initial venture of the three-cylinder 2–8–0 engine No 461 built at Doncaster in 1918, the Gresley three-cylinder engines of various types had the very simple layout of the mechanism advocated by Holcroft.

But when it came to a discussion of Gresley's paper, Clayton, with the experience of the SE & CR 2–6–0 No 822 in mind, rather 'rocked the boat'. He drew attention to a feature of the engine working which had given them a good deal of trouble on the Southern, namely the over-running of the inside valve. It has since been proved that, unless the conjugated gear is very well maintained and wear in the various pin joints kept to the very minimum by constant attention to the bearings, this over-running can be the cause of serious trouble and even complete failure. During the Second World War, the maintenance of locomotives with the conjugated valve gear on the LNER naturally deteriorated, not so much in respect of the work put into the locomotives when they were under overhaul as by the very long mileages they were required to run between visits to works, and the lesser amount of attention that was given to engines in the course of ordinary day-to-day maintenance at the sheds. When wear develops in the pin joints, it naturally affects the outside valve gear as much as the inside one. If over-running of the valve occurs outside it is faithfully reproduced inside by the combination levers and its effect is magnified. The over-running inside causes the inside cylinder to receive a greater amount of steam per stroke than the setting of the reversing lever would warrant, and this meant that the inside cylinder was inclined to do far more than its fair share of the work. This effect, combined with the particular form of big-end used on the LNER, led to quite a lot of serious failures.

At the time of his paper to the Institution of Mechanical Engineers in 1925, Gresley was inclined to pass off this trouble lightly and there is no question whatever that any ill-effects due to this inherent defect in the valve gear were successfully minimized under ordinary conditions of shed and works maintenance of the locomotives. The Gresley express locomotives were undoubtedly among the most successful of any running in Great Britain in the years before the Second World War. On the Southern, the work of engine No 822, and the corresponding 2–6–4 'K' class, was certainly appreciated, but was not such as to warrant the building of more locomotives with three cylinders and a conjugated valve gear. The building of engines 822 and 890 was, however, a very interesting intermediate step in the gradual evolution of Maunsell's locomotive practice, and it was perhaps characteristic of his work as a whole that when the need arose for more locomotives of three-cylinder design, he decided to use three sets of valve gear and so avoid the inherent complications of the conjugated motion.

CHAPTER SIX

THE 'KING ARTHURS' AND THEIR EARLIER WORK

The years immediately following the grouping of the railways in 1923 witnessed a steady increase in passenger-train loads in most parts of Great Britain. On the Southern, the traffic manager intimated that locomotives would be required capable of maintaining a start-to-stop average speed of 55 mph with train loads up to 500 tons. This envisaged the restoration of the crack timings of London & South Western days between Waterloo and Bournemouth, Waterloo and Salisbury and Salisbury and Exeter, but with 500-ton trains, as compared with the maximum of about 350 tons worked prior to the deceleration made during the First World War. On the Tonbridge and Chatham main lines of the Eastern Section, the operation of much heavier trains than those of pre-war days was also contemplated, though the severe nature of much of those roads would require some relaxation, either of average speed or load, from the 500-tons-55-mph standard laid down for the Western Section. Authority was given for twenty engines of an entirely new type to be built and, by the close of 1923, preliminary designs for the locomotive that eventually emerged as the 'Lord Nelson' were in hand.

But production of a locomotive of an entirely new design and, moreover, one which came to include several novelties in construction, is not a rapid process, and events combined to compel the building of new express passenger engines at an earlier date. For one thing, the Western Section was short of really capable engines. The passenger stud was headed by the twenty two-cylinder 4–6–0s of Robert Urie's 'N15' class; then there were the ten Drummond four-cylinder 4–6–0s of class 'T14' ('Paddle-boats'); ten Urie 6-ft 4–6–0s (class 'H15'); ten 6-ft Drummond four-cylinder 4–6–0s (448–457

class, used mainly west of Salisbury) and six Drummond
4–6–0s 330 to 335, with 6-ft wheels, one of which had been
rebuilt by Urie as a two-cylinder engine. An order for ten
6-ft 4–6–0s of similar design to the 'N15' was in course of
completion at Eastleigh in 1923, and these engines were put
into passenger traffic as soon as they were run in.

Prior to grouping, an order had been given to Eastleigh
Works for the reconstruction of the 448–457 series of four-
cylinder Drummond 4–6–0s, as two-cylinder engines; but at
the end of 1923 no steps had been taken to put the work in
hand, and, in view of the shortage of express engines,
Maunsell decided to modify the original plan, and to replace
the Drummond engines by new 6 ft 7 in 4–6–0s with the
'N15' boiler. At the same time, the front-end was to be
modelled on Ashford lines. Under Clayton's close supervision a new cylinder design was worked out, including large
ports, large steam-chest volume and long-travel valves,
while the cylinders themselves were made $20\frac{1}{2}$-in diameter
by 28-in stroke, to work in conjunction with a higher boiler
pressure than that used in the LSWR 'N15's – 200 instead of
180 lb per sq in. The decision to replace rather than rebuild
the Drummond engines meant that the latter could remain
in traffic through the summer of 1924, when the motive-
power situation was expected to be critical. Only the
tenders, and such items as the engine bogies, were to be used
in the replacements.

From the motive-power point of view, one major difficulty
was that the Urie 'N15' class of 6 ft 7 in 4–6–0s was proving
a disappointment. Complaints were received by the chief
mechanical engineer of the unsatisfactory working of these
engines; they were massive, built in the battleship tradition
of the Drummond school, but, although they could run very
fast on occasions, they were never really free in steaming
and could not sustain a high output of power. Recorders
taking notes of the running of these engines from the carriage, and having no access to footplate data, were often
perplexed at the apparently poor work. Some of these
recorders sought to put the blame upon the enginemen, for

slack or inefficient working; but while this stigma might have applied to some railways, no line of the 1920–25 period was better served by its drivers and firemen than the Western Section of the Southern. The footplate traditions built up in the days of Dugald Drummond had been sustained and strengthened in Urie's time; no body of men had been better schooled in the art of handling their engines than those of the LSWR and one may be fairly sure that no one could have got better work out of the Urie 'N15's than the top-link drivers at Nine Elms, Salisbury and Exmouth Junction.

But still the work as a whole was disappointing; on one particular journey engine No 753, with a load of no more than 280 tons, was in such straits for steam when passing Oakley summit that no higher speed than 47 mph was run for miles on the ensuing downgrade towards Andover – with the train already behind time. It was on account of erratic and indifferent work of this kind that the running department approached Maunsell, and early in 1924 a comprehensive series of tests was begun upon engine No 742, while running in ordinary passenger service between Waterloo and Salisbury. On a typical run made with the engine in its original condition, with 5⅛-in diameter blast-pipe top, the boiler pressure could not be maintained higher than 140 lb per sq in throughout the critical uphill section from Weybridge to the deep cutting west of Pirbright Junction. And on what is normally a fast section, from Farnborough to Basingstoke, pressure fell to 100 lb per sq in. On these trials the engine was indicated, and it has been suggested that there was a close connexion between these trials in the spring and summer of 1924, and the appearance of the new 4-6-0s early in 1925. Actually, there was very little connexion. Maunsell had to 'make something' of the Uries, and the road trials of 742 were still in full swing when the front-end design of the new 4-6-0s was complete, in April 1924.

Modification to the Urie 'N15' first took the form of increasing the area of the steam and exhaust ports, and the provision of ⅛-in exhaust clearance. This improved the steam flow through the cylinders, but still the steaming remained

indifferent; the smokebox arrangements for the new 4–6–0
(which included modified chimney and blast-pipe), were
then applied to 742, and proved extremely successful, so
much so that on a typical run during the final series of tests
the boiler pressure was consistently maintained at 170 to
180 lb per sq in for 75 miles on end, during which time the
indicated horsepower was continually over 1,000 and rising
at times to over 1,200. The engine was indeed transformed,
and, it should be noted, without alteration to the valve
motion, which had a travel of $5\frac{1}{8}$ ins in full gear, and a steam
lap of one inch. The trials on the modified 742 provided a
gratifying vindication of the boiler and smokebox modifications proposed for the new engines, and work at Eastleigh
was pushed ahead in earnest. Simultaneously, arrangements
were made for bringing the remaining Urie 'N15's into line
with No 742.

In the early autumn of 1924 plans for the summer service
of 1925, discussed between the various officers concerned,
made it clear that the stock of express locomotives would be
inadequate to meet the programme. The design of a new
locomotive to meet the '500-ton-55-mph' standard was
progressing, but as there was no prospect of the first of these
engines appearing before 1926, it was decided to put on
order a further twenty of the Maunsell 'N15's and have
them built by contractors. Drawings were available, patterns
could be lent, and there was a prospect of having some at
least of these engines before the summer service started.
But the preliminaries were going to take time. Holcroft has
told me how, in mid-October, when the urgent need arose,
Clayton and he worked late into the evenings drafting the
specification to be sent out with the invitation to tender;
even so, after allowing time for the various firms to make
their estimates, more than a month had elapsed and it was
not until December that the order for twenty locomotives was
placed with the North British Locomotive Company. The
'Scotchmen', as these latter engines became known on the
Southern, were built in record time, and the first four
engines were delivered in May 1925. In the meantime, East-

leigh had completed in February 1925 the first of the new engines; the Eastleigh batch took the numbers of the Drummond 4–6–0s which they replaced.

Prior to the completion of these engines, the Board had decided that, in future, all express passenger locomotives of the Southern would be named and, in view of the company's close association with the West of England, it was decided that the 'N15' class should be named after personalities and places connected with the legend of King Arthur and the Round Table.

There is an amusing story to be told about this introduction of names for express locomotives on the Southern. The decision was from the top management and Maunsell had, of course, to be informed. Sir John Eliot was then public relations officer of the Southern and was given the task of breaking the news. After listening to the plan for naming the engines after characters and places in the legend of King Arthur, Maunsell, in a flash of his typical Irish humour, said: 'Tell Sir Herbert I have no objection, but I warn you it won't make any difference to the working of the engine!' As a piece of publicity it was a stroke of genius, for these fine names brought that touch of individuality that mere numbers can never convey, and at once the engines of the 'King Arthur' class became firm favourites with the travelling public. The first of the Eastleigh engines, No 453, was named *King Arthur*, but while the rest of the 448–457 series, and the 'Scotchmen', were with one exception named after the knights of the Round Table, the Urie 'N15's which were also included in the class, were named after other associations with the legend. No 742, for example, became *Camelot*. The exception among the new engines was No 454, named *Queen Guinevere*.

The names and numbers of the first three batches of the 'King Arthur' class engines were as follows:

736	*Excalibur*	739	*King Leodegrance*
737	*King Uther*	740	*Merlin*
738	*King Pellinore*	741	*Joyous Gard*

742	*Camelot*	749	*Iseult*
743	*Lyonesse*	750	*Morgan le Fay*
744	*Maid of Astolat*	751	*Etarre*
745	*Tintagel*	752	*Linette*
746	*Pendragon*	753	*Melisande*
747	*Elaine*	754	*The Green Knight*
748	*Vivien*	755	*The Red Knight*

Eastleigh replacements of the Drummond 6-ft 4–6–0s ('G14' class):

448	*Sir Tristram*	453	*King Arthur*
449	*Sir Torre*	454	*Queen Guinevere*
450	*Sir Kay*	455	*Sir Lancelot*
451	*Sir Lamorak*	456	*Sir Galahad*
452	*Sir Meliagrance*	457	*Sir Bedivere*

Engines built by North British Locomotive Ltd, 1925:

763	*Sir Bors de Ganis*	778	*Sir Pelleas*
764	*Sir Gawain*	779	*Sir Colgrevance*
765	*Sir Gareth*	780	*Sir Persant*
766	*Sir Geraint*	781	*Sir Aglovale*
767	*Sir Valence*	782	*Sir Brian*
768	*Sir Balin*	783	*Sir Gillemere*
769	*Sir Balan*	784	*Sir Nerovens*
770	*Sir Prianius*	785	*Sir Mador de la Porte*
771	*Sir Sagramore*	786	*Sir Lionel*
772	*Sir Percivale*	787	*Sir Menadeuke*
773	*Sir Lavaine*	788	*Sir Urre of the Mount*
774	*Sir Gaheris*	789	*Sir Guy*
775	*Sir Agravaine*	790	*Sir Villars*
776	*Sir Galagars*	791	*Sir Uwaine*
777	*Sir Lamiel*	792	*Sir Hervis de Revel*

The 'King Arthurs' rank among the really great designs of the day. It should be emphasized, too, that the completion of engine No 453 took place three months before the historic locomotive exchange of May 1925, between the Great Western 'Castles' and the LNER 'A1' 'Pacifics' – an event which is often quoted as the starting point in modern British locomotive development. The refinements of front-end design, including a valve travel in full gear of as much as $6\frac{9}{16}$ ins, were incorporated on a locomotive built in the massive traditions of Eastleigh; in this latter respect Finlayson put on the Drummond cab and made the width over the platforms to the South Western standard and, therefore, too wide to run on the Central and Eastern sections. The 'Scotchmen' were built to the composite loading gauge, and had Urie tenders and cabs similar to those of the 'N' class 2-6-0s. For the nominal tractive effort of 25,320 lb at 85 per cent boiler pressure, the total engine weight of 81 tons was perhaps on the heavy side – one ton more, in fact, than that of the Great Western 'Castles', having a tractive effort of 31,625 lb. Clayton once tackled Finlayson on this very point, asking why he could not get the weight down a little; but old Jock would not be drawn further than to remark that he supposed 'the spec-eefic gr-r-ravity of steel was differ-r-rent at Swindon'.

At first, the distribution of the new engines at the various sheds was fairly clearly defined by batches. The 'Eastleigh' 'Arthurs', Nos 448–457, were seen on the West of England trains as they were mostly shedded at Salisbury and Exmouth Junction; Nos 763–772 went to Stewarts Lane, for the Continental boat expresses: Nos 773–782 were at Nine Elms, and 783 to 792 at Bournemouth. It was with these last ten locomotives that I enjoyed most of my earlier experiences with the 'King Arthur' class. Looking back over the many logs I compiled between 1925 and 1930, I cannot say that any of them contained very outstanding or spectacular work. They were quietly efficient. The Bournemouth drivers of those days seemed content to work easily uphill, and to allow their engines to run freely on the easier stretches. I travelled frequently, too, behind Nine Elms men on the Sunday evening train then leaving Bournemouth at 7.5 PM. It was always very heavy, and again the usual practice was to go quietly up from Southampton to Litchfield, and then to run very fast east of Basingstoke.

The capacity of the 'King Arthurs' for very fast and heavy work was shown in some trials with engine No 451, *Sir Lamorak*, on which indicator diagrams were taken. On November 20th, 1925, with the normal ten-coach train of the 'Atlantic Coast Express', the driver was instructed to work the engine 'a bit heavy', in order to get some good fat diagrams; the result was an arrival at Salisbury 16 minutes early, catching the station staff totally unprepared to deal with the train! An abbreviated log of this journey, as recorded from the footplate by Mr Holcroft, is given below.

SR WATERLOO–SALISBURY

Load: 10 coaches, 281 tons tare, 295 tons full
Engine: 'N15' 4–6–0 No 451, *Sir Lamorak*

Distance miles		Sch. min	Actual min	Average speeds mph
0·0	Waterloo	0	0	—
3·9	Clapham Junction	7	6½	36·5
24·4	Woking	28	25½	64·6
47·9	Basingstoke	54	45½	70·4
66·4	Andover	73	61	71·8
83·8	Salisbury	92	76	69·4

As a complement to the foregoing effort, with a fairly light train, the same engine put up some magnificent running on another indicator trial with the 11 AM from Waterloo to Salisbury on which a load of fourteen coaches was taken, 440 tons tare. The run was made in 93 minutes start to stop, and the following data show that the performance of the engine was highly efficient:

Trial Run: 13th April, 1926

Load tons tare	440
Average speed mph	54·0
Average indicated horsepower	1,113
Average gradient, rising	1 in 3,160
Coal consumed lb per train mile	42
Coal per IHP (lb)	2·2
Calorific Value of coal in BThU per lb	13,690

The indicated horsepower quoted above is the mean of sixteen cards taken during a period of 86 minutes. The regulator was full open for the whole of that time and the actual maximum IHP recorded was 1,241 at 59 mph, when the engine was working in 22½ per cent cut-off. Although this test was carried out without a dynamometer-car, and without the precision characterizing present-day indicator trials, there is no reason to doubt the general run of the results. The overall performance as represented by the coal consumption per IHP hour is certainly excellent.

About the same time, a very interesting exchange of 'King Arthur' class engines took place between the Eastern and the Western sections of the Southern Railway. It was desired to compare the relative difficulties of working on the Salisbury and Dover roads, and so one engine was chosen from Stewarts Lane and one from Nine Elms sheds, and these two were worked with their regular crews on both routes. After preliminary exchanges to enable the drivers to learn the 'foreign' roads, each engine made six trials on each road. The two engines were taken for trial without any special preparation, and while this ensured that the tests were conducted under ordinary service conditions it was unfortunate that the Stewarts Lane engine, No 768, had trouble with the exhaust injector; also, the superheat reached was low, about 580 to 590 degrees Fahrenheit instead of 600 to 650 degrees. The Nine Elms engine, No 778, on the other hand, did splendidly throughout, and handsomely beat No 768 on her own section. The results so far as coal consumption was concerned are given in the table overleaf.

On one run with the 'Atlantic Coast Express', No 768 worked a train of 418 tons tare and about 430 tons gross to Salisbury in 91 minutes in spite of a permanent-way check between Oakley and Overton. The passing times were 7¼ minutes to Clapham Junction, 29¼ minutes to Woking, 54 minutes to Basingstoke, and 72½ minutes to Andover. Cut-offs were varied between 23 and 27 per cent, but it was only between Woking and Battledown Junction that the regulator was full open. The engine steamed well throughout, with pressure never less than 190 lb sq in, but the superheat temperatures were mostly below 600 degrees Fahrenheit. The details below suggest that the Dover road is the harder of the two, seeing that the driver most familiar with

'N15' TRIALS ON EASTERN AND
WESTERN SECTIONS

Route	Engine No	Average load tons tare	Coal used per double trip including standing (lb)	Coal per Train mile (lb)	Booked average speed mph
Victoria–Dover	768	412	9,237	59·5	45·9
	778	410	7,588	48·6	45·9
Waterloo– Salisbury	768	414	8,905	53·2	54·5
	778	420	8,084	48·2	54·5

it showed a considerably heavier coal consumption 'at home' than over the strange route. On the other hand, the Nine Elms driver was remarkably consistent in his coal consumption; even the slower timing of the 'Golden Arrow' indicates clearly the less favourable nature of the Eastern Section road. Personally, I never found performance on the boat trains very enterprising, and the accompanying log of the 10.45 AM in 1926 is perhaps typical (see Table 8 opposite).

During the coal trials against engine No 778, the Stewarts Lane engine, No 768, made a much better run than the one tabulated, though the timing was done in less detail. With a load of 418 tons tare, and about 450 tons gross, Tonbridge was passed in 49¾ minutes after two permanent-way checks. Then came some fine running, with a time of 20¼ minutes from Paddock Wood to Ashford and 9½ minutes on to Sandling Junction – total 85½ minutes from Victoria; and with a brisk finish Dover was reached in 98¼ minutes. The engine was run with full regulator throughout from Tonbridge to Sandling Junction and the cut-offs were 33 per cent in accelerating from the Tonbridge slack, 25 from Paddock Wood, 27 from Chart Siding, 30 from Ashford and 33 per cent from Smeeth. This was heavy for a 'King Arthur' and,

TABLE 8

SR 10.45 AM CONTINENTAL BOAT EXPRESS

Load: 412 tons tare, 435 tons full
Engine: 'N15' 4–6–0 No 768, *Sir Balin*

Distance miles		Schedule min	Actual min sec		Speeds mph
0·0	VICTORIA	0	0	00	—
4·0	Herne Hill	9	9	15	—
5·7	Sydenham Hill	—	12	55	26
8·7	Beckenham Junction	17	17	20	—
12·6	Bickley Junction	24	23	40	32
14·9	Orpington	29	28	15	—
17·7	Knockholt	33	33	10	27½
21·7	Dunton Green	—	38	55	57½
23·2	Sevenoaks	40	40	40	47
28·1	Hildenborough	—	45	50	70½
30·6	TONBRIDGE	48	48	45	slack
35·9	Paddock Wood	54	55	20	61½
40·5	Marden	—	59	55	57
43·0	Staplehurst	61	62	35	—
46·3	Headcorn	—	65	55	—
51·5	Pluckley	—	72	10	47
57·2	ASHFORD	75	78	10	61½
61·5	Smeeth	—	82	40	—
64·3	Westenhanger	—	87	10	47
66·5	Sandling Junction	87	88	40	
71·0	FOLKESTONE CENTRAL	—	93	15	
72·0	Folkestone Junction	93	94	15	
78·0	DOVER MARINE	102	101	40	

in view of the coal consumption, rather suggests that this particular engine was not in the best of condition.

Some years afterwards, when travelling by the up 'Atlantic Coast Express', I was interested to see this same engine back on at Exeter, and in the hands of Driver Davey, of Exmouth Junction, she made one of the finest runs I have ever clocked with a 'King Arthur'. The log is detailed in the

accompanying Table 9. We began steadily up that difficult
start of 1 in 100 up to Exmouth Junction and then, with the
engine going in complete silence, we swept down the 1½
miles of 1 in 100 past Pinhoe to reach 68 mph at Broad Clyst.

TABLE 9

SOUTHERN RAILWAY: EXETER–SALISBURY

12.30 PM 'Atlantic Coast Express'

Load: 13 coaches, 416 tons tare 445 tons full
Engine: 'N15' class, 4–6–0 No 768, *Sir Balin*

Distance miles		Schedule min	Actual min sec		Speeds mph
0·0	EXETER	0	0	00	—
1·1	Exmouth Junction	3	4	00	—
4·8	Broad Clyst		8	45	68
12·2	SIDMOUTH JUNCTION	17	18	12	33½/60
16·8	Honiton		24	35	30½
18·0	*Milepost 153½*		27	10	25½
23·8	Seaton Junction		33	35	82
27·0	Axminster		36	02	74
32·1	Chard Junction		40	57	56
38·3	*Milepost 133¼*		48	37	42
40·1	Crewkerne		50	40	82
45·3	*Milepost 126¼*		54	57	61½
48·9	YEOVIL JUNCTION	57	58	10	75
53·5	Sherborne		62	20	62
56·1	*Milepost 115½*		65	45	32
59·6	TEMPLECOMBE	69	70	35	75
64·1	*Milepost 107½*		74	37	50
66·4	*Gillingham*		76	55	65½
70·5	Semley		82	05	35¼
79·8	Dinton		91	12	75
85·5	Wilton		96	05	slack
88·0	SALISBURY	98	99	20	

On the long ascent to Honiton Tunnel – 13·2 miles of it with
only two very short breaks – the big load of 445 tons told
against the engine, but it was nevertheless very fine work to
climb from Broad Clyst to Milepost 153½ at an average
speed of 43 mph, and the attainment of 60 mph on the mile
of 1 in 100 descent after Sidmouth Junction showed that
there was no nursing of the engine. Once into Honiton
Tunnel, with the heavy pulling over, the run became a

characteristically exciting experience, with very rapid accelerations from each successive summit, and the speed often all but doubled in 2½ to 3 miles. Crewkerne was a case in point, where the engine accelerated from 42 to 82 mph in 2¾ miles. It will be seen that the average speed from Milepost 153½ to Wilton, 67·5 miles, was 58·8 mph.

In referring to 'King Arthur' performance over the Salisbury–Exeter line it is sometimes imagined that the fast climbing of many of the steeper banks is entirely due to impetus. Table 10 is a really excellent example of a start

TABLE 10

SOUTHERN RAILWAY:
12.24 PM SEATON JUNCTION–EXETER

Load: 12 coaches, 362 tons tare, 385 tons full
Engine: 'N15' class 4–6–0, No 455, *Sir Lancelot*

Distance miles		Actual min sec		Speeds mph
0·0	SEATON JUNCTION	0	00	—
0·8	*Milepost 148½*	2	30	21
1·8	*Milepost 149½*	5	15	22
2·8	*Milepost 150½*	7	53	23
3·8	*Milepost 151½*	10	15	26
4·8	*Milepost 152½*	12	32	26
5·8	*Milepost 153½*	14	40	29
7·0	Honiton	16	15	58
10·3	*Milepost 158*	19	05	78¼
11·6	SIDMOUTH JUNCTION	20	45	—
—		—		
0·0		0	00	
3·7	Whimple	5	40	65½
7·4	Broad Clyst	8	35	79
9·3	Pinhoe	10	10	62½
11·1	Exmouth Junction	12	25	—
12·2	EXETER	14	55	

against the worst of all these banks with engine No 455, *Sir Lancelot*. The way the engine gathered speed with its load of 385 tons, against the 1 in 80, was most impressive; and then, as usual, came the customary swift downhill accelerations. The train was well on time, or no doubt still faster work would have been done from Honiton. On the other

hand, the Urie engines never seemed quite so strong on the
banks as the 'King Arthurs' proper, although they, too, ran
very fast downhill. In the Thirties, I travelled several times
behind No 744, *Maid of Astolat*, and she twice came within
an ace of 90 mph between Honiton and Exeter. The run
recorded in Table 11 shows part of a trip on the 3 PM from

TABLE 11

SOUTHERN RAILWAY:
TEMPLECOMBE–SIDMOUTH JUNCTION

Load: 10 coaches, 323 tons tare, 350 tons full
Engine: Urie 'N15' 4–6–0, No 744, *Maid of Astolat*

Distance miles		Actual min sec		Speeds mph
0·0	TEMPLECOMBE	0	00	—
1·5	*Milepost* 113½	5	08	33
6·1	Sherborne	10	03	83½
—	Wyke Crossing	—		75
10·7	YEOVIL JUNCTION	13	37	79
12·9	Sutton Bingham	15	31	64½
14·3	*Milepost* 126½	16	58	56
16·0	Hardington Box	18	33	71
19·5	Crewkerne	21	43	58
21·6	*Milepost* 133¼	24	20	34½
27·5	Chard Junction	30	06	77½
32·6	Axminster	33	53	85
35·8	Seaton Junction	36	24	68
38·6	*Milepost* 150½	39	40	36
40·6	*Milepost* 152½	43	57	23½
41·6	*Milepost* 153½	46	16	28¼
42·8	Honiton	47	45	60
46·1	*Milepost* 158	50	30	82
47·4	SIDMOUTH JUNCTION	52	15	

Waterloo when we reached well over 80 mph on each of the
principal descents, and very nearly bagged a fourth at
Yeovil Junction. But up Honiton bank, whereas No 455, in
starting a heavier train from a dead stop at Seaton Junction,
reached 26 mph on entering Honiton Tunnel, No 744 had
fallen to 23½ at this point, even though she passed Seaton
Junction at 68 mph!

A mixed-traffic version of the 'King Arthur' class was

introduced in 1927. This followed to some extent the L & SWR 'S15' class of 1920; but the Maunsell 'S15's, of which fifteen were built in 1927 and another ten were added in 1936, had a valve motion interchangeable with that of the 'Arthurs' and proved equally successful in their particular sphere. Their numbers were 823–837 (1927 batch) and 838 to 847. They worked the heavy night express goods trains between Nine Elms and Exeter, and between Nine Elms and Southampton with the corresponding up trains. I had a short, though excellent, trip on the footplate of No 827 with the up evening Exeter fitted goods, when we had forty-four wagons on from Templecombe eastwards. Like all modern mixed-traffic engines, the 'S15's were called upon to do relief passenger and excursion work on Saturdays in the summer; they did it remarkably well, despite having coupled wheels of no more than 5 ft 7 ins diameter. The leading dimensions of the Maunsell 'S15's are given in the Table in Appendix I; by way of contrast the L & SWR variant had 21-in by 28-in cylinders and 180-lb pressure, against 200. The numbers of these latter engines were 496–515.

A further fourteen 'King Arthurs' were built at Eastleigh in 1926 for the Brighton Section. To suit the existing turn-tables, these engines were fitted with six-wheeled tenders in place of the big double-bogie Urie type fitted to the 763–792 series.

Engines built at Eastleigh in 1926 for Central Section:

793	Sir Ontzlake	800	Sir Meleaus de Lile
794	Sir Ector de Maris	801	Sir Meliot de Logres
795	Sir Dinadan	802	Sir Durnore
796	Sir Dodinas Le Savage	803	Sir Harry le Fise Lake
797	Sir Blamor de Ganis	804	Sir Cador of Cornwall
798	Sir Hectimere	805	Sir Constantine
799	Sir Ironside	806	Sir Galleron

In later years, many of these engines originally allocated to Continental boat-train workings received six-wheeled tenders and on two runs that I enjoyed over the Brighton line before electrification both the 'King Arthurs' concerned

had begun their careers as boat-train engines. In a further
table I have set out details of two runs on the world-famous
'Southern Belle', the inspiration for so many other all-

TABLE 12

THE 'SOUTHERN BELLE'

5.35 PM Brighton–Victoria

Engine No Engine Name Number of Cars Load tons gross		764 Sir Gawain 9 350			766 Sir Geraint 10 385	
Distance miles	Sch. min	Actual min sec		Speeds mph	Actual min sec		Speeds mph
0·0	BRIGHTON	0	0 00	—	0 00	—
1·3	Preston Park		3 30	—	3 40	—
4·7	Clayton Tunnel South		8 25	47	8 45	45
9·8	Keymer Junction	13	13 20	69	13 40	70½
			p.w.s.		—	
12·9	Haywards Heath		16 20	20	16 30	61
16·8	Balcombe		22 15	52½	20 40	52
—			—		p.w.s.	
19·0	Balcombe Tunnel		24 45	54½	23 40	35
21·4	THREE BRIDGES	25	27 07	66	26 20	60
24·9	Horley		30 15	70½	29 25	75
29·0	Earlswood		34 12	60	33 00	62
32·1	Quarry Box	36	37 30	51½	36 13	54½*
35·9	Coulsdon North	40	41 37	—	40 40	—
37·4	Purley		42 47	70½	42 05	74
40·4	EAST CROYDON	45	45 35	—	44 40	—
44·3	Streatham		50 00	64½	49 15	58
46·0	Balham	52	51 55	—	51 40	—
48·2	CLAPHAM JUNCTION	55	54 20		54 05	
50·9	VICTORIA	60	59 55		59 30	
	Net times		58		58½	

* Minimum speed 45 mph in Quarry Tunnel.

Pullman trains, not merely in accommodation but in name
– 'Bournemouth', 'Thanet', 'Devon', the 'Eastern Belle'
of the LNER, and even Mr Punch's ever-memorable 'Suffix
Belle', which covered the 91½ miles from High Dudgeon to

Pelting St Giles in 63 minutes and on which passengers were not allowed to bring their own food! However, to return to the Brighton line, the two runs I made were both on Saturday evenings in the early spring when the patronage of the train was modest. Both engines did well, though clearly having a good deal in reserve. While the Brighton 4–6–4 tanks always gave the impression of having to be 'pushed' a little to reach speeds of 70 mph downhill, the 'Arthurs' streaked away in complete silence.

TABLE 13

SOUTHERN RAILWAY:
8.4 AM WHITSTABLE–CANNON STREET

Load: 10 coaches, 322 tons tare, 345 tons full
Engine: 'N15' class 4–6–0 No 772, *Sir Percivale*

Distance miles		Actual min sec		Speeds mph
0·0	WHITSTABLE	0	00	
4·1	Graveney Siding	6	25	56
7·1	Faversham	10	00	30*
11·1	Teynham	14	40	70½
14·4	Sittingbourne	17	34	50 (min)
20·2	Rainham	23	27	62½
24·8	CHATHAM	28	19	—
25·4	Rochester	29	09	35*
32·2	Sole Street	42	09	27½
35·7	Fawkham	46	28	67
38·6	Farningham Road	48	52	77½
41·4	Swanley Junction	51	37	53½
44·3	St Mary Cray	54	24	67½
45·7	St Mary Cray Junction	56	07	30*
47·6	Elmstead Woods	59	07	50½
50·7	Hither Green	62	08	69
—		sigs checks		
56·0	LONDON BRIDGE	75	01	
56·7	CANNON STREET	77	17	

Schedule: 74 min. Net time: 72 min. * Speed restrictions.

Lastly, to complete a survey of 'King Arthur' performance in their earlier days, there is a run that I timed over the Chatham line in 1934. For a short time I was travelling regularly between Cannon Street and Whitstable, and made a number of runs on the 8.4 AM up. The run detailed in Table 13 is typical of the locomotive work involved. More often than not, checks occurred in the London suburban area, though we usually came through St Mary Cray Junction on time. Operating in the London area had not then reached the very high level of efficiency that now exists. Prior to reaching the suburban area, *Sir Percivale* had done quite well, touching 70½ mph on the short descent through Teynham and mounting the 1½ miles of 1 in 110 after Sittingbourne at a minimum speed of 50 mph. On the dead level to Gillingham, however, we did not exceed 62½ mph and the 5 miles of Sole Street bank, almost entirely at 1 in 100, witnessed a minimum speed of 27½ mph. While this was leisurely compared with West of England standards nothing faster was needed, and we had the usual 'King Arthur' dash downhill afterwards, with a top speed of 77½ mph at Farningham Road.

Lastly, reference must be made to the coal trials carried out in 1925 with engine No 453, *King Arthur*, to ascertain what difference in consumption might be expected with various classes of fuel. A very full account of these trials was given by Mr Holcroft in an article published in *The Engineer* for December 18th, 1925, and from it the following points may be mentioned. Welsh and Yorkshire grades of coal were examined and in every instance the engine crews were carefully schooled to ensure that the most efficient firing technique was adopted for the fuel concerned. The tests were made on the 'Atlantic Coast Express' between Waterloo and Salisbury with tare loads varying between 310 and 350 tons, and it can generally be said that there was no appreciable difference. On the outward journey, consumption varied between 34·1 and 41·4 lb per train mile, and on the easier return trip the variation was between 29·1 and 36·9 lb – if one evidently exceptional trip be excepted on which 47·2 lb per train mile was used.

CHAPTER SEVEN

4·4·0 DEVELOPMENT AND PERFORMANCE

At the time of the grouping of the railways in January 1923, the South Eastern & Chatham had an order outstanding for fifteen new 4–4–0 express engines of similar weight and capacity to the 'L' class. Following the successful rebuilding of the Wainwright 'D' and 'E' 4–4–0s, as described in Chapter Four, a new design would have followed on the same lines. However, no complaints had been received from the running department about the original 'L' class 4–4–0s as they were capable of dealing successfully with the existing loads and timings. A scheme for improving the valve gear had been worked out by the chief mechanical engineer's department; at the time, however, the shops were so busy with routine repairs that the plan was pigeon-holed. When the fast 80-minute expresses between Charing Cross and Folkestone Central were put on, in the summer of 1922, the running department pressed for more class 'L' 4–4–0s. This cut across Maunsell's standardization policy in which it was proposed to use the 'K' class 2–6–4 tanks for work of this kind. Twenty of these latter engines had actually been authorized, but in the difficult circumstances following the end of the First World War there had been a long delay in getting them started. In any case, on fast runs of almost seventy miles in length their tank capacity would have left very little margin.

So far as the new 4–4–0s were concerned, grouping had the effect of postponing their construction indefinitely, and for the first five years of its operation the 80-minute Folkestone service was run by the original 'L' class 4–4–0s. Providing the loads did not much exceed 200 tons, they could manage this 52 mph booking satisfactorily. With short-lap valves and a somewhat hamstrung front-end, these

'L' class engines had to be run at about 40 per cent cut-off
with a narrow regulator opening. They were well suited to
the haulage of heavy loads at 45 to 50 mph, but faster
running was obtained only by lengthening the cut-off, to
provide more exhaust opening, and this of course meant
working with a partly-closed regulator. They showed up
better on the Hastings line, on which the severity of the
curvature in places entailed many speed restrictions to
40 mph or so. There were few opportunities on that route for
sustained fast running, such as that regularly made between
Westenhanger and Tonbridge on the mail line.

For some reason, which those who were most familiar
with the 'L' class never seemed able to fathom, No 761 was
the freest-running of the lot, and in *The Railway Magazine*
for September 1922 details were given of a run with this
engine, and a load of 215 tons gross, on which speed
averaged 66 mph from Smeeth to Paddock Wood, with
maximum speeds of $72\frac{1}{2}$ mph through Ashford and again at
Headcorn. But even on this run, when time was kept to
Charing Cross, the engine was nearly a minute down on
schedule on passing Tonbridge – 40·5 miles from Folkestone
Central in 41 minutes 55 seconds. Recovery took place on
the hilly stretch up to Knockholt, where, of course, the
engine was easily master of so relatively light a train. There
were occasions, as at holiday weekends, when train loads
were much heavier, and then it was only in cases of exceptionally competent driving that time was kept. The following are examples of running on the 80-minute Folkestone
trains in the years 1923, 1924 and 1925:

Engine No	775	761	775	777
Loads tons tare/full	310/340	255/275	263/285	312/340
Direction	Down	Up	Up	Up
Net over time: min	83	$81\frac{3}{4}$	79	88

The run up of No 775 was certainly a very fine one, with
Tonbridge (40·5 miles) passed in 41 minutes 15 seconds from
the start and speed averaging 68 mph from Smeeth to

Paddock Wood; but the other journeys tell their own tale. What finally forced the issue was the introduction of heavy corridor stock in place of the old SE & CR non-corridors. This sent the regular load of certain trains over the 300-ton mark, and made an improved type of locomotive essential.

When authority was given to go ahead, the need had become so urgent that time did not permit of a thorough redesign to produce an engine on 'E1' lines. Ashford was not able to undertake the work, and the new engines had to be built by contractors. The course adopted was to use the existing drawings, patterns and templates, and introduce only those modifications which could be readily accommodated. It was not possible, without redesigning the cylinders, to give longer steam-chests with direct ports and $1\frac{5}{8}$-in lap as on the 'E1' rebuilds. In accordance with the scheme which had been pigeon-holed some years earlier, the valve travel was increased to the maximum the existing design of steam-chest would permit by adjustment of the eccentrics and alteration of the rocking-lever arms. Thus the steam lap was increased from $\frac{7}{8}$ in to $1\frac{3}{16}$ ins. Another improvement was to use the class 'N' chimney and smokebox arrangement. This was tried out first on one of the existing 'L' 4-4-0s, No 779, and the proportions were settled by experiment before incorporation in the 'L1' design. In the way the 'L1' was developed from the 'L' there is quite a striking parallel to the case of the 'King Arthur', developed from the L & SWR 'N15' of Urie design.

The changes common to both developments are set out below, and it is important to emphasize that the guiding principles of both are to be seen in the first design of Maunsell's team, the 'N' class 'Mogul' of 1917:

1. Built at short notice to satisfy an urgent traffic need.
2. 'N' class smokebox tried out first on existing engine.
3. Boiler pressure raised by 20 lb per sq in.
4. Cylinder diameter reduced.
5. Valve travel and lap increased.
6. Maunsell superheater.

The rearrangement of the cab was much more extensive in the case of the 'L1', than on the 'King Arthur'. Instead of the large toolboxes with wooden tops, which were built up over the trailing coupled wheels and made standing room limited on the 'L' class engines, the 'L1's had tip seats for the driver and fireman, as on the 'E1', 'D1', and 'N' classes. Thus the driver could stand directly behind the front window, in a comfortable stance, instead of having to lean across the toolbox; the fireman, too, had more room to swing his shovel. The tenders were similar to those of the 'N' class.

Fifteen engines, Nos 753 to 759 and 782 to 789, were built by the North British Locomotive Co in 1926. Originally, all engines of the constituent companies of the Southern Railway retained their old numbers. To avoid confusion these numbers were prefixed according to the works at which they were maintained. Thus engines of the former SE & CR had the prefix 'A'; Brighton engines were 'B', and the ex-LSWR types were prefixed 'E'. New locomitives of types derived from pre-grouping designs were numbered in the corresponding series, so that the 'King Arthurs', derived from the L & SWR 'N15' class, were prefixed 'E', while the 'L1' 4–4–0s were prefixed 'A'. At a later date the ex-SE & CR engines had 1,000 added to their numbers, and the ex-Brighton types 2,000; so that the 'L1' class eventually became 1753 to 1759 and 1782 to 1789.

The new 4–4–0s were an immediate success, and although their nominal tractive effort was no greater than that of the 'L' class, and the boiler was the same in each case, they were able to manage the 80-minute Folkestone trains with loads of 300 tons, against the 200–225 tons which represented about the maximum with which timekeeping could be relied upon with the older engines. Excellent runs have, on the other hand, been recorded with 'L1' class engines loaded up to no less than 350 tons. One such run I noted personally remains vividly in my memory for the silence in which the engine, No 787, worked into speed between Ashford and Tonbridge. On this journey there was a heavy slack through

Ashford, but afterwards we put up an average of 67·8 mph over the 10·4 miles from Headcorn to Paddock Wood with a load of 355 tons. The following examples of speed over the racing stretch from Smeeth to Paddock Wood are taken from *The Railway Magazine* and are typical of 'L1' class performance.

Engine No	753	783	755	784	758
Load tons gross behind the tender	275	305	305	320	340
Average speed for 25·6 miles	70·7	72·0	70·2	68·4	72·0
Maximum speed	75	75	74	74	76½

In view of the great success of the 'L1' engines, it might be imagined that some alterations would be made to the original 'L' class as opportunity permitted. So far as I am aware, however, no change was made to the valve motion, though as some of the 'L' class acquired Maunsell chimneys there may have been changes in the smokebox. Be that as it may, in the years just before the Second World War the 'L'

TABLE 14

SOUTHERN RAILWAY: MINSTER–ASHFORD

(8.11 AM Ramsgate to Ashford)
Load: 4 coaches, 128 tons tare, 135 tons full
Engine: 1744, class 'L' 4–4–0

Distance miles		Sch. min	Actual min sec	Speeds mph
0·0	MINSTER	0	0 00	
5·0	Grove Ferry		6 12	45*
7·1	Chislet		8 25	75
9·1	Sturry		10 00	76
11·5	CANTERBURY WEST	13	12 34	
0·0		0	0 00	
3·0	Chartham		4 55	58
5·2	Chilham		7 10	60
9·9	Wye		11 48	74
			sigs	
14·2	ASHFORD	20	17 55	

* Slack over reverse curve.

TABLE 15
SOUTHERN RAILWAY:
WHITSTABLE–BROMLEY SOUTH

Date Engine No Class Load tons E/F		June 1939 1762 'L' 221/230		August 1935 1786 'L 1' 323/350	
Distance miles	Sch. min	Actual min sec	Average speed mph	Actual min sec	Average speed mph
0·0 WHITSTABLE	0	0 00 sigs	—	0 00	—
7·1 Faversham	10	12 23	34·4	10 17	41·2
11·1 Teynham		17 45	44·8	15 18	47·9
14·4 Sittingbourne	18	20 45	66·0	18 14	67·3
17·5 Newington		24 00	57·3	21 40	54·3
20·2 Rainham		26 28	65·8	24 20 sigs	60·8
23·2 Gillingham		29 14	65·3	28 10	47·0
24·8 CHATHAM	30	31 14	48·0	31 10	32·0
25·4 Rochester		31 56	51·2	31 57	45·8
26·2 Rochester Bridge		33 02	43·5	33 07	41·2
28·2 Cuxton Road		36 12	37·9	36 07	40·0
32·2 Sole Street	43	42 45	36·6	43 15	33·6
33·2 Meopham		44 05	45·0	44 48	38·9
35·7 Fawkham		46 28	62·9	47 32 sigs	54·3
38·6 Farningham Road		48 56	70·2	51 14 sig stop	47·1
41·4 Swanley Junction	53	52 02 p.w.s.	54·2	63 50	—
44·3 St Mary Cray		55 36 sigs	48·7	67 32	47·0
45·7 St Mary Cray Junction		58 08 sigs	32·9	69 20	43·3
46·5 Bickley Junction	59	61 42	13·5	70 05	63·9
47·1 Bickley		63 00	27·6	70 48	51·2
48·2 BROMLEY SOUTH	62	64 56	—	72 35	—
Net times		57·1/4 min		58·1/4 min	

class engines were putting up some very fast running on occasions. A remarkable example is that on the 8.11 AM from Ramsgate to Ashford. I have tabulated the log of the run as between Minster and Ashford (Table 14) and those who do not know this route will probably be surprised to learn that the general tendency of the gradients is rising, all the way! After a very rapid start on the level, speed was eased to 45 mph at Grove Ferry over the curves; but in the next 2¼ miles speed was worked up to 75 mph and was held at 75–6 mph up the 1 in 579 to Sturry. Then, between Canterbury and a point some 1½ miles beyond Chilham, the gradients are steadily rising; indeed this stretch ends with 1½ miles at 1 in 200–176–200. Here a speed of 60 mph was sustained till the crest was reached and the engine streaked away to 74 mph on the level at Wye. This was a most exhilarating little run.

An interesting direct comparison between classes 'L' and 'L1' might be made from the two runs from Whitstable to Bromley tabulated opposite (Table 15). Certainly on the basis of these times the 'L1' did, with 350 tons, much the same as the 'L' did with 230. But without knowing how the two engines worked one cannot draw any reliable conclusions. To Mr S. A. W. Harvey I am indebted for an analysis of all the runs he has clocked with superheater 4-4-0s of the inside-cylinder varieties on Sole Street bank. This analysis (Table 16) makes most interesting reading. The long incline

TABLE 16

4-4-0 Performance on Sole Street bank

CUXTON ROAD BOX–SOLE STREET: 4 miles

Engine Class	'D1'	'E1'	'L'	'L1'
Number of runs timed	11	17	47	11
Average load tons gross	225	230	250	320
Average speeds mph	31·4	32·0	31·2	28·9
BEST RUN:				
Load tons tare	275	255	280	350
Time min sec	7 08	6 27	7 13	7 08
Average speed mph	33·6	37·2	33·3	33·6

TABLE 17

SOUTHERN RAILWAY: 9.15 AM CHARING CROSS–FOLKESTONE

Run No Engine 'L1' class Load E/F (tons)			1 1786 230/250		2 1758 239/255		3 1788 336/350	
Distance miles		Sch. min	Actual min sec	Average speeds mph	Actual min sec	Average speeds mph	Actual min sec	Average speeds mph
0·0	WATERLOO JUNCTION	0	0 00		0 00		0 00	
1·2	LONDON BRIDGE	4	2 48	25·7	2 44	26·3	3 10	22·7
4·2	New Cross	8	6 57	43·3	6 44	45·0	7 23	42·8
					p.w.s.			
6·5	Hither Green	11	9 33	53·1	10 20	32·0	10 10	49·6
8·3	Grove Park		11 47	48·2	12 50	43·3	12 53	39·9
9·6	Elmstead Woods		13 38	42·2	14 45	40·3	15 25	30·8
10·6	Chislehurst	16½	15 00	43·9	16 07	43·9	17 15	32·7
13·1	Orpington	19½	18 24	44·1	19 20	46·7	21 15	37·5
14·6	Chelsfield		20 10	51·0	21 00	50·5	23 25	41·6
15·9	Knockholt		21 55	44·6	22 35	49·3	25 10	44·5

			74 minutes		73 minutes		77½ minutes	
19.9	Dunton Green		26 09	56·6	26 42	58·4	29 30	55·5
21.4	Sevenoaks	29	27 33	64·3	28 02	67·4	30 57	62·1
26.3	Hildenborough		32 26	60·0	32 32	65·4	35 27	65·4
28.8	TONBRIDGE	36½	35 05	56·5	34 55	62·8	37 53	61·7
			p.w.s.		sigs			
34.1	Paddock Wood	42½	41 01	53·6	41 30	48·3	43 30	56·7
38.7	Marden		46 07	54·1	47 45	44·2	47 25	70·3
41.2	Staplehurst		48 52	54·5	50 30	54·5	49 45	64·5
44.5	Headcorn		51 47	67·9	54 35	48·5	52 40	71·6
					sigs			
49.7	Pluckley		56 15	70·0	62 40	38·6	57 30	64·5
					p.w.s.			
55.4	ASHFORD	62	61 04	71·1	68 45	56·2	62 55	63·2
59.7	Smeeth		64 54	67·3	72 55	62·0	67 05	62·0
63.5	Westenhanger		68 50	58·1	76 35	62·1	71 10	55·8
64.7	Sandling Junction	72	70 17	49·8	77 53	55·5	72 35	50·9
67.4	Cheriton Junction		73 05	57·8	80 25	64·0	75 15	60·8
68.5	Shorncliffe		74 15	56·7	81 20	72·0	76 15	66·0
69.2	FOLKESTONE	77	75 38	—	82 52	—	77 28	—
	Net times		74 minutes		73 minutes		77½ minutes	

is commenced at reduced speed – usually about 30 mph through Rochester – and impetus would not ordinarily be exhausted by the time Cuxton Road box was passed. But the average speed over the four miles from this signal-box to Sole Street Station gives a very good guide to the sustained effort on the bank. In this analysis, forty-seven runs with 'L' class engines give results little better than those of the superheater 'D1' and 'E1' rebuilds, and the best 'L' ascent is eclipsed by the best 'E1' effort. But on every account the 'L1' performances are the best of all; the climbing of engine No 1786 with 350 tons, Mr Harvey's best, was certainly excellent. I have worked out the point-to-point average speeds on the comparative runs of engines 1762 and 1786, as Mr Harvey was not able to clock maximum and minimum speeds.

Dealing now more particularly with the performance of the 'L1' class, I have tabulated three runs on the pre-war 9.15 AM from Charing Cross to Folkestone Central (Table 17). This train included a stop at Waterloo Junction in the 80-minute timing, and when the loads reached as much as 350 tons some hard running was needed. On run No 1, engine No 1786 with 250 tons started well, passing Hither Green 1½ minutes ahead of time. This gain was held to Paddock Wood, but it will be seen that the mere keeping of point-to-point bookings involved some fine work uphill. From my own experience of running over this route, I should think that the minimum speed anywhere up to Knockholt was not below 40 mph. Downhill speeds were moderate; but after the permanent-way slack there was some excellent going from Staplehurst to Westenhanger, where speed averaged 67 mph. On No 2 run, engine No 1758 lost a minute through the early permanent-way check, but by still finer climbing and a fast descent from Sevenoaks Tunnel to Tonbridge she had actually overtaken No 1786 at this point. More checks followed and Ashford was passed 6¾ minutes late; but a fine concluding effort was made, and although Ashford was evidently passed at slower speed than usual, a minute was regained before Folkestone. On the last run, the load told heavily against No 1788 on the rise to Knockholt. The driver was probably disinclined to 'push' the engine too hard in the early stages in order to conserve his water supply. Certainly the climb out to Orpington was not up to the standard of engine No 1786 on Sole Street bank. But from Knockholt the running of No 1788 on the 9.15 AM to Folkestone was excellent, with an average speed of over 60 mph through from Knockholt to Shorncliffe, and one of 63·7 mph over the generally-rising gradients from Paddock Wood to Westenhanger.

In the last year of the Southern Railway, 1947, I enjoyed an excellent run on the footplate of an 'L1', No 1758, on the 4.57 PM mail train up from Ashford, running to London Bridge via Redhill. The load was a moderate one of 275 tons gross behind the tender, and with it the engine ran very freely. The driver made frequent changes in cut-off to suit the rise and fall of the road and this took us along at a fine even pace, as the effects of each rise were anticipated and cut-off lengthened before speed had begun to fall. Once into speed, the cut-off was varied between 22 and 28 per cent, and our progress was such that Milepost 35¾ (a mile short of Paddock Wood), 20·4 miles from Ashford, was passed in 21¾ minutes from the start. Beyond this point a long engineers' slack delayed our run into Tonbridge. From the restart, up steadily-rising gradients of 1 in 266 and 1 in 251, 30 per cent cut-off was used at first, with the regulator wide, though not fully open. Edenbridge, 9·2 miles, was passed in 13¼ minutes, at 54 mph, but after this, with the train getting ahead of time, the steaming was eased. Altogether, I found No 1758 a very lively and good steaming engine. After Redhill, with load reduced to 180 tons, the effort required was relatively small.

CHAPTER EIGHT

THE 'LORD NELSONS' TO 1938

The announcement by the traffic manager in September 1923, that the future standard for heavy main-line express trains was to be 500 tons, and that these trains would require to be worked at start-to-stop average speeds of 55 mph – alike on the West of England and Bournemouth routes, on the Kent Coast lines, and with the Continental boat express – came as a challenge to the chief mechanical engineer's department. In 1923, there were no Southern Railway locomotives that could approach this target, even in the most favourable circumstances; but one gathers from some of those most intimately concerned that the task of producing a new design to meet these requirements was undertaken with relish. Yet for some time the circumstances of the day imposed many handicaps and delays.

It was in mid-October 1923 that instructions were given to proceed with twenty new engines, and preliminary investigations began at once at Ashford. At that time, the Great Western 'Castle' and LNER 'Pacifics' of Gresley and Raven design were the most powerful express passenger locomotives on British railways, and the new Southern locomotives would clearly have to be of roughly the same capacity to meet the new traffic requirements. Two questions at once arose; should the new engine be of the 4–6–0 or the 4–6–2 type; should it have three cylinders, or four? Maunsell was open-minded; but Clayton was very impressed by the 'Castle' and thought that a 4–6–0 with narrow firebox would do the job, and be cheaper to build. While the quality of coal likely to be available on the Southern would not be up to that regularly used on the Great Western, the distances to be run on the Southern were not so long, and in Clayton's opinion a wide firebox was not called for on this account. Regarding the number of cylinders, experience with the

SE & CR 2–6–0 engine, No 822, had pointed clearly to the advantages of six exhaust beats per revolution, instead of four. But Clayton was so impressed with Churchward's practice as to favour four cylinders, though the GWR 'Castles' and 'Stars', with normal crank setting, gave only four beats per revolution.

Clayton's junior partner, H. Holcroft, following up his work on three-cylinder locomotives had, in 1920, carried his advocacy still further with a paper on 'Four-Cylinder Locomotives', read before the Institution of Locomotive Engineers. In that paper he had put forward a proposal for cranks at 135 degrees, giving eight exhausts per revolution; with this was coupled the design of a conjugated valve gear, so that only two sets of motion would be needed for the four cylinders. Use of the 135-degree setting would enable Clayton to have four cylinders, but at the same time to gain the advantage of softer blast and more even turning moment. To put the 135-degree crank arrangement to the test, though without conjugated valve gear, one of the remaining 6-ft Drummond four-cylinder 4–6–0s, No 449, which had earlier been fitted with a superheated boiler, was selected for trial. A set of coupled wheels was prepared at Eastleigh, in which the angle of cranks of the driving wheels was altered to 135 degrees, and the balance weights suitably adjusted in all wheels of the set. After the performance of the engine had been recorded with the cranks at the normal 180-degree setting, the engine was lifted in the shops and the set of wheels with the 135-degree setting substituted; and with this sole alteration No 449 was sent back into traffic. The resulting performance was so much in favour of the alteration that it was decided to adopt the 135-degree crank setting for the new engines.

Further work on the new four-cylinder 4–6–0 was deferred during the summer of 1924. At the time, the new chief mechanical engineer's headquarters office at Waterloo was in process of establishment, with accompanying upheaval in the personal affairs of all concerned, house removals, and so on. In the early autumn of 1924, however, work began in earnest on the scheming-out of the design, but before giving his final decision on the type of engine Maunsell was anxious to obtain some first-hand observations of the locomotive work on other lines. So, on October 1st, 1924, Clayton rode from Paddington to Plymouth on No 4076, *Carmarthen Castle*, with the 'Cornish Riviera Express'. Ten days later he rode on a Gresley 'Pacific', with the 'Flying Scotsman'. Any doubts that might have existed were dispelled by Clayton's footplate trips on these two engines, and the definite decision was taken to make the new Southern engine a four cylinder 4–6–0. These observations of Clayton's on the relative merits of two famous designs were to be amply confirmed less than a year later, in the interchange trials of 1925. At that time, however, the Gresley 'Pacifics' had the original valve gear, and it was not until 1926 that modifications were made which transformed their general running and greatly reduced their coal consumption. As to the 'Castle', it is well known how, by direct interchange, the influence of Swindon practice spread to the LNER and to the LMSR; Southern footplate experience on No 4076 put the finishing touch on a process that had begun with the appointment of Pearson to the SE & CR in 1914, and which had been fostered by Clayton's contact with Churchward over the proposed standard locomotive designs during the First World War.

Design work on the new engine was again held up in the late autumn of 1924, when the pressing needs of the traffic department for the summer service of 1925 made it necessary to abandon for a time the plan to have twenty new engines authorized to the '500-ton-55-mph' specification. The preparation of detail drawings for a new engine, and the subsequent making of patterns and templates, would alone occupy some twelve months, whereas adding to the number of an existing design would enable construction to start, once the necessary material was on hand. A further batch of improved 'N15' class 4–6–0s ('King Arthurs') was, therefore, built by outside contractors. But once the detailed contract specifications for these engines had been prepared attention was once again turned to the new four-cylinder

4–6–0, and after running conditions on all routes concerned
had been examined on the '500-ton-55-mph' basis, it was
estimated that a locomotive capable of a sustained output of
1,500 indicated horsepower would meet the case. The leading dimensions were settled as: cylinders 16½-in diameter
by 26-in stroke; coupled wheels, the standard 6 ft 7 ins, and
a working pressure of 220 lb per sq in. This provided a
nominal tractive effort of 33,500 lb, the highest of any
British express passenger engine at that time. Piston valves
with long lap were, of course, included – 1½ ins lap and 6½ ins
travel in full gear.

But although the general outline of the design came from
an appraisal of the Great Western 'Castle', very little
similarity can be seen in the working-out of the details – far
less than in the 'N' class 'Moguls', as compared with the
GWR '43XX' type. In the new Southern 4–6–0, all four
cylinders were practically in line. This gave very short and
direct steam passages but, with a divided drive, resulted in
the outside connecting rods being 11-ft centres against
6 ft 11 in centres for the inside ones. Four separate sets of
valve gear were used. The original length of boiler between
tube-plates in the Waterloo design was shortened at the
request of Eastleigh, for the practical reason of making the
tube length the same as that of the 'King Arthurs' and so
avoiding the need to stock an additional size of tube. Consequently, the boiler barrel was one foot shorter than that of
the 'Castle' although, in the Belpaire firebox, that rounding
of the outer shell, so carefully developed at Swindon, was to
a large extent reproduced. The trapezoidal shape, tapering
inwards from the front, was not adopted, and with a straight
barrel the water space outside the tubes at the firebox tube-
plate was considerably less than on the 'Castle'. A regulator
in the dome, and the introduction of the feed through clack
valves on the side of the boiler, served to emphasize the lack
of similarity between the Eastleigh and the Great Western
designs. The degree of superheat was also considerably
higher in the Maunsell engine.

Very great care was taken in design to keep the weight

down and Clayton had to exercise strict supervision at
Eastleigh to prevent the traditional heavy-handedness of
the ex-LSWR draughtsmen from getting the upper hand.
Certain parts which would normally be left as forged, or
cast, were machined to keep the weight down, but when the
prototype engine came well within the estimated figure this
latter refinement was not applied to the further fifteen
engines of the class. The connecting rods and motion were
made very light by the use of 'Vibrac' high-tensile alloy
steel. The extent to which weight was kept down is shown
by a comparison between the new engine and the 'King
Arthur'. Although the latter's nominal tractive effort was
only 76 per cent of that of the new design, the weight of
engine only in working order was 81 tons, against no more
than $83\frac{1}{2}$ tons for the new design. After the hurried sub-
stitution of 'King Arthurs' for the twenty new engines
authorized in October 1923, no further authority had been
given for new locomotive construction, but in 1925 the
directors sanctioned the building of fifteen express engines
for the Central Section. It was decided to build fourteen of
these to the 'King Arthur' class at Eastleigh, equipping
them with six-wheel tenders for the shorter runs, thus
affording an opportunity for the fifteenth engine of this
order to be made the prototype of the new four-cylinder
design.

All in all, the new 4–6–0 represented a thoroughly original
and handsome design, and as it had the highest tractive
effort of any British passenger engine, the Southern Railway
publicity department made the most of their opportunities in
boosting 'the most powerful British locomotive'. And the
very name bestowed on it, *Lord Nelson*, was symbolical of
Southern readiness to take on all comers. A first-class impression was certainly created, both in railway circles and
outside, and it was significant that in the late autumn of
1926, when locomotive affairs had reached something of a
crisis on the LMSR, the Southern was called into consultation
on the design of the 'Royal Scot' engine and a complete set of
the 'Nelson' drawings was supplied at their request. Neverthe-

less, this new LMS engine, a well-designed multi-cylinder 4-6-0 with a tractive effort of more than 30,000 lb, was largely inspired by the successful running of another Great Western 'Castle', this time on the LMS main line.

The *Lord Nelson* was completed at Eastleigh in August 1926, and from then until April 1927 she was engaged in work of an experimental kind, so far as the engine itself was concerned, though the trials were conducted on service trains with consistently reliable timekeeping. At an early date it was clear she was an extremely free-running engine, as speeds of 90 mph were touched on several occasions: and although much of this early work was done with poor quality foreign coal, due to the prolonged coal strike of that year, the steaming was good, including that on such a heavy duty as the 10.45 AM 'Golden Arrow', from Victoria to Dover.

Between Waterloo and Salisbury, trial runs were made in December 1926, with the normal ten-coach formation of the 'Atlantic Coast Express', 316 tons tare. On a down journey, the engine was worked in 16 per cent cut-off throughout; with one brief intermission, near Hook, the regulator was kept full open on the gradually-rising stretch of line leading to the summit, 53½ miles out of Waterloo. This point was passed in 57 minutes and Porton (78·3 miles) was passed in 80 minutes. Adverse signals delayed the finish, with a dead stop for 1¾ minutes, but arrival in Salisbury was a little before time, in 90¼ minutes from Waterloo (83·8 miles). On the following day, on a test with the up train, the departure from Salisbury was 10¼ minutes late and opportunity was taken to make some fast running. The adverse length to Oakley, 31·4 miles from Salisbury, was made in 33½ minutes, after which 37·6 favourable miles on to Esher occupied no more than 29½ minutes – an average of 76½ mph. This might have been still faster, as the engine attained 90 mph with ease; but at that time the standard of permanent-way construction and maintenance on the constituent sections of the Southern Railway had not reached the high levels afterwards sustained, and the engine tended to pitch at low rail joints. The regulator had accordingly to be eased at times. On this trip, 66 miles were run in the first hour from Salisbury, and in spite of three signal checks Waterloo was reached in 83 minutes (83·8 miles).

On these two trips water consumption was 31 gallons per train mile westbound and 30 gallons eastbound. The estimated coal consumption was 37 lb per train mile, westbound, and 34½ coming up, in both cases using imported coal. On the up journey, the cut-off was between 20 and 25 per cent up the initial stiff climb to Grateley, and 15 per cent thereafter. One point noticeable during the early trial runs of the *Lord Nelson* was the response of the engine to different methods of driving. The Western Division men, working faithfully in the Drummond tradition, used a wide-open regulator and early cut-offs; men from the former SE & CR handling the engine on heavy boat trains, rarely opened the main regulator valve more than halfway, and kept cut-off at about 25 to 30 per cent. Yet there seemed little to choose between the results obtained. This was the same also with the 'King Arthurs', and was later to be shown on the 'Schools' class 4–4–0s. Purely from the user's point of view, there is a great deal to be said for an engine that responds equally well to the vagaries of individual enginemen.

In running the winter ten-coach load of the 'Atlantic Coast Express' the engine was, of course, working well below its maximum designed capacity, and by far the most interesting among these early trials was one on Sunday, April 10th, 1927, when a special train of sixteen coaches, 521 tons tare, was run from Waterloo to Exeter, and indicator diagrams were taken. The following particulars relate to the Waterloo–Salisbury section of this run:

Distance	83·8 miles
Booked time	90 minutes
Actual time	96¼ minutes*
Average indicated horsepower	1,292
Average cut-off with full regulator	22 per cent
Average boiler pressure	210 lb per sq in

* Includes one signal stop and two severe crossover slacks.

Average steam-chest pressure	200 lb per sq in
Coal used per train mile	66·5 lb
Water used per train mile	44 gallons*
Coal per sq ft of grate area per hr	105 lb
Coal per IHP hour	2·68 lb

Some very fine work was involved subsequently in running the 75·8 miles from Salisbury to Sidmouth Junction in 87¼ minutes, including the ascent of 4½ miles on a 1 in 80 gradient from Seaton Junction to Honiton Tunnel. South Wales coal was used, having a calorific value of 13,500 B.Th.U. per lb. A study of the indicator results shows how closely the design target of 1,500 IHP was realized in service. A number of readings in the 47–55 mph range were obtained between 1,400 and 1,500 IHP using cut-offs of 23 to 25 per cent, while at 15 per cent values of 1,350, at 70 mph, 1,400 at 74 mph, and 1,325 at 84 mph were registered.

In all-round service, however, the 'Nelson' boiler was never quite so free in steaming as that of the 'King Arthurs'; yet when the locomotives were competently handled their running could be exceptional. They were, however, the only Southern express engines in which the firegrate was partly level and partly sloping. While generation after generation of Great Western enginemen had learned to fire such a grate with conspicuous success, there were, on the Southern, ultimately only sixteen engines of the 'Lord Nelson' class, and all the enginemen concerned did not have the opportunity to become wholly familiar with them. Very similar troubles were experienced on the former London & North Western Railway when the 'Claughton' class was first introduced in 1913. When Maunsell was thoroughly satisfied with the prototype, ten further engines of the 'Lord Nelson' class were built at Eastleigh in 1928–9, and five more towards the end of 1929. The only alteration made was a slight modification of the inside cylinders to give a better

---

* Includes water used for train heating, but does not include steam recovered through exhaust steam injector.

lead to the exhaust steam at the base of the blast-pipe. These engines were named after famous British admirals of the past and, as a whole, the class ranked very high in popular esteem.

The names and original numbers of these engines are:

850	*Lord Nelson*	858	*Lord Duncan*
851	*Sir Francis Drake*	859	*Lord Hood*
852	*Sir Walter Raleigh*	860	*Lord Hawke*
853	*Sir Richard Grenville*	861	*Lord Anson*
854	*Howard of Effingham*	862	*Lord Collingwood*
855	*Robert Blake*	863	*Lord Rodney*
856	*Lord St Vincent*	864	*Sir Martin Frobisher*
857	*Lord Howe*	865	*Sir John Hawkins*

During Maunsell's time, five engines of the class were subjected to various modifications:

(*a*) No 859, *Lord Hood*, was fitted with 6 ft 3 in coupled wheels instead of 6 ft 7 ins, to see if a smaller driving wheel would be beneficial in working of Continental boat trains on the heavily-graded Eastern Section.

(*b*) No 860, *Lord Hawke*, was fitted with a boiler barrel longer than standard, providing additional heating surface of 131 sq ft. This was actually the original Waterloo design, with a 10-in longer tube than that common to the standard 'Nelsons' and the 'King Arthurs'.

(*c*) No 857, *Lord Howe*, was fitted with round-topped firebox and combustion chamber. This alteration, however, had no bearing on the 'Nelson' design itself. In 1933, a 'Pacific' was under consideration, and No 857 was made the 'guinea pig' for trying out some new practices proposed for the 'Pacific' boiler, including a combustion chamber.

(*d*) No 865, *Sir John Hawkins*, had the crank setting altered from 135 degrees to the conventional 90 degrees.

This alteration was typical of Maunsell's willingness to try out practical suggestions put to him for improvements in design; in this case, the idea was that a four-cylinder engine with cranks at 90 degrees might accelerate a train better than one having a 135-degree setting. Negative results, as in the alterations to engines 859 and 860, served to confirm his faith in the original design.

(e) No 862, *Lord Collingwood*, was fitted with Kylchap blast-pipe and double chimney. For some reason, this change seems to have been markedly unsuccessful. Yet another variation had been considered in 1931, of converting a 'Nelson' into a four-cylinder compound, with 250-lb pressure and poppet-type valves. But although authority was actually given to carry out this conversion it was not proceeded with.

None of the experimental modifications of 'Lord Nelson' class engines showed any particular advantage over the standard design; in fact, two of the poorest runs I ever experienced were with engine No 859 on the up 'Golden Arrow' and with No 865 on the down 'Bournemouth Belle'. Despite the 6 ft 3 in coupled wheels of No 859, the climbing from Tonbridge to Sevenoaks Tunnel, with no more than 377 tons tare, was such that 17¼ minutes were spent over this 7½ miles of ascent. Yet on the previous day the same engine had done excellently on the outward bound 'Golden Arrow', running at 72 mph steadily on track level with a trailing load of 445 tons. On the other hand, none of the modified engines was altered back to its original condition. Despite the variation in their tractive performance on the road, the 'Nelsons' were extremely reliable from the running-shed point of view, and in the discussion upon Mr C. S. Cocks' paper before the Institution of Locomotive Engineers in 1948 high tribute was paid to their freedom from trouble and lightness in maintenance by Mr Pelham Maitland, who, as Nine Elms shed superintendent, had all of them in his immediate charge at some time or another.

Details of three interesting runs on the up 'Atlantic Coast Express' are given in Table 18. The first was the Press run with engine No 850, in 1926, when it was new and its capabilities were being displayed for the first time. The ascent of Porton bank was taken very quietly, with speed falling to 37 mph on the four miles of 1 in 169–140 gradient; furthermore, the maximum of only 74 mph at Andover was, if anything, below usual standards for the 'Atlantic Coast Express'. But then, after a minimum speed of 59 mph up the three miles of 1 in 178 from Andover to Milepost 62½ the engine was allowed to run, and the average speed over the 48·5 miles from Oakley to Clapham Junction was 70·8 mph. From information communicated to various Press representatives after this run, it seems that the engine made this high-speed running under relatively easy steam. I clocked both the second and third runs in the year 1931, and they are of additional interest since they concern engine No 860, *Lord Hawke*, which had a boiler barrel longer than standard. On the No 2 run, the start out of Salisbury was altogether more vigorous than that of No 850 on the 'show' run of 1926; the time to Porton was two minutes less, and with a minimum speed of 43 mph on the bank and a maximum of 77½ mph through Andover, No 860 was three minutes ahead at this latter point. The continuation was, however, slow, and eventually the driver did not have enough in hand to offset the effects of a permanent-way check, so that we were 1½ minutes late in. Run No 3 could be described as a normal 'Nelson' effort on the up 'Atlantic Coast Express'. The start was not so brisk as on the second run but, once past Grateley, No 860 was run in much more enterprising style.

For a time, engines of the 'Lord Nelson' class worked through from Waterloo to Exeter, with a change of crew at Salisbury; but on the Western end of the line they never seemed to come into their own. They ran extremely fast on the favourable stretches, but from records published from time to time in *The Railway Magazine* the uphill work was rarely, if ever, up to the best 'King Arthur' standards. The run recorded in Table 19, with engine No 850, is about the

TABLE 18

SOUTHERN RAILWAY: 'ATLANTIC COAST EXPRESS'

Distance miles		Sch. min	1 850 Lord Nelson 388 / 415		2 860 Lord Hawke 419 / 450		3 860 Lord Hawke 416 / 445	
	Run No / Engine No / Engine Name / Load (tons empty) / Load (tons full)		Actual min sec	Speeds mph	Actual min sec	Speeds mph	Actual min sec	Speeds mph
0·0	SALISBURY	0	0 00	—	0 00	—	0 00	—
1·1	Tunnel Junction		4 10		3 30	—	4 05	—
5·5	Porton		11 20	37	9 15	47½	10 15	45
8·1	Amesbury Junction		15 20	41½	12 45	43/47	13 50	41½/46
11·0	Grateley		19 05	50	16 10	51½	17 10	53½
17·4	Andover	22	24 45	74	21 45	77½	22 25	79
21·2	Milepost 62¼		28 15	59	25 10	52	25 55	53½
22·7	Hurstbourne		29 30	66	26 50	60	27 25	62½
24·6	Whitchurch		31 20	61	28 55	51½	29 25	56
31·4	Oakley		38 05	60	36 25	63½	36 35	64½
33·5	Worting Junction	39	40 05	—	sigs slight		38 35	67
36·0	BASINGSTOKE	41½	42 10	77½	38 40	53	40 45	75
41·6	Hook		46 40	71½	41 15	67	45 15	65½
47·3	Fleet		51 15	77½	46 25	64½	50 25	70½
50·6	Farnborough		54 00		52 00	64½	53 27	64½
52·8	Milepost 31		56 00	69	55 15	62	55 37	59
59·4	WOKING	62½	61 15	80½	57 25	61	61 55	69
64·7	Weybridge		65 20	71½	63 15	74	p.w. slack	40
70·5	Hampton Court Junction	73	70 15	68	68 00	62/66	68 50	58
76·5	Wimbledon		76 00		p.w.s. bad 82 45		73 45	67
79·9	CLAPHAM JUNCTION	84	79 05		86 35		79 30	62½
							sigs	
83·8	WATERLOO	92	85 30		93 30		90 10	

best I have seen with a 'Nelson' between Salisbury and
Exeter. At the 'high spots' – Gillingham, Sherborne, Axminster, Sidmouth Junction and Broad Clyst – it will be seen

TABLE 19

SOUTHERN RAILWAY: SALISBURY–EXETER

Load: 12 coaches, 389 tons tare, 410 tons full
Engine: 850, *Lord Nelson*

Distance miles		Sch. min	Actual min sec	Speeds mph
0·0	SALISBURY	0	0 00	
2·5	Wilton		6 25	—
—			p.w. slack	
8·2	Dinton		15 55	—
12·5	Tisbury		21 25	55
17·5	Semley		27 35	43½
21·6	Gillingham		31 00	81
28·4	TEMPLECOMBE	33	37 10	—
30·8	Milborne Port		40 00	46 (min)
34·5	Sherborne		43 15	83½
39·1	YEOVIL JUNCTION	44	46 45	73/77
41·3	Sutton Bingham		48 50	51 (min)
47·9	Crewkerne		55 20	72
49·7	*Milepost* 133¼		58 05	30
55·9	Chard Junction		64 00	78
61·0	Axminster		68 00	80
64·2	Seaton Juction		70 30	67
70·0	*Milepost* 153½		81 35	21 (min)
71·2	Honiton		83 10	60
75·8	SIDMOUTH JUNCTION	85	86 55	84
79·5	Whimple		89 50	72 (min)
85·1	Pinhoe		93 45	90 (max)
86·9	Exmouth Junction	95	95 20	—
88·0	EXETER	98	97 45	

Net time: 94½ minutes.

that speeds were 81, 83½, 80, 84 and 90 mph respectively;
but the uphill speed of 30 mph at Hewish summit, and 21
mph at Honiton Tunnel did not suggest any real mastery of
the load, though without a record of the engine working one
cannot attach too much significance to the details of passing
times and speeds.

A criticism of policy rather than of engineering design has been made that, in the season of heaviest traffic and with only sixteen engines available, there were insufficient to make up links composed entirely of 'Lord Nelson' class engines either on the boat trains, or on Western Division workings from Waterloo. During the winter months there were usually sufficient 'Nelsons' at Stewart's Lane to work all the regular boat trains. The utilization was not high, normally consisting of a single return trip to Dover, or Folkestone Junction, six days a week for each engine in the link. At one time it was intended there should be a total of thirty-one, but the directors cut the order for the third batch from twenty to five, owing to heavy expenditure on electrification schemes. Consequently, with only sixteen engines, instead of thirty-one, loadings had to be arranged so that the trains were within the capacity of 'King Arthurs', in the event of 'Nelsons' not being available. This meant that the larger engines were always working within their optimum capacity, except when the additional tractive effort was employed to make up lost time.

Yet on the everyday form displayed in the years 1932–7 on trains within 'King Arthur' capacity, it seems very doubtful if the 'Nelsons' could regularly have risen to the heights of performance put up in the trial run of April 10th, 1927 – in other words, the 500-ton-55-mph standard. This falling-off in form may have been due to a reduction in the lead of the valves from $\frac{1}{4}$ in to $\frac{1}{8}$ in, made incidentally rather than deliberately so far as the 'Nelsons' were concerned. It will be told in a later chapter why this change was made on the 'Schools' class 4–4–0s. The two classes had parts in common, and Eastleigh took it upon themselves to make the change on the 'Nelsons', too, with apparently detrimental results. The $\frac{1}{4}$-in lead was restored in Bulleid's modification to the front-end of the 'Nelsons'. It must remain a matter for conjecture whether, if the Southern had gone some way towards the LNER 'big engine' policy, and built, say, sixty instead of sixteen 'Nelsons', the widespread familiarity with their running would have resulted in better all-round performance. As it was, they were not 'anybody's' engines; with expert driving and firing it seemed that there was no limit to their achievement, but in less expert hands they were liable to fall below the average of 'King Arthur' performance. The extensive alterations made to their front-end after Maunsell's retirement, to bring them up to date with current practice after some twelve years' service, are referred to in a later chapter.

CHAPTER NINE

NEW THREE-CYLINDER DESIGNS

By the year 1928, the gradual development of fast passenger train services on many parts of the Southern Railway system led to a demand for more locomotives of an intermediate character. The duties were of the kind for which Pearson in SE & C days had advocated the use of tank engines. One is inclined to think that he viewed the proposition from the 'shop' angle, rather than that of the running man; there were, for example, no tenders to fill up the works sidings! But his frequent assertions that tank engines did not need turning were not borne out in practice. On the Southern, as everywhere else, enginemen, if they had the time and opportunity, would invariably turn their engines rather than run bunker-first for any appreciable distance. There was also the factor of water capacity. While tank engines may have managed the lightly loaded Portsmouth expresses of the Brighton in pre-grouping days, it was a different matter altogether with the heavy Isle of Wight boat trains over the steep gradients of the Portsmouth direct line.

Not long after the construction of the prototype 'K' class engine No 790, a test was made in October 1917 with the 1.40 PM boat train non-stop from Charing Cross to Folkestone Junction, 70·9 miles. The load consisted of four Pullman cars, six non-corridor bodies and a six-wheeled van, 310 tons tare. The scheduled time of 102 minutes was kept, in spite of a bad signal check at Hildenborough; but so far as water supply was concerned it was a close thing. An inspector was riding on the footplate, and a very careful watch was kept throughout; but after leaving Charing Cross with full tanks they finished with only 150 gallons left. This showed a total consumption of 1,850 gallons, or 26 to the mile. While this was quite good in the haulage of a train that probably weighed quite 340 tons gross, the average speed of

this wartime service – barely 42 mph – was low compared
with what would be required in normal express service. In
later years, the 'K' class engines managed the Cannon
Street–Ashford non-stop run quite comfortably, though this
distance of 55 miles allowed a consumption of about 35
gallons per mile – a very big difference from 26. Furthermore, on the 1917 run with the 1.40 PM boat train, steam-
heating was not in use. So, after some consideration, the
new intermediate passenger engines of 1928 were built as a
tender-engine version of class 'K' – a 2–6–0 with 6-ft
coupled wheels, designated class 'U'.

The design is generally similar to the 'N' class mixed-
traffic engines, though with 6-ft coupled wheels against
5 ft 6 ins, and a large number of parts are interchangeable.
The 'U' class engines were permitted to run up to a maximum speed of 70 mph, and they were well-suited to all
classes of passenger working, excepting only the heaviest
and fastest duties, which were allocated to 4–6–0s. Thirty
engines of this class were built new in 1928–31, and carried
the running numbers 1610–1639. After the Sevenoaks
disaster of 1928, when one of the 'K' class 2–6–4 tanks was
derailed at full speed, these tank engines were eventually
converted to class 'U'. It is sometimes assumed that class
'U' came into being as a result of Sevenoaks. This is not so;
the decision to build no further 'K' tanks, and to have
6-ft 2–6–0s instead, was taken some time previously, and the
first engines of class 'U' were actually in service before the
accident to the 'K' class tank engine occurred.

The three-cylinder 2–6–4 tank No 890, class 'K1' did,
however, become the prototype of the three-cylinder 2–6–0
passenger engines. Like the other 2–6–4 tanks, she was
rebuilt in 1928 and at first retained the conjugated valve
gear. The 'U1' class proper, comprising twenty engines built
at Eastleigh in 1931 and numbered 1891 to 1910, had three
independent sets of Walschaerts valve gear. Reference to
them is rather anticipating the general theme, but it is con-
venient to deal with the entire group of engine classes that
were derived from the South Eastern & Chatham prototype

2–6–0 and 2–6–4 tank. As the remainder of the group were of the three-cylinder type, some reference is needed as to how the second phase of the three-cylinder propulsion came into being on the Southern Railway.

This second phase was notable for the introduction of the 'Schools' class express passenger 4–4–0s in 1930, of which a good deal more will be said in the next chapter. In that class, three cylinders were used so that a higher tractive effort might be obtained without greater adhesion weight, through utilizing the more even turning effort on the driving axle resulting from six exhausts per revolution. So far as the 6-ft 2–6–0s were concerned, it was hoped to get more rapid acceleration from rest, since in theory one could develop a higher tractive effort without risk of slipping. The 'U1' engines had cylinders of 16-in diameter by 28-in stroke, against 19 ins by 28 ins in class 'U', and the nominal tractive effort at 85 per cent boiler pressure was 25,385 lb against 23,865 lb. The long piston stroke in relation to cylinder diameter made the 'U1' engines very suitable to working with short cut-offs, and while, officially, they were permitted to run up to a maximum of only 70 mph, in actual fact they often ran a great deal faster. Among notes of a large number of runs kindly put at my disposal by Mr S. A. W. Harvey there are two cases of 80 mph, and many examples of free running up to 75 or so.

Both in Maunsell's time and since, engines of class 'U' and 'U1' undertook much of the less spectacular passenger working. They had the Waterloo–Portsmouth service before the introduction of the 'Schools' on to that route, and at one time the 5.5 PM from London Bridge to Eastbourne was a regular 'U1' job. The reduced width over the cylinders also made it possible to use the 'U1' engines on the Hastings line, but the numerous curves caused undue flange wear, and the same trouble was experienced west of Exeter, where some of these engines were used for a short time. But they did much of their best and most reliable work on 'semi-fasts', particularly on the Chatham main line. The 'semi-fast' is a mere figure of speech in the case of these 2–6–0s;

between stops their running was fully up to the Kent Coast
express standards. In more recent times 'U' and 'U1' class
engines have undertaken the working of through trains
from the Northern and Western lines to the Kent coast. One
summer Saturday in 1950, for example, No 31907 took over
the haulage of a Wolverhampton–Ramsgate train, nominally
non-stop from Banbury to Ramsgate via Maidstone, Ashford and Canterbury. Actually, the Western Region handed
over to No 31907 at Kensington (Addison Road), and the
'non-stop' run was further interrupted at Maidstone where
the engine was watered and remanned. As a further example
of their good work, No 31894 had the 12.15 PM Birmingham
express out of Brighton, and with a heavy train of 350 tons
ran the 40·4 miles to East Croydon in 50½ minutes despite
2½ minutes lost by diversion to the relief line at Coulsdon
North.

One of the fastest runs of which I have details was made in
1938 by 'U1' engine No 1907 on the 1.3 PM from Bromley
South to Chatham with a heavy load of 360 tons. The severe
uphill start to St Mary Cray Junction, 2½ miles, including
1½ miles at 1 in 95–100 from the immediate start, was
covered in 7¼ minutes. Then some really fast running followed, with an average of exactly 60 mph from St Mary
Cray Junction to Sole Street, 13·5 miles. Although this
stretch includes the fine racing descent to Farningham Road
where 76 mph was attained, there is more adverse than
favourable going. The crest of the bank, near Sole Street,
was cleared at the exceptional speed of 56 mph. A top speed
of 76 mph was again reached, descending to the Medway
Valley, and Cuxton Road signal-box, 20 miles, was passed
in 24¼ minutes from Bromley South. Despite a signal check
at Rochester Bridge, Chatham, 23·4 miles, was reached in
30¼ minutes start-to-stop. With such a load as 360 tons this
was an excellent piece of work and shows that the 'U1'
engines were capable of express passenger performance
beside their more regular duties on semi-fast trains. On the
Portsmouth direct line, when 98 minutes was the allowance
for non-stop trains over the 73·6 miles from Portsmouth

Town to Waterloo, the 'U1' engines handled trains up to 350 tons successfully. Records available show that on this line they were restrained more nearly to their official maximum speed of 70 mph on falling grades, whereas in later years, when the timing was cut to 90 minutes, the 'Schools' class ran frequently up to 85 mph on favourable stretches. At the same time, while both the 'U' and 'U1' engines are classified as 'passenger', they are often used on freight trains.

Some typical examples of 'U1' running principally on the Chatham line are:

Route	Engine No	Load tons gross	Mileage	Actual time min sec		Net time min	Max speed mph
Chatham–Bromley	1908	305	23·4	32	55	33	72
Rochester–Bromley	1890	355	22·8	36	50	36¾	68
Chatham–Bromley	1897	265	23·4	35	30	35½	70
Victoria–Chatham	1902	290	34·3	52	02	51	66
Ashford– Paddock Wood	1907	235	21·3	24	53	24¾	68
Sevenoaks– London Bridge	1907	235	20·2	27	35	26¾	65
Bromley–Faversham	1908	340	41·0	57	01	52¾	72

Over the switchback road of the North Kent line these are excellent runs for a relatively low-powered locomotive. Their 'express passenger' capabilities over a more favourable road are well illustrated by the run from Ashford to Paddock Wood.

The detailed logs of three runs from Bromley South to Chatham, with loads of more than 300 tons are given in Table 20. Of these the first, behind No 1897, was unchecked. Speed rose to 74 mph at Farningham Road, but after passing Sole Street on time at 47 mph the engine was run very easily down to Rochester, and speed at no time exceeded 50 mph. By contrast, No 1901 lost two minutes by adverse signals in the early stages and did not exceed 70 mph at Farningham Road; then, after passing Sole Street at 46,

the engine was let fly and speed touched a full 80 mph before
Cuxton Road. The third run was the best of the three.
No 1907 lost about a minute by adverse signals before
Bickley Junction, but then she ran splendidly. A speed of

TABLE 20
SOUTHERN RAILWAY:
BROMLEY SOUTH–CHATHAM

		Run No Engine No Load tons tare Load tons full		1 1897 304 325		2 1901 320 345		3 1907 340 360	
Distance miles			Sch. min	min	sec	min	sec	min	sec
0·0	BROMLEY SOUTH		0	0	00	0	00	0	00
—				—		—			sigs
1·7	Bickley Junction		5	5	03	5	25	6	00
3·9	St Mary Cray			7	42	8	12	8	55
6·8	Swanley Junction		11	10	48	11	28	12	00
—						sigs			
9·6	Farningham Road			13	28	15	55	14	35
12·5	Fawkham			16	05	19	20	17	00
15·0	Meopham			19	08	23	05	19	40
16·0	Sole Street		21	20	23	24	25	20	43
20·0	Cuxton Road Box			24	58	28	10	24	15
22·0	Rochester Bridge		29½	27	40	30	55	27	07
22·8	Rochester			28	50	32	12	28	30
—					—		—		sigs
23·4	CHATHAM		32	30	23	33	20	30	22
	Net time, min				30½		31½		28¾

76 mph was attained through Farningham Road; Sole Street
was cleared at 56, and 76 mph was reached again on the
descent to Rochester. A further example of high-speed
running by a 'U1' is given in the tabulated details of the
8.20 PM up from Faversham, in 1939, as between Rochester
and Bromley South (Table 21). Considering the load, the
ascent of Sole Street was quite undistinguished, but then the
engine raced away to reach 80 mph at Farningham Road.
This characteristic of moderate uphill work and very fast

running on favourable stretches was common to many engines with modern long-travel valves, and Walschaerts gear; the 4-4-0s with Stephenson's gear tended to show up better on the banks.

TABLE 21

SOUTHERN RAILWAY:
ROCHESTER–BROMLEY SOUTH

Load: 225 tons tare, 245 tons full
Engine: 1909 class 'U1' 2-6-0

Distance miles		Sch. min	Actual min sec	Speeds mph
0·0	ROCHESTER	0	0 00	—
0·8	Rochester Bridge		2 20	—
2·8	Cuxton Road Box		6 45	—
6·8	Sole Street	14	14 42	31
7·8	Meopham		16 10	60
10·3	Fawkham		18 45	
13·2	Farningham Road		21 07	80
—			p.w.slack	—
16·0	Swanley Junction	24	24 45	—
18·9	St Mary Cray		28 40	—
21·1	Bickley Junction	31	31 35	—
—			sigs	
22·8	BROMLEY SOUTH	34	34 45	

In more recent times during the period of the summer service, engines of this class were occasionally drafted from the Eastern Section of Southern Region to the Nine Elms shed for working the Saturdays-only service from Waterloo to Lymington. On this duty the main-line engine was turned at Brockenhurst, and the turntable there cannot accommodate any longer engine and tender than the 'U1'. I was able to observe the working of this particular service from the footplate, and the engine was, by a coincidence, the same one that featured in several fine pre-war journeys mentioned earlier in this chapter, No 1907 – then renumbered 31907. The trains concerned were the 9.42 AM down from Waterloo, and the 1.46 PM up from Brockenhurst. The

scheduled times and the actual performances may be summarized as follows:

	Down	Up
Length of trip, miles	92·9	92·9
Total booked time, min	140	138
Booked running time, min	126	127
Number of booked stops	5	3
Average speed mph	44·5	44·2
Total actual time, min	151½	154½
Total running time, min	138½	146
Net running time, min	127	126½
Average speed mph	44·2	44·3
Number of signal checks	4	3
Number of signal stops	2	2
Load of train, tons tare	324	324
Load of train, tons gross	370	365

The performance can, therefore, be considered as a satisfactory one on an overall basis, but circumstances combined
to make it a great deal better than would otherwise appear.
First of all, the engine had last been shopped for general
repairs in June 1950, twenty-six months prior to the date of
my trip; since this general overhaul she had covered a little
over 75,000 miles. In spite of this, however, her general
condition was good; she rode easily and well, up to the
maximum attained speeds of 70 and 72 mph and the only
indication of mounting mileage was a certain amount of play
between the axleboxes and guides, apparent when running
with steam shut off.

The major factor that governed the finer points of performance was that neither the driver nor the fireman had
previously ever worked on an engine of this class. The 'U1'
is, however, a very simple and straightforward one to
manage, and the driver quickly adopted full-regulator working with the gear well linked up, running mostly at 20 per cent
cut-off. The fireman, like many a keen youngster with whom
I have ridden, tended to overfire at times and to have a core
of partly burnt coal just under the door. With so heavy a
train, a fairly thick fire was necessary and when it was well

burned through the engine steamed very freely. All in all, the crew did very well, and that they were able to do so, as strangers, on an exacting duty, is much to the credit of the design. The train itself, it should be added, was loaded almost to capacity; with corridors and guards vans accommodating many passengers there must have been at least 800 on board during the outward trip, hence the heavy increase of gross load behind the tender over tare load.

While quite a number of logs have been compiled with trains hauled by engines of class 'U1', the two-cylinder variety class 'U' do not seem to have come within the ken of 'stop-watchers' to anything like the same extent. The run of No 1635, recorded by Mr S. A. W. Harvey and shown in Table 22, is probably not a very good example of their work, though it is interesting in another way as being routed via the Catford loop line. As far as Shortlands, where the Chatham main line is rejoined, No 1635 had done adequately with this substantial train, though the loop is graded somewhat more easily than the main line by avoiding the heavy ascent from Brixton to Sydenham Hill Tunnel. But after Shortlands the work was disappointing. At St Mary Cray, where the 'U1' No 1907 was doing 68 mph, No 1635 was doing no more than 54, speed fell to 34 at Swanley, where No 1907 was doing 58 and the top speed through Farningham Road was only 62 mph. Then there was a distinct improvement, as Sole Street was cleared at 44 mph; but this really came too late and the train was nearly three minutes late into Chatham.

By contrast, another engine of the class in her 2–6–4 tank days made a smart run on the 3.15 PM express from Victoria to Eastbourne. The load, it is true, was no more than 250 tons and again No 799, *River Test*, went easily uphill. But this time there was some fast work on the favourable stretches, with speeds of 75 mph at both Horley and Haywards Heath, and Lewes (50·2 miles) was reached practically on time in 65½ minutes from Victoria, despite three slight signal checks. The net time was 62 minutes. This run was timed by Mr Cecil J. Allen.

The last variety of what may be termed the Southern
'Mogul' family was the class 'W' 2–6–4 goods tank engine
of 1931. This was a reversion to the style of the 'K' tanks,
but with 5 ft 6 in coupled wheels. To provide a high and even

TABLE 22

SOUTHERN RAILWAY: VICTORIA–CHATHAM

Load: 309 tons tare, 340 tons full
Engine: 1635, class 'U' 2–6–0

Distance miles		Sch. min	Actual min	sec	Speeds mph
0·0	VICTORIA	0	0	00	—
0·7	Grosvenor Road 'B' Box		2	45	—
2·3	Clapham		6	35	36
3·2	Brixton	7½	8	25	32
5·2	Peckham Rye		11	40	44
6·1	Nunhead	12½	13	00	36
8·0	Catford		16	25	50
8·9	Bellingham		17	35	—
10·4	Ravensbourne		19	40	36
11·1	Shortlands	20½	20	55	40
12·0	BROMLEY SOUTH		22	10	—
13·7	Bickley Junction	24½	25	50	30
15·9	St Mary Cray		29	10	54
18·8	Swanley Junction	30½	33	00	34
21·6	Farningham Road		36	40	62
24·5	Fawkham		40	10	—
27·0	Meopham		44	10	—
28·0	Sole Street	41	45	35	44
32·0	Cuxton Road Box		49	45	68
34·0	Rochester Bridge	49½	52	10	
35·4	CHATHAM	52	54	50	

starting torque, the engines were fitted with three cylinders,
with details and motion interchangeable with class 'U1'.
The nominal tractive effort at 85 per cent boiler pressure
was the high one of 29,452 lb and rendered the class very
suitable for short hauls with heavy trains, as with inter-
region freights between Old Oak Common and Hither Green
yards. As in the 'U1' class, all three cylinders drove on to the
middle pair of coupled wheels. Such cross-London routes
involve sharp gradients leading to flyover junctions which

may well have to be climbed immediately after a signal stop. Good braking is likewise needed for the descents and not only had the coupled wheels a high percentage brake force, but the bogie was braked – an unusual feature in the later days of steam. The class 'W' engines have been most successful in dealing with this particular traffic. To summarize the 'Mogul' group: the same design of boiler, with 200 lb per sq in working pressure was used on classes 'N', 'N1', 'U', 'U1' and 'W'; the cylinders and motion of the three-cylinder 'N1' engines, of which five were built in 1930, were the same as 'U1' and 'W'. The prototype three-cylinder engines 822 (class 'N1') and 890 (class 'K1') originally had conjugated valve gear; this was later removed, though the 'K1' engine, after conversion to the 2–6–0 type and transference to class 'U1' ran for some time with the original valve gear. Eventually the 'Mogul' family on the Southern consisted of 172 engines; 80 of class 'N', 6 of 'N1', 50 of class 'U', 21 of class 'U1' and 15 of class 'W'.

There is a further interesting three-cylinder design to be mentioned at this stage, the 'Z' class 0–8–0 shunting tank. The need was felt for a small number of powerful engines for work in hump, and other marshalling yards, and to have sufficient side-play at the leading and trailing wheels to permit of a $4\frac{1}{2}$-in chain curve being negotiated. A good design was worked out making extensive use of standard parts. Thus the cylinders are interchangeable with classes 'N1' and 'U1' and the boiler is a Brighton standard. The grate area is small, only 18·6 sq ft, but the aim of the design was to provide a boiler of large steam and water capacity, to store heat for periods of waiting and to minimize blowing off. With 4 ft 8 in coupled wheels, three cylinders and the high nominal tractive effort of 29,380 lb at 85 per cent boiler pressure, these engines did their work with quiet efficiency.

Their quietness, indeed, was much appreciated by those who lived near heavily-worked marshalling yards; the 'Z' class engines were practically immune from slipping, and the softness of their exhaust was noticeable. Some of these engines were in service at the important marshalling yard beside the main line at Eastleigh. There, trains had to be shunted against a rising gradient of 1 in 250; but the 'Z' class engines experienced no difficulty in propelling the heaviest loads the operating department liked to run. At this yard, the engines were continuously in steam for a week at a time, yet despite this high utilization they were remarkably free from running troubles. The 'Z' class engines were built at Brighton Works in 1929 and were numbered 950 to 959.

CHAPTER TEN

THE 'SCHOOLS' CLASS

The 'Schools' class, introduced in 1930, was the last Maunsell design of express passenger locomotive actually to be constructed, and in many ways it was the finest of them all. It is perhaps an exaggeration to say that the outstanding position these engines achieved in the British railway world arose almost by accident, yet one can be fairly sure that when the design was on the drawing-boards those responsible hardly foresaw that these engines would one day virtually supersede the 'King Arthurs' on an express service so fast and heavy as that between Waterloo and Bournemouth.

The origin of the 'Schools' class lay in a request by the traffic manager for a locomotive on the lines of the *Lord Nelson*, but suitable for intermediate passenger duties; to work train loads of 400 tons at an average speed of 55 mph. After some investigation, the chief mechanical engineer's department found that the desired result could be obtained very simply by using three cylinders of 'Nelson' dimensions instead of four, and four coupled wheels instead of six. Cylinders, wheels, motion (other than length of rods), were the same on both 4–6–0 and 4–4–0. It was at first proposed to carry the interchangeability of 'Nelson' and 'Schools' parts still further by using 'Nelson' flanged plates for the boiler; but the weight came out too heavy, and a shortened version of the 'King Arthur' boiler was used instead. Another advantage arose from the use of a round-topped boiler, in that the cab sides could be raked inwards so as to clear the restricted loading gauge of the Hastings line.

The basic dimensions of the design were, therefore; three cylinders 16½-in diameter by 26-in stroke; four coupled wheels 6 ft 7 in diameter; total heating surface 2,049 sq ft (against 2,215 in the 'King Arthur') and grate area 28·3 sq ft. This latter was the same as on the later 'King Arthurs', and on the 'S15' mixed traffic 4-6-0s. On these latter engines, the water space round the firebox was increased as compared with that of the earlier 'King Arthurs', which had grates of 30 sq ft. On the 'Schools', however, the boiler pressure was increased from the 200 of the 'King Arthurs' to 220 lb per sq in, and this gave a nominal tractive effort practically equal in the two classes. The adhesion weight of the 'Schools' was, however, no more than 42 tons against 60 in the 4-6-0s, and the ratio of 598 lb of tractive effort per ton of adhesion weight on the 'Schools' against 422 lb per ton made it necessary to be careful when starting the 'Schools' from rest. The actual nominal tractive efforts were 25,320 lb for the 'King Arthur' and 25,130 for the 'Schools', both at 85 per cent working pressure. The 'Schools', named after well-known public schools of the South Country, were immediately accepted by the public as a handsome and powerful addition to the Southern locomotive stud, though at first few foresaw the potentialities that were eventually to be realized in these engines.

On the basis of nominal tractive effort, the 'Schools' were the most powerful 4-4-0s ever built in Great Britain. As previously mentioned, the total heating surface was 2,049 sq ft, made up as follows:

Large tubes	399 sq ft
Small tubes	1,205 sq ft
Firebox	162 sq ft
Total evaporative	1,766 sq ft
Superheater	283 sq ft
Combined total	2,049 sq ft

The small tubes were of 1¾-in outside diameter, with a length of 12 ft 3⅜ ins between the tube-plates. This compared with 2-in diameter small tubes on the 'King Arthur', and a distance of 14 ft 2 ins between tube-plates. Both boilers steamed very freely, even though very often fired with inferior fuel in their later days. The piston-valves, as in the

'Lord Nelson', were of 8-in diameter with a steam lap of $1\frac{1}{2}$ ins and a travel of $6\frac{1}{2}$ ins on full gear. As originally designed, the lead was $\frac{1}{4}$ in.

The 'Schools' ranked among many modern steam locomotives with well-designed valve gear, on which it seemed to make very little difference in actual running whether they were driven with the gear linked up inside 20 per cent cut-off and the regulator opened wide, or whether they were driven first valve of the regulator only and cut-off 30 per cent or perhaps even more. With a relatively small tender carrying no more than five tons of coal and 4,000 gallons, it might be thought that their range of operation would have been limited on a line having no water troughs; in fact, Mr C. S. Cocks in his paper 'A History of Southern Railway Locomotives in 1938', read before the Institution of Locomotive Engineers in 1948, definitely stated that this was so, and added: 'Had large tenders or water scoops been available there is not the slightest doubt that these locomotives would undertake work of a more exacting nature.' In view of what they actually did achieve on the Bournemouth route prior to the outbreak of war in 1939, and which is referred to later, one would be intrigued to discover what duties Mr Cocks had in mind.

At first, the 'Schools' were used on the Hastings line and on the 80-minute Charing Cross–Folkestone expresses. The 1930 batch consisted of only ten locomotives, but thereafter five were built in 1932, ten in 1933, six in 1934 and nine in 1935, and their use was extended to the North Kent line and to Portsmouth direct line, via Guildford and Haslemere, on which they worked the 90-minute expresses with great distinction.

The names and numbers of the 'Schools' class engines were:

900	Eton	904	Lancing
901	Winchester	905	Tonbridge
902	Wellington	906	Sherborne
903	Charterhouse	907	Dulwich

908	*Westminster*	924	*Haileybury*
909	*St Paul's*	925	*Cheltenham*
910	*Merchant Taylors*	926	*Repton*
911	*Dover*	927	*Clifton*
912	*Downside*	928	*Stowe*
913	*Christs Hospital*	929	*Malvern*
914	*Eastbourne*	930	*Radley*
915	*Brighton*	931	*Kings Wimbledon*
916	*Whitgift*	932	*Blundells*
917	*Ardingly*	933	*Kings Canterbury*
918	*Hurstpierpoint*	934	*St Lawrence*
919	*Harrow*	935	*Sevenoaks*
920	*Rugby*	936	*Cranleigh*
921	*Shrewsbury*	937	*Epsom*
922	*Marlborough*	938	*St Olave's*
923	*Bradfield*	939	*Leatherhead*

The following table shows some results of indicator trials from which the performance table on page 128 has been prepared:

Cut-off	Regulator opening	Speed mph	IHP
Full gear	Full	10	600
31%	Part open	31½	1,020
28%	Full	39½	1,125
25%	Full	37	1,050
25%	Full	45	1,120
25%	Full	46½	1,175
25%	Full	48	1,110
25%	Full	50½	1,130
20%	Part open	69	1,035
20%	Part open	77	1,010
Mid gear	Full	53½	675

From the plotted points, making due allowance for the 'scatter' noticeable in the graphical results of road tests, it has been deduced that the optimum output in 25 per cent cut-off takes place at about 68 mph at which point 1,285 IHP is attained, with full regulator. An interesting feature of the above results is the indicated horsepower of 675 obtained in mid gear. On the road, drivers usually started their trains on a relatively short cut-off, to avoid slipping. I have seen drivers put their reversers into mid gear and then slowly increase cut-off as the engine got under way. The reversing gear is one of the very easiest to adjust; and many of the men I have ridden with worked the reverser frequently. Others maintained an unchanged cut-off from start to finish. The lead of $\frac{1}{4}$ in on the valves occasionally caused difficulty through the engine stopping 'blind', and being unable to move in forward gear when the regulator was re-opened. At London Bridge, in particular, this gave trouble with heavy west-bound trains as, owing to the proximity of points in rear, setting-back was not permitted. Accordingly, the lead was reduced to $\frac{1}{8}$ in and this difficulty was considerably lessened.

I was able to witness, at first hand, a good deal of the day-to-day work of the 'Schools' on the Folkestone trains in 1934–6 and summary details of all my runs up to the end of June 1936 are included in the two accompanying Tables 23 and 24. On the down journeys, mostly made on the 12.55 PM Saturday train, there was no time to be booked against any engine, despite gross loads up to a maximum of 420 tons. In the up direction, however, engine No 915, *Brighton*, lost time on two occasions, once by as much as $3\frac{1}{2}$ minutes. On two occasions I was privileged to ride on the footplate and saw some contrasting styles in enginemanship. On No 921, *Shrewsbury*, Driver Hoskins of Ramsgate, with the 5.10 PM up from Folkestone, ran almost entirely on the first port of the regulator, and used cut-offs varying between 25 and 31 per cent. He made the splendid run tabulated on the first column of my summary table. Engine 921 had the best of reputations, and many years later when I was discussing some details of this run with Mr T. E. Chrimes, then motive power superintendent of the Southern, he referred to her as 'the fastest thing on wheels'! In complete contrast to Driver Hoskins' methods, which were the most generally favoured among the Ramsgate drivers of those days, Driver

TABLE 23
SOUTHERN RAILWAY: CHARING CROSS–FOLKESTONE

Engine No / Name / No of Cars / Tons E/F	Sch.	916 Whitgift 9 282/300	920 Rugby 9 289/305	912 Downside 9 288/305	919 Harrow 9 288/305	921 Shrewsbury 11 354/385	921 Shrewsbury 11 354/385	921 Shrewsbury 12 386/410	912 Downside 12 387/420	915 Brighton 10 321/345
Charing Cross	0 0	0 00	0 00	0 00	0 00	0 00	0 00	0 00	0 00	0 00
Waterloo Junction	—									2 43
										3 30
New Cross	9	sigs 10 09	sigs 9 49	sigs 10 15	sigs 10 35	sigs 11 12	sigs 10 53 sigs	sigs 11 52	sigs 11 40	10 44
Knockholt	—	25 48	p.w.r. 27 31	p.w.r. 26 40	25 22	26 33	27 09	28 10	27 00	26 23
Tonbridge	38¼	p.w.r. 38 02	41 04	p.w.r. 46 03	38 32	p.w.r. 41 20	39 52	p.w.r. 45 53	39 55	39 11
Paddock Wood	44¼	43 15	47 09	51 13	44 00	48 30	45 40	51 57	46 02	44 35
Ashford	65	62 33	66 56	71 12	63 10	68 53	65 22	72 18	66 07	63 44
Sandling Junction	75	p.w.r. 75 10	76 33	80 25	72 02	78 26	p.w.r. 77 21	81 52	75 57	p.w.r. 75 09
Folkestone	80	80 08	81 35	84 58	76 55	83 12	82 19	86 55	81 00	80 00
AVERAGES										
New Cross–Knockholt	—	44·8	39·6 (checked)	42·7	47·4	45·6	43·1 (slightly checked)	42·9	45·6	44·8
Paddock Wood–Ashford	62·2 mph	66·2	64·7	65·3	66·7	62·8	64·8	62·9	63·4	66·8
Tonbridge–Sandling	59·0 mph	64·1 (net)	60·8	62·8	64·3	58·1	60·7 (net)	59·8	59·7	63·4 (net)
NET TIME:		75½	78	77½	75½	78½	77½	79	78¾	76¾

TABLE 24

SOUTHERN RAILWAY: FOLKESTONE–CHARING CROSS

Engine No / Name	Sch.	921 Shrews-bury	910 Merchant Taylors	910 Merchant Taylors	919 Harrow	915 Brighton	915 Brighton	912 Down-side	912 Down-side	917 Ard'gly
No of Cars Tons E/F		9 282/300	9 288/305	9 288/305	9 287/305	9 287/305	10 324/345	10 323/345	11 354/390	11 356/390
0·0 Folkestone	0	0 00	0 00	0 00	0 00	0 00	0 00	0 00	0 00	0 00
			p.w.r.				p.w.r.			
13·8 Ashford	16½	16 40	17 52	17 14	16 24	17 26	18 46	16 11	16 42	17 00
35·1 Paddock Wood	34½	34 20	35 26	35 02	34 30	36 04	36 45	34 08	34 45	34 30
40·4 Tonbridge	39½	39 07	40 45	40 10	39 31	41 20	41 41	39 16	39 47	39 09
			p.w.r.							
47·8 Sevenoaks	51½	49 50	54 01	51 15	51 45	54 16	54 48	50 11	50 45	50 29
53·3 Knockholt		56 56	60 26	57 17	58 30	61 10	60 48	56 35	56 56	56 51
62·7 Hither Green	66	65 12	68 23	66 12	67 08	69 23	69 15	65 30	65 39	65 06
		p.w.r.	p.w.r.				sigs	sigs		
69·2 Waterloo Junction	76	76 20	78 55	75 55	76 35	79 28	80 26	76 35	75 30	74 49
69·9 Charing Cross	80	80 02	82 55	80 00	80 45	83 40	84 23	80 45	80 15	79 27
AVERAGES:										
21·3 Ashford–Paddock Wood	71·0	72·4	72·8	71·8	70·7	68·6	71·0	71·3	70·8	73·2
12·9 Tonbridge–Knockholt		45·8	39·3	45·2	40·8	39·0	40·5	44·7	45·1	43·8
Net time to Waterloo		74	75½	76	76½	79½	77	75½	75½	74¾

TABLE 25
SOUTHERN RAILWAY:
11.50 AM WATERLOO–PORTSMOUTH

Load: 10 cars, 326 tons tare, 350 tons full
Engine: 3-cylinder 4–4–0 No 924, *Haileybury*

Driver: May
Fireman: Mintram } Fratton shed

Distance miles		Sch. min	Actual min sec	Speeds mph
0·0	WATERLOO	0	0 00	—
1·3	Vauxhall		3 27	
3·9	Clapham Junction	7	7 00	—
5·6	Earlsfield		9 17	52
7·3	Wimbledon		11 15	55
—	Raynes Park			57
—			p.w.s.	—
9·8	Malden		14 25	25
12·0	Surbiton		17 47	50
13·3	Hampton Court Junction	17½	19 11	59
14·4	Esher		20 18	60
17·1	Walton		22 55	64½
19·1	Weybridge		24 54	60
				67
21·7	Byfleet		27 20	64½
—			—	61 (min)
24·4	Woking	28½	30 00	30
26·8	Worplesdon		35 15	61
—	*Milepost 28½*		—	52
—			sigs	
30·3	Guildford	36	37 57	—
31·5	Shalford Junction		39 49	51½
33·5	Farncombe		42 10	54
34·5	Godalming		43 14	59
				56
36·3	Milford		47 08	58
38·5	Witley		47 52	43
—			—	58½
41·0	*Milepost 41*		51 04	36
42·5	*Milepost 42½*		54 00	26
43·0	Haslemere	54½	54 55	—
46·9	Liphook		58 40	71/69
—				74
—			p.w.s.	15
51·5	Liss		64 40	60
—	Stodham Crossing		—	68
54·9	Petersfield	67	67 55	59
—				63½

TABLE 25—*continued*

Distance miles		Sch. min	Actual min sec	Speeds mph
57·3	Buriton Siding		70 26	55½
58·0	*Milepost 58*		71 14	50
61·2	Idsworth Crossing		75 25	68½ (max)
63·3	Rowlands Castle	77½	77 25	45
			sigs slight	60 (max)
66·4	Havant	81	81 11	30
67·2	Bedhampton		82 18	50
—			sigs	60 (max)
69·5	Farlington Junction		84 53	—
			prolonged signal stops	
72·8	Fratton	88	109 05	
—			sigs	
73·6	PORTSMOUTH	90	114 00	

Net time: 83½ mins.

Keel, on the 12.55 PM down worked No 916, *Whitgift*, on short cut-offs, and used absolutely full regulator for the harder stretches, as from New Cross right up to Knockholt. This was another excellent engine, and she responded to the driver's artistic use of the lever and regulator with a fast and economically-made run. His running cut-offs varied between 17 and 29 per cent and on the fast stretch east of Tonbridge he varied the regulator opening between the first port, full open, and about two-fifths of the main valve.

Although a great deal of fine running was made on the Eastern Section lines, the finest work done by the class was undoubtedly accomplished by the ten locomotives allocated first to Fratton shed, and afterwards transferred to Bournemouth Central after the electrification of the Portsmouth line. These engines were Nos 924–933. The Portsmouth route is extremely hilly, including severe ascents on 1 in 80 through both the North Downs and the South Downs; there are many regular service slacks, such as those at Woking Junction, Guildford and Havant, and yet the 73·6 miles between Waterloo and Portsmouth were booked to be covered nonstop in 90 minutes. On this service the maximum tonnage

TABLE 26

SOUTHERN RALWAY: PORTSMOUTH–WATERLOO
(10.16 am SUNDAY TRAIN)

Load: 11 cars, 360 tons tare, 395 tons full
Engine: 3-cylinder 4–4–0 No 925, *Cheltenham*

Driver: P. Stares }
Fireman: W. Hall } Fratton shed

Distance miles		Sch. min	Actual min sec	Speeds mph
0·0	PORTSMOUTH	0	0 00	—
0·8	Fratton	2	1 56	
—			p.w.r. sev. sigs	
4·1	Farlington Junction		8 15	
—			sigs	
6·4	Bedhampton		12 20	
—			sigs	
7·2	Havant	9½	14 08	
8·6	*Milepost* 65		16 52	36
9·6	*Milepost* 64		18 24	42
10·3	Rowlands Castle		19 28	41
10·6	*Milepost* 63		19 53	41
11·6	*Milepost* 62		21 16	45
12·4	Idsworth Crossing		22 18	—
12·6	*Milepost* 61		22 36	45
13·6	*Milepost* 60		23 58	40
14·6	*Milepost* 59		25 41	31
15·6	*Milepost* 58		28 00	24¾
16·3	Buriton Box		29 08	50½
18·7	Petersfield	27½	31 21	75
—	Stodham Crossing		—	83½
22·1	Liss		33 59	74
24·6	*Milepost* 49		36 20	52½
25·6	*Milepost* 48		37 24	60
26·7	Liphook		38 32	56
—			—	64½
29·6	*Milepost* 44		41 25	62
30·6	Haslemere	41	42 33	50
—	*Milepost* 42½		—	48½
—			—	68/74
35·1	Witley		46 56	p.w. 30
37·3	Milford		49 43	65
39·1	Godalming		51 26	eased
40·1	Farncombe		52 25	60
—			—	62 (max)
—			p.w.s.	15
42·1	Shalford Junction		54 39	—

TABLE 26—*continued*

Distance miles		Sch. min	Actual min sec	Speeds min sec
43·3	Guildford	55	57 10	
44·8	*Milepost* 28¾		60 06	34½
46·8	Worplesdon		62 22	66
49·2	Woking	63	65 06	30 slack
51·9	Byfleet		68 00	67
—			—	71½
54·5	Weybridge		70 14	68½
56·5	Walton		71 58	75
59·2	Esher		74 06	77½
60·3	Hampton Court Junction	73½	74 59	73
61·6	Surbiton		76 03	71½
			p.w.s.	20
63·8	Malden		78 05	
66·3	Wimbledon		80 44	53
68·0	Earlsfield		83 29	61½
69·7	Clapham Junction	83	85 09	
			sig stop	
72·3	Vauxhall		90 43	
			sigs	
73·6	WATERLOO	90	93 58	

Net time 82 mins. Engine worked on 29 per cent cut-off throughout.
Train packed. Many passengers standing in corridors.

handled by the 'Schools' was 350 tare, representing eleven heavy corridor coaches. Despite the difficulties of the route, engines of the 'School' class kept excellent time and usually had several minutes in hand. On two footplate journeys I was privileged to make in 1936, first engine No 924, with ten coaches, made a net time of 83 minutes, while No 925, with the maximum permitted load, achieved some still faster times, even though the train was so crowded with passengers as to represent a gross load of 395 tons behind the tender.

The full logs of these two brilliant runs are shown in Tables 25 and 26. I was not able to make the runs except at a week-end in the summer, and while this had the advantage of ensuring a good load and good rail conditions, the line was apt to be congested, especially in the approaches to Portsmouth Harbour Station. On the down run, I travelled by the

11.50 PM from Waterloo and Driver May was most apologetic at the start. Two relaying slacks were in operation, the second a very bad one on the fastest stretch of all between Liphook and Liss. He had hoped to show off the paces of the engine, but had to shut off steam after a speed of 74 mph had been attained just after Liphook. But so fine was the running elsewhere that Rowlands Castle was passed on time. From Bedhampton, however, we had to join in the queue and eventually reached Portsmouth 24 minutes late. Some years later, when riding on an oil-fired 'T9' 4-4-0 from Salisbury into Portsmouth, I travelled with another fireman of the same name as he who did so well on No 924. Naturally, I asked if they were relations; they were father and son, but I also learned to my sorrow that the elder Mintram gave his life during the Second World War, while serving with the Royal Navy.

On the following morning, a Sunday, I came up with the 10.16 AM train, another 90-minute service, and witnessed some running that was, if anything, even more brilliant (Table 26). Our driver went by the nickname of 'Blinder' Stares; but I hasten to add that while he ran very hard on the open stretches, as from Buriton Tunnel to Haslemere, and from Woking to Hampton Court Junction, he was scrupulously careful in observing the speed restrictions. The long, sustained excitement of this journey arose from the loss of 4½ minutes out to Havant, by adverse signals, and the recovery of time in the face of two severe permanent-way checks, at Shalford Junction and Malden. Another extraordinary feature of the run was that the driver set his lever in 29 per cent cut-off and never once changed it from start to finish. The regulator was opened to the full extent of the first valve on the hardest stretches, but never on the second valve, and the speed-worthiness of the engine in these circumstances was astounding – not only in the swift dash through Petersfield, but in our glorious sprint on the main line east of Woking.

It is now more than thirty years since I made this journey on the footplate. It was a hot sunny morning in late June

TABLE 27
WATERLOO–SOUTHAMPTON: 79·2 MILES

Engine No Engine Name	932 Blundells	925 Cheltenham	931 Kings Wimbledon	925 Cheltenham	926 Repton	932 Blundells	926 Repton	927 Clifton
No of coaches	12	13	14	14	14	15	15	15
Gross tons behind tender	415	445	480	485	490	510	525	525
Actual time (minutes)	82½*	88¼	87½	87¼	91¼	86½	87½	88
Net time (minutes)	83†	87	84	84½	88	86½	87½	87½
Net average speed (mph)	57·3	54·7	56·7	56·2	54·1	55·0	54·3	54·3

* Passing time. † Equivalent time to stop.

and conditions were sweltering in that cab. When we arrived in Waterloo I stopped for some minutes leaning over the cab-side, talking to Stares and watching the crowd of passengers we had brought surging towards the barriers. Suddenly a lady passenger, evidently mistaking me for the fireman and taking unjustified pity on my blackened and sweat-covered face, thrust an orange into my hand saying, 'Here, eat this!'

It was, however, on the long steady gradients of the one-time London & Southampton Railway that the capacity of the 'Schools' was most clearly demonstrated. Here there is no opportunity for charging the gradients at high speed and relying to some extent upon impetus. Nothing can make up for sheer solid worth, in the form of high continuous steaming capacity. Table 27 on the previous page gives summary details of eight runs with the Bournemouth expresses. The schedule time for this run was then 87½ minutes, and it does seem incredible that 4–4–0 locomotives of no more than 67 tons total engine weight and 42 tons adhesion could have made such runs with fifteen-coach trains of 500 tons and more. These were no isolated efforts. Run after run in similar style was recorded by many different observers, and I shall not forget one in the late winter of 1938–9 against a furious south-westerly gale when No 933 hauling a thirteen-coach train of 445 tons reached Southampton in 90¼ minutes or 89 minutes net – a trifling loss of 1¼ minutes.

When it comes to a more detailed analysis of the eight journeys tabulated, the performance of the locomotives becomes even more striking. The journey may be sub-divided as shown in Table 28.

On the eight runs previously mentioned, the time over the 43 miles from Hampton Court Junction to Litchfield signal-box ranged from 43 to 48 minutes. The last named was the journey on which the net time to Southampton was the longest of all, 88 minutes. Some impression of the sustained power output involved can be gained from the further table herewith, on which the average speeds from Hampton Court Junction to Litchfield and the estimated drawbar horsepower are set out. Judging from recent tests of locomotives published by the Railway Executive, the simple and well-known Johansen formula for train resistance: R (in lb per ton) $= 4 + 0.025v + 0.00166v^2$, where v is the speed in miles per hour, gives results that seem rather on the high

TABLE 28

Miles	Section	Road characteristics	Booked speed (mph)
13·3	Waterloo–Hampton Court Junction	Inner suburban area restrained speed	44·3
43·0	Hampton Court Junction–Litchfield Box	Steady climb on average gradient of 1 in 675	56·1
17·3	Litchfield Box–Eastleigh	Fast descent on gradient of 1 in 250	67·0
5·6	Eastleigh–Southampton	Speed restrictions, easy running to finish	42·0

side, and in calculating figures for the accompanying tables values have been taken of 10 lb per ton at 60 mph and 9 lb at 55 mph.

From the table of indicated horsepower with full regulator and working in 25 per cent cut-off, the anticipated output at 55 mph is 1,230 and at 60 mph 1,270 hp; from Table 29 it would indeed seem that on the runs 4, 6 and 8 the locomotives were steaming up to, if not beyond this high standard. It is of interest to analyse still further the run of engine No 932, *Blundells*, in column 6 overleaf, when the 43.0 miles from Hampton Court Junction to Litchfield were covered at an average speed of 58·6 mph.

After this fine exhibition of sustained hard steaming on a long, rising stretch the engine was taken at high speed down the 1 in 250 descent, covering the 15·5 miles from Michel-dever to Eastleigh at an average speed of 77·5 mph and sustaining a maximum of 82 mph. Eastleigh, 73·6 miles from

TABLE 29

Run No	1	2	3	4	5	6	7	8
Engine No	932	925	931	925	926	932	926	927
Load tons gross behind tender	415	445	480	485	490	510	525	525
Average speed (mph)	59·8	55·9	57·1	58·3	53·7	58·6	54·8	55·8
Average estimated DHP	935	885	985	1,040	895	1,095	1,000	1,034

Waterloo, was passed nearly two minutes early, in 77¾ minutes and quite easy running followed into Southampton. Although this run was the most praiseworthy of all, the whole collection of eight forms a remarkable tribute to the efficacy of the 'Schools' as motive-power units, units that, in relation to their total engine weight of 67 tons, must rank as among the most outstanding ever to run in Great Britain.

TABLE 30

Miles	Section	Gradient average	Average speed (mph)	Average estimated DHP
5·8	Hampton Court Junction to Weybridge	1 in 1,800 rising	63·9	1,040
11·9	Weybridge to Milepost 31	1 in 240 rising	57·4	1,250
11·2	Milepost 31 to Hook	1 in 1,950 rising	60·1	930
14·1	Hook to Litchfield	1 in 490 rising	56·8	1,150

On the footplate, despite a rather attenuated cab, they were most comfortable to ride, easy on the track and kind to their privileged guests. Some of the fastest running I have personally recorded on them has been made while the engine was riding so steadily that I had no need to hold the cab-side or support, and was able to make all my notes standing. Some of these engines had multiple-jet blast-pipes and large-diameter chimneys, following similar alterations made to the Nelsons'. While I have noted some very excellent performances with engines so modified, insufficient data is available by which to judge whether any substantial improvement has been made by this change, either in the maximum power output or in economy. At the time of this change, the locomotives concerned were fitted with steam-chest pressure gauges. In pre-war days, observers on the footplate were often curious to know the effective regulator opening, when remarkable feats of running were achieved. Since the war, on engines fitted with multiple-jet blast-pipes, I have seen the steam-chest pressure gauge registering 195 lb per sq in with the regulator apparently no more than about half open.

An interesting high-speed performance was made with one of the modified engines when No 931, *Kings Wimbledon*, worked the Saturday section of the 'Atlantic Coast Express' leaving Waterloo at 10.24 AM in such style that Andover 66·4 miles from the start, was passed in 58¾ minutes with a load of 305 tons; the 38 uphill miles from Esher to Oakley, on a rising gradient averaging about 1 in 610, were covered in 30¾ minutes – 74 mph average. This is roughly equivalent to an output of 1,000 DHP and reference to the table of IHP shows that at 74 mph, with full regulator and 25 per cent cut-off, an output of about 1,270 to 1,280 might be expected. The difference of 270 to 280 horsepower, representing the frictional loss, seems rather on the low side for a speed of 74 mph, and suggests that on this fast run No 931 may have been steamed rather heavier than the rate corresponding to 25 per cent. On a recent run with No 930, *Radley*, the driver worked his engine in 32 per cent cut-off, with almost full regulator on the climb from Tonbridge to Sevenoaks Tunnel, without any loss of pressure, or falling of water level in the boiler. At the same time, the low internal resistance of these engines, due to even turning moment, favours the development of a high drawbar horsepower in relation to IHP. The success of the 'Schools' is due to high mechanical, as well as thermal efficiency. It only remains to add that the 'Schools' have always been universal favourites with the men, at whatever depots they have been stationed. The design will certainly go down in history as one of the masterpieces of British locomotive practice.

CHAPTER ELEVEN

LOCOMOTIVE PERFORMANCE 1935-9

Day-to-day running on the Southern Railway had reached a high level of efficiency by the later Maunsell years. On most routes the timings had been gradually accelerated, while loads were showing a constant tendency to rise. Moreover, the standards of general operating had been improved out of all recognition, and even on summer Saturdays punctuality was well maintained on the lines out of Waterloo. Colour-light signalling was to some extent responsible for this improvement; but all concerned with the running of trains seemed to be 'on their toes', and delays to express passenger trains were regarded as serious matters. In one respect, of course, the Southern was fortunate. All its constituents were pre-eminently passenger lines; at times of heavy pressure the freight trains could be run almost entirely at night, and there was little in the way of complicated cross-country connexions to be made. In this chapter I have brought together a number of typical runs, most of which I clocked personally, to indicate the kind of performance put up in ordinary service. The only occasion on which the driver was aware that his work was being recorded in detail was a post-war journey on the 11.30 AM to Southampton, when I was on the footplate. With my own runs I have included some further journeys with 'King Arthur' class engines, details of which were published at various times in *The Railway Magazine* by Mr Cecil J. Allen.

Taking the Eastern Section first, there are two runs (Table 31) on the up 80-minute Folkestone expresses, contrasting the work of the 'School' class engines in light and heavy loading conditions. The run with the seven-coach train was made in early spring, and even with this relatively light load the exacting nature of the 76-minute booking to Waterloo is apparent; for with three permanent-way checks

TABLE 31
SOUTHERN RAILWAY:
FOLKESTONE–CHARING CROSS

Engine No Engine Name Load tons tare Load tons full		921 Shrewsbury 224 235			917 Ardingly 356 390	
Distance miles		Sch. min	Actual min sec	Speeds mph	Actual min sec	Speeds mph
0·0	FOLKESTONE	0	0 00	—	0 00	—
1·8	Cheriton Junction		3 47	41	4 31	39
4·5	Sandling Junction	7½	7 10	51	8 23	47½
5·7	Westenhanger		8 43	53	9 54	49½
9·5	Smeeth		12 06	75	13 32	71
13·8	ASHFORD	16½	15 25	82	17 00	76½
16·0	Chart Siding		17 08	73½	18 49	69
19·5	Pluckley		19 54	80/76	21 47	75/72
24·7	Headcorn		23 52	82	25 59	79
28·0	Staplehurst		26 21	77	28 38	74
30·5	Marden		28 21	72	30 45	70½
—			p.w.s.	30	—	
35·1	Paddock Wood	34½	32 55	—	34 30	75
38·9	Milepost 31		38 18	53	37 49	64½
—			—	60	—	67½
40·4	TONBRIDGE	39½	39 54	40*	39 09	40*
42·9	Hildenborough		43 28	45½	42 18	43
44·8	Weald Box		46 15	40½	45 19	35½
47·2	Tunnel exit		49 50	40½	49 33	34
			p.w.s.		—	
47·8	SEVENOAKS	51½	51 17	25	50 29	—
49·3	Dunton Green		53 18	57½	52 09	—
53·3	Knockholt		57 55	47½	56 51	44
56·1	Orpington	60	60 29	76½	59 34	71½
58·6	Chislehurst	62½	62 27	79	61 39	74
59·6	Elmstead Woods		63 16	73	62 28	73
60·9	Grove Park		64 18	75½	63 31	75
62·7	Hither Green		65 50	—	65 06	—
65·0	New Cross		69 02	—	68 15	—
			p.w.s.	25	—	
68·0	LONDON BRIDGE	73	74 07	—	72 36	—
—			sigs	5	—	
69·2	WATERLOO JUNCTION	76	77 32		74 49	
—			79 54		76 12	
69·9	CHARING CROSS	80	82 45		79 27	

* Permanent speed restrictions.

in operation we did not keep time. Even so, there was some very fast running. After an acceleration to 53 mph up the initial 1 in 266 to Sandling Tunnel, the engine averaged 77·5 mph over the 21 miles from Smeeth to Marden, with maximum speeds of 82 mph at both Ashford and Headcorn. The check at Paddock Wood was a bad one, and we were barely on time through Tonbridge; but the second check at Sevenoaks was less severe, and with high speed down from Knockholt we were through New Cross on time. The two concluding delays, however, put us 1½ minutes out on arrival at Waterloo. The net time was no more than 72 minutes, an excellent run. On the second run, with the 6.5 PM Sunday evening train, Driver Morley, of Ramsgate, made a splendid run with a 390-ton load. It is strange, too, that one of the very few runs I have experienced over this route without a single check should have been made on a Sunday. The effort was sustained throughout: a fine start, an average of 73·5 mph from Smeeth to Paddock Wood and a good climb to Knockholt. We were a minute early at Hither Green and, with smart station working at Waterloo, we reached Charing Cross nicely inside the 80-minute booking.

In the reverse direction, a run I made on the Night Ferry service in February 1937, not long after its introduction, gave me a locomotive performance that, within my own experience, was quite exceptional in its vigour (Table 32). The train was always very heavy, and often beyond the un-aided capacity of a 'Nelson'. When this was the case, it was double-headed with two 4–4–0s, nearly always an 'L1' leading, and either an 'L' or an 'E1' as assistant. But on this trip we had a relatively 'light' load of 424 tons tare, and engine No 854, *Howard of Effingham*. The work was pleasant-ly vigorous from the start, with such speeds as 55 mph through Bromley and a minimum of 34½ at Bickley Junction. Then we became involved in signal checks, and took 49½ minutes to pass Tonbridge. When, to follow this, there came a severe relaying slack at Marden I was nearly tempted to give up timing and attend to some urgent notes I had brought with me to do on the journey if the railway interest

TABLE 32

SOUTHERN RAILWAY:
VICTORIA–DOVER MARINE
(10.0 PM NIGHT FERRY SERVICE)

Load: 424 tons tare, 440 tons full
Engine: No 854 *Howard of Effingham* ('Nelson' class)

Distance miles		Actual min sec	Speeds mph
0·0	VICTORIA	0 00	
4·0	Herne Hill	9 10	
5·7	Sydenham Hill	12 39	27
7·8	Kent House	15 58	56
10·0	Shortlands	18 30	50
10·9	Bromley	19 32	55
12·6	Bickley Junction	22 15	34½
14·9	Orpington	25 43	44½
		sigs sev.	
17·7	Knockholt	30 50	5
21·7	Dunton Green	36 33	65
		sigs sev.	
23·2	Sevenoaks	39 23	15
28·1	Hildenborough	46 35	70½
30·6	TONBRIDGE	49 30	40 (slack)
35·9	Paddock Wood	56 03	67½
—		p.w.s. sev.	15
40·5	Marden	63 20	43
43·0	Staplehurst	66 17	63
46·3	Headcorn	69 19	69
—		—	66
51·5	Pluckley	74 00	71½
55·0	Chart Siding	77 56	67
57·2	ASHFORD	78 51	75
61·5	Smeeth	82 28	68/69½
65·3	Westenhanger	85 57	61½
66·5	Sandling Junction	87 07	65
69·2	Cheriton Junction	89 25	76½
—		—	eased
71·0	FOLKESTONE CENTRAL	90 58	63
72·0	Folkestone Junction	91 54	64½
76·1	Shakespeare's Cliff Halt	96 18	
78·0	DOVER MARINE	99 40	

Net time: 89½ minutes.

flagged. But when No 854 got away to 69 mph on the level at
Headcorn, and then did not fall below 66 mph on the rise to
Chart Siding – several miles at 1 in 277–287 – I was glad I
had persevered a bit longer. We swept through Ashford at
75 mph and cleared Westenhanger at 62½ mph. The result
was that, despite 10 minutes delay on the road, we reached
Dover in a shade under 100 minutes – 89½ minutes net. The
running between Staplehurst and Folkestone was a grand
example of what the original 'Nelsons' could do when
expertly handled.

One really needs to see the Hastings line from the footplate to appreciate the difficulties in running imposed by the
curvature. The overall speeds have never been spectacular,
but the haulage of holiday trains loading up to nearly 400
tons gross weight provided the 'Schools' with some of their
most exacting duties. When I made the run shown in Table
33, on the 7.17 PM from St Leonards to Charing Cross,
through carriages were still being run to and from Bexhill;
we took eight coaches from Hastings, and attached another
three at Crowhurst. With the lighter load of 270 tons gross,
we attained 36 mph up the 1 in 100 from West St Leonards,
and then after the downhill spurt from Battle to Roberts-
bridge we did well up to Wadhurst with our 370-ton load.
The engine was accelerated to 57 mph from the start in 3½
miles of level road and then went up seven miles of stiff
ascent, mostly at 1 in 100–132, without falling below 39
mph. The climbing on the main line inward from Tonbridge
was rather below the best standards of the 'Schools' on the
Folkestone trains, though, to be sure, *Leatherhead* was
running this Hastings train on time. But the trip ended with
a fast spell down from Knockholt, and a maximum speed of
80½ mph.

Switching over now to the Western Section, I have included details of the work on the 5.25 PM from Haslemere to
Waterloo to show the excellent standards of running prevail-
ing generally on the Southern Railway in the years just
before the Second World War (Table 34). The big Drummond 'D15' engine, No 465, was then in her intermediate

TABLE 33

SOUTHERN RAILWAY:
7.17 PM ST LEONARDS–LONDON BRIDGE

Load: 8 cars, 250 tons tare, 270 tons full
Engine: No 939, *Leatherhead* ('Schools' class)

Distance miles		Actual min sec		Speeds mph
0·0	WEST ST LEONARDS	0	00	—
0·8	*Milepost* 60	2	48	—
1·8	*Milepost* 59	4	35	32½
2·8	*Milepost* 58	6	27	36
3·2	Crowhurst	7	18	

Load: 11 cars, 344 tons tare, 370 tons full

0·0	Crowhurst	0	00	—
2·0	Battle	5	00	—
—			—	62½
—		slight slack		—
4·9	Mountfield Halt	8	03	47 (min)
			—	69 (max)
8·0	ROBERTSBRIDGE	11	50	
0·0		0	00	
2·2	Etchingham	3	55	50
3·6	*Milepost* 46	5	36	57
5·8	Ticehurst Road	8	05	50½
8·6	*Milepost* 41	11	47	39
10·3	Wadhurst	14	22	41
—			—	50 (max)
12·9	Frant	17	54	41 (min)
15·2	TUNBRIDGE WELLS	21	17	
0·0		0	00	
1·5	High Brooms	3	51	
—			—	54 (max)
4·9	TONBRIDGE	8	33	39 slack
5·9	*Milepost* 28½		—	44
7·4	Hildenborough	12	13	38
9·3	Weald Box	15	30	32½
11·7	Sevenoaks Tunnel out	19	58	32½
12·3	SEVENOAKS	21	03	—
0·0		0	00	
1·5	Dunton Green	3	09	48
5·5	Knockholt	8	57	35
8·3	Orpington	11	50	69
10·8	Chislehurst	13	59	73
11·8	Elmstead Woods	14	48	75
13·1	Grove Park	15	48	80½
14·9	Hither Green	17	28	(slack)
17·2	New Cross	20	50	
		sigs		
20·2	LONDON BRIDGE	26	40	

TABLE 34

SOUTHERN RAILWAY:
5.25 PM HASLEMERE–WATERLOO

Load: 9 cars, 292 tons tare, 310 tons full
Engine: No 465 Drummond 6 ft 7 in (4–4–0) class 'D15'

Distance miles		Actual min sec		Speeds mph
0·0	HASLEMERE	0	00	—
0·5	*Milepost 42½*	2	27	—
		—		72 (max)
4·5	Witley	6	47	57
6·7	Milford	8	48	75
8·5	Godalming	10	50	
1·0	Farncombe	3	02	
—		sigs & p.w.s.		
3·2	GUILDFORD	6	45	
1·5	*Milepost 28¾*	4	13	30
3·5	Worplesdon	6	49	58
5·9	WOKING	9	55	40 (slack)
8·6	Byfleet	13	04	61
		—		66
11·2	Weybridge	15	37	61
13·2	Walton	17	31	64½
15·9	Esher	19	57	68
17·0	Hampton Court Junction	20	55	66
		p.w.s.		
18·3	Surbiton	22	22	—
20·5	Malden	25	49	56 (max)
		sigs dead slow		
23·0	Wimbledon	30	02	5
24·7	Earlsfield	32	51	50 (max)
26·4	CLAPHAM JUNCTION	35	01	40 (slack)
29·0	Vauxhall	38	25	52
30·3	WATERLOO	40	45	

Net time: 36½ minutes.

state, exactly as rebuilt by Urie and fitted with the Eastleigh superheater; she had quite a big train for the Portsmouth line, and was driven with great determination. The
trip began, so far as I was concerned, with a fast run down
from Haslemere touching 75 mph at Milford; then after the

stops at Godalming, Farncombe and Guildford we ran right
up to the standards of the 90-minute Portsmouth trains on
the non-stop run to Waterloo. Speed rose to 68 mph on the
level at Esher, and after the check at Surbiton the engine
was put to it hard to reach 56 mph in just over two miles.
Then came a signal check at Wimbledon, but the driver still
tried hard; and after Clapham Junction we accelerated to
52 mph at Vauxhall, and made what is easily my record
time of 2 minutes 20 seconds from there into Waterloo. The
up Portsmouth expresses in the 90-minute steam days were
allowed 35 minutes pass-to-stop from Guildford to Waterloo; the net time of No 465, $36\frac{1}{2}$ minutes start-to-stop is
roughly equal to this.

I have referred fairly extensively to the work of the 'Schools'
on the Bournemouth expresses, in Chapter Ten. The engines of that class which were then stationed at Bournemouth
took a share in the working of the cross-country trains
destined for Newcastle on the one hand, and Birkenhead on
the other. The Birkenhead–Bournemouth expresses rarely got
a chance to show their paces over the Great Western line
between Reading and Didcot, and the through service
worked by Southern engines between Bournemouth and
Oxford formed a good mileage job rather than a high-speed
turn. Apart from the working of those Waterloo–Bournemouth trains which stopped at Southampton – and working
them with loads up to fifteen coaches of the heaviest stock –
the running of the 'Bournemouth Limited' in two hours non-
stop was perhaps the finest job the 'Schools' ever did.
Bournemouth expresses non-stop from Waterloo in two
hours were no novelty; but before the introduction of the
'Schools' every engine working on these trains had a large
bogie tender, and in Drummond's day, when the loads were
about 270 tons, time was sometimes lost through drivers
having to conserve their water supply. Yet here in the
'Schools' was an engine with a six-wheeled tender carrying
five tons of coal and 4,000 gallons of water against the
corresponding amounts of five tons and 5,000 gallons on the
bogie tenders of the 'King Arthurs'. I have shown in Table

35 an excellent example of running on the 8.40 AM up two-hour train, with the normal maximum load of eleven coaches. I am not aware that this train was ever 'strengthened' at times of heavy traffic, but, on this particular run, time was kept in spite of a full seven minutes lost by out-of-course slowings. Careful attention was also paid to the permanent speed restrictions, over curves and junctions, and, in the log, reductions will be noted to 50 mph at Christchurch, 30 at Totton Viaduct, 15 over Northam Junction and 60 at Worting Junction. While it would be asking for trouble to exceed the limits at Totton and Northam by very much, Christchurch and Worting are places where a driver who was running well up to the limit might be tempted to run faster to gain a little time. But the whole performance of No 930, *Radley*, gave the impression that the situation was very comfortably in hand.

The recovery from the Christchurch slack to 53 mph at Hinton Admiral was made up markedly-rising gradients, including one half-mile at 1 in 137; and the minimum of 47 mph up the last mile at 1 in 119–103 was excellent. Then over the Forest section, though checked to 25 mph on the most favourable stretch of all, through Brockenhurst, the engine recovered splendidly to reach 72 mph between Lyndhurst Road and Totton. Then, after a clear run through Southampton, we were pulled up dead by signal at St Denys, and on getting away again had only 80 minutes left in which to run the 77·2 miles to Waterloo. This was successfully done, despite a permanent-way check to 20 mph in the middle of another very fast stretch near Hook. Even with this hindrance, which cost at least 2½ minutes, we passed Clapham Junction, 73·3 miles, in 74 minutes. Speed was held steadily at 50 mph up the long 1 in 250 from Eastleigh up to Litchfield Tunnel, and after recovery from the check near Hook a fine average speed of 76 mph was made over the 26 miles from Farnborough to Wimbledon. This net time of 112 minutes, with its average speed of all but 58 mph, was made on a consumption of about 3,500 gallons of water – 32 to the mile. This was a characteristic, rather than an

TABLE 35
SOUTHERN RAILWAY:
8.40 AM BOURNEMOUTH–WATERLOO

Load: 11 coaches, 352 tons tare, 375 tons full
Engine: No 930, *Radley* ('Schools' class)

Distance miles		Actual min sec	Speeds mph
0·0	BOURNEMOUTH	0 00	—
1·8	Pokesdown	4 22	
—		—	66
3·7	Christchurch	6 32	50 (slack)
—		—	48½
6·9	Hinton Admiral	10 24	53
—		—	47
9·4	New Milton	13 27	51½
12·4	Sway	16 31	62½/60
—	Lymington Junction	p.w. slack	25
15·2	BROCKENHURST	19 55	58/54
—		—	64½
19·9	Beaulieu Road	24 44	61/67½
22·6	Lyndhurst Road	27 12	65½
24·7	*Milepost 83¼*	29 07	72
25·4	Totton	29 52	30 (slack)
28·7	SOUTHAMPTON CENTRAL	34 16	51
29·8	Northam Junction	36 09	15 (slack)
30·8	St Denys arr	38 52	sig stop
	dep	39 35	
34·4	EASTLEIGH	46 17	50½
38·2	Shawford	50 49	50½
41·3	WINCHESTER	54 33	50
43·4	Winchester Junction	57 07	49
46·1	Wallers Ash Box	60 25	50
49·8	Micheldever	64 52	50
51·8	Litchfield Box	67 14	51
55·3	Wootton Box	71 00	64½
—		—	69
57·6	Worting Junction	73 06	60 (slack)
60·1	BASINGSTOKE	75 20	76
—		—	79
65·7	Hook	79 44	74
—	*Milepost 41*	p.w.s.	20
68·2	Winchfield	83 32	50
71·5	Fleet	86 57	64½
74·7	Farnborough	89 52	69
—	Sturt Lane Junction	—	72
77·0	*Milepost 31*	91 49	69
79·9	Brookwood	94 14	77
83·6	WOKING	97 05	80½

TABLE 35—*continued*

Distance miles		Actual min sec	Speeds mph
86·1	Byfleet	98 56	82
88·8	Weybridge	100 58	77
90·8	Walton	102 28	81
93·6	Esher	104 34	78
95·9	Surbiton	106 23	74
98·2	Malden	108 15	72½
100·7	Wimbledon	110 23	69
102·5	Earlsfield	111 56	
104·1	CLAPHAM JUNCTION	113 37	
106·6	Vauxhall	116 35	
108·0	WATERLOO	119 30	

Net time: 112 minutes.

exceptional performance, and testifies to the splendid working efficiency of the 'Schools' class engines.

On the down West of England expresses between Waterloo and Salisbury I was generally unfortunate in my personal experiences. Either the loads were light, or delays were encountered. One Saturday in 1936 I travelled by the 10.35 AM from Waterloo, then allowed only 86 minutes to Salisbury. Engine No 780, *Sir Persant*, with a 380-ton train, made a grand start passing Weybridge in 23¼ minutes; but delays at Woking and Basingstoke were so bad that eventually we took 101 minutes to Salisbury. I have tabulated two runs with identical loads (Table 36). The 'King Arthur' effort, with engine No 450 was on the 3 PM from Waterloo, allowed 88 minutes, while the 'Nelson' trip was on the Sunday 'Atlantic Coast Express'. These two runs are extremely interesting as showing the superiority of the 'Nelson' over the 'Arthur' on a road where there is little 'give and take'. *Sir Kay* was being well driven, and in relation to its size put forth a fine output of power; but on the long grind from Weybridge to Oakley *Lord St Vincent* just streaked ahead and in almost complete silence. Then at Andover, where the 'King Arthur' could have piled on some real speed, there came a permanent-way check right in the

TABLE 36

SOUTHERN RAILWAY: WATERLOO–SALISBURY

Engine No Engine Name Load tons tare Load tons full	450 Sir Kay 419 450		856 Lord St Vincent* 420 450	
Distance miles	Actual min sec	Speeds mph	Actual min sec	Speeds mph
0·0 WATERLOO	0 00	—	0 00	—
—	—	—	sigs	—
3·9 CLAPHAM JUNCTION	7 25	—	8 55	—
7·3 Wimbledon	11 30	53	13 32	51
12·0 Surbiton	16 42	57	18 43	60
—	p.w. slack	25	—	—
14·4 Esher	21 00	—	20 59	66
19·1 Weybridge	27 17	59	25 21	61½
21·7 Byfleet	30 00	57	27 43	67½
24·4 WOKING	32 55	53	30 19	61
28·0 Brookwood	37 13	49¼	34 11	54½
31·0 Milepost 31	40 51	50	37 35	51½
33·2 Farnborough	43 16	59	40 01	60½
36·5 Fleet	46 35	62	43 10	67
39·7 Winchfield	49 51	56½	46 06	60½
42·2 Hook	52 22	64½	49 32	69
47·8 BASINGSTOKE	57 52	56	53 38	63½
50·3 Worting Junction	60 44	50	56 11	54
52·4 Oakley	63 07	—	58 28	—
55·6 Overton	66 22	63½	61 35	66
59·2 Whitchurch	69 38	71	64 38	75
61·1 Hurstbourne	71 16	76½	66 06	80½
62·6 Milepost 62½	72 30	69	67 14	77½
—	p.w. slack	77	—	—
66·4 ANDOVER JUNCTION	75 42	30	69 55	91
67·8 Red Post Junction	78 25	48½	—	—
72·8 Grateley	84 43	43	75 01	58½
75·7 Amesbury Junction	88 11	60	77 51	66
78·3 Porton	90 33	79	80 06	86½
82·7 Tunnel Junction	94 08	—	83 15	—
83·8 SALISBURY	96 19		85 32	

* Original condition: before Bulleid rebuilding.

dip. The way the engine fought back, and mounted the 4½ miles of 1 in 264–165 to Grateley at a minimum speed of 43 mph was excellent, but the train was nevertheless 8¼ minutes late into Salisbury. There was no margin to offset delays with a load of this magnitude. As if to heighten the contrast, *Lord St Vincent* got a clear road; we swept through Andover at 91 mph, cleared Grateley summit at 58½ mph, and reached 86½ mph down Porton bank. In consequence, we ran into Salisbury some 4½ minutes early. So far as the work of No 450, *Sir Kay*, was concerned, I was very interested to find that it compared closely with the 'all-out' performance of the new diesel-electrics Nos 10201 and 10202. In 1952, I was privileged to travel on the latter engine, and in starting westward from Andover the climbing to Grateley involved an effort just about equal to that of *Sir Kay*.

In the latter days of the Maunsell régime, all my eastbound journeys from Salisbury were with 'N15' class engines, and I have set out in Table 37 the details of two interesting trips alongside that Southern 'record of records' over this route, with engine No 777, *Sir Lamiel*, details of which were published in *The Railway Magazine* by Mr Cecil J. Allen. I remember discussing this run with Mr Holcroft, and he, who knew the capacity of the 'King Arthurs' as well as anyone, was frankly incredulous. His only explanation was that there must have been a strong following wind! Certainly, the results were astonishing, with an average speed of 80·2 mph over the 54·4 miles from Andover to Surbiton! My own runs were nothing like so spectacular, but both included some very fine performances. *Sir Galahad*, in particular, did some terrific work from Grateley summit, touching 85 mph at Andover and never falling below 60 mph all the way up to Oakley. This stage of the run makes an interesting comparison with the runs of No 860, *Lord Hawke*, included in Chapter 8. We might eventually have made a really fast overall time on this run, but it was a hot, thundery afternoon and at Hook we ran into a torrential rainstorm which made sighting the signals difficult. The driver accordingly eased up, and when we later passed into clear weather the

TABLE 37

SOUTHERN RAILWAY : SALISBURY–WATERLOO

Engine No Engine Name Load tons tare Load tons full	777 Sir Lamiel 328 345		456 Sir Galahad 419 450		776 Sir Galagars 419 445		751 Etarre 447 490	
Distance miles	Actual min sec	Speeds mph	Actual min sec	Speeds mph	Actual min sec	Speeds mph	Actual min sec	Speeds mph
0·0 SALISBURY	0 00	—	0 00	—	0 00	—	0 00	—
1·1 Tunnel Junction	3 04	—	3 48	—	3 49	—	4 24	—
5·5 Porton	8 22	53	10 37	36	9 50	39	11 59	29
11·0 Grateley	14 00	66	18 13	53½	17 00	53½	21 00	46
17·4 ANDOVER JUNCTION	18 43	88½	23 16	85	22 16	78½	26 38	75
21·2 Milepost 62½			26 21	61½	25 34	62	30 10	53
22·7 Hurstbourne	22 52	70½	27 42	68½	26 51	68½	31 43	60
24·6 Whitchurch	24 24	76½	29 28	62	28 35	64	33 48	54
28·2 Overton	27 20	72½	32 57	63½	31 53	65	37 53	53
31·4 Oakley	29 54	79	36 04	62	34 50	69	41 29	59

33·5	Worting Junction	31	33	75	38	02	69	36	39	71	43	39	64
36·0	BASINGSTOKE	33	26	88½	40	05	75	38	36	82½	45	52	67½
					storm								
41·6	Hook	37	25	80	44	53	63	42	46	78	50	26	65
44·1	Winchfield	39	15	82	47	14	63	44	38	76	52	34	69
47·3	Fleet	41	33	85	50	08		47	12	79	55	15	75
50·6	Farnborough	44	00	80½	53	05	69	49	50	75	58	06	68
52·8	*Milepost* 31			76½	55	01	68	51	39	72	60	06	65
55·8	Brookwood	47	56	83½	57	36	76½	53	59	80	62	43	72½
					sigs								
59·4	WOKING	50	26	88½	61	25	30	56	41	80½	65	41	75
62·1	Byfleet	52	15	90	64	35	60	58	41	82	67	51	74
64·7	Weybridge	54	05	82	67	18	53	60	41	69	70	00	86½
69·4	Esher				72	02	62½			71	74	05	72
71·8	Surbiton	59	28	76½	74	27	56	66	47	67	76	14	63
76·5	Wimbledon	63	20	69	79	32	58½	71	21	58	80	45	64
79·9	CLAPHAM JUNCTION	66	27		83	17		75	07		84	27	
					sigs						sigs		
83·8	WATERLOO	72	41		93	12		80	40		96	17	
	Net times (minutes)	72¾			87½			80¾			91½		

effort from the engine was not renewed with anything like the same vigour. The run ended in something of an anti-climax, with signal delays inwards from Woking.

In almost every respect this run of mine with *Sir Galahad* was eclipsed by a wonderful performance recorded in June 1939 by Sir James Colyer-Fergusson with engine No 776, *Sir Galagars*. Driver Payne of Nine Elms was at the regulator, and leaving Salisbury seven minutes late he did his level best to be 'on time' at Waterloo. Some very hard running was involved with no lower speed than 64 mph on the rising gradient between Hurstbourne and Oakley. The driver told my friend afterwards that he had to 'push' the engine rather more than he liked to make such a long sustained effort; but the 'pushing' was certainly to some purpose when it is seen that the average speed over the 35·8 miles from Basingstoke to Surbiton was 76·2 mph. Payne was one of the most expert and enterprising Southern drivers of his day, and this run probably represents something very near the maximum that could be got out of an 'Arthur' in such conditions of loading.

Speaking of drivers, I should mention that it was Alderman of Nine Elms who made the record run with No 777, while on my run with No 456 the driver was Johnson of Salisbury shed. On the 6.19 PM Sunday evening express, with a packed train of fourteen bogies, Driver Silk of Nine Elms did some fine work with one of the Urie engines No 751, *Etarre*. As might be expected, the start was much slower than that of *Sir Galahad* – in fact No 751 was 5¾ minutes behind time at Basingstoke. But a splendidly-sustained effort followed with this 490-ton train. Speed averaged 70·7 mph over the 35·8 miles from Basingstoke to Surbiton and, passing Clapham Junction in 84½ minutes from the start, we could have finished comfortably in 91 or 92½ minutes.

This last run with *Etarre* was a fine example of what the Urie 'N15' engines could do after their smokebox arrangements had been modified by Mr Maunsell. In 1945, I had an excellent run on the footplate of No 747, *Elaine*, on the 11.30 AM from Waterloo on which we took an identical load of 490 tons. With stops at Basingstoke, Micheldever and Winchester, there was not much chance of sustained running; but the engine worked well and ran fast down from Micheldever. I was particularly interested to see her complete immunity from slipping when starting away. At Basingstoke, Winchester and again at Southampton, while the reverser stood in full forward gear the regulator was put straight over to the full open, and the engine moved cleanly away without any suspicion of slip.

And so I come last of all, and perhaps most appropriately, to the West of England line between Salisbury and Exeter. Nowhere else did the Maunsell locomotives perform with more consistent brilliance than here. In the period now under review, the 'King Arthurs' had the course to themselves, and it was remarkable that while they seemed to have little margin in hand with 450-ton trains on the more level section of line east of Salisbury, on the Exeter road they would often pull off average speeds of nearly 60 mph from the start to stop on the westbound run. I have shown details, in Table 38, of four journeys over this most exciting course. The runs with engines Nos 779, 453 and 768 were published in *The Railway Magazine*, while the first of the four, with a Urie engine, was an experience of my own – the continuation of the unlucky run with No 780 down from Waterloo, on the 10.35 AM Saturday train. On a fast run over this route, one could usually expect to clock six separate maxima of 80 mph or more, at Gillingham, before Templecombe, at Sherborne, near Axminster, before Sidmouth Junction, and at Broad Clyst. On Runs 2 and 3 the 'six' did not materialize as No 779 reached only 79 mph at Axminster, and No 453 did 79 mph at both Gillingham and before Templecombe. Only 79! – but with No 779 on a run including such first-rate hill-climbing that Exmouth Junction, 86·9 miles, was passed in $85\frac{1}{2}$ minutes, and only a slight signal check at the finish prevented a 60 mph start-to-stop run.

As to the individual features of these four splendid runs, the Urie engine, *Maid of Astolat*, was consistently slower on

TABLE 38

SOUTHERN RAILWAY: SALISBURY–EXETER

Run No		1		2		3		4	
Engine No		744		779		453		768	
Engine Name		Maid of Astolat		Sir Colgrevance		King Arthur		Sir Balin	
Load tons tare		361		388		420		421	
Load tons full		380		415		450		455	
Distance miles		Actual min sec	Speeds mph	Actual min sec	Speeds mph	Actual min sec	Speeds mph	Actual min sec	Speeds mph
0·0	SALISBURY	0 00	—	0 00	—	0 00	—	0 00	—
2·5	Wilton	6 34	—	5 35	—	6 20	—	6 15	—
8·2	Dinton	13 43	58½	11 40	63	13 15	57	13 05	59
12·5	Tisbury	18 30	54	15 55	—	17 55	—	17 50	53
17·5	Semley	24 21	45¼	21 05	52	23 35	45	23 50	42
21·6	Gillingham	27 57	83½	24 25	82	27 10	79	27 30	82
23·9	Milepost 107½	29 46	66	26 18	63	29 05	60	29 19	64
28·4	TEMPLECOMBE	33 23	82	29 55	82	32 45	79	32 55	82
30·8	Milborne Port	36 06	48½	32 30	51	35 25	49	35 30	50
34·5	Sherborne	39 27	82	35 37	85	38 40	82	38 45	85
39·1	YEOVIL JUNCTION	43 12	75	39 10	—	42 15	—	42 10	77
41·3	Sutton Bingham	45 20	48	41 05	56	44 15	50	44 05	54
47·9	Crewkerne	52 08	68	47 05	71	50 50	66	50 15	71
49·7	Milepost 133¼	54 49	32½	49 15	42	53 23	36	52 45	37
55·9	Chard Junction	60 48	77¼	54 50	—	59 17	—	58 25	80
61·0	Axminster	64 42	65	58 40	79	63 08	80	62 00	86½
64·2	Seaton Junction	67 21	19	61 20	—	65 45	—	64 30	71½
69·0	Milepost 152½	76 10	26	68 50	25	73 40	23	71 30	26½
70·0	Milepost 153½	78 43	60	71 01	29	75 50	27	73 31	32
71·2	Honiton	80 15	83½	72 25	—	77 25	—	74 50	62
75·8	SIDMOUTH JUNCTION	84 03	69½	76 10	80	81 05	82	78 35	82
79·5	Whimple	87 03	82½	79 15	68	84 00	71½	81 50	65
83·2	Broad Clyst	89 40	88	82 00	—	86 35	86	84 30	76
86·9	Exmouth Junction	92 45	62½	85 35	80	89 25	—	87 45	83
				sigs					
88·0	EXETER	94 51	—	88 10	—	92 00	—	90 00	—

the banks, although her downhill speeds were some of the highest, including the 88 mph at Broad Clyst. One would have thought that in heavy slogging, as between Seaton Junction and Honiton Tunnel, there would have been no difference between the Urie and the Maunsell engines; but the work of No 744 was quite typical, and not a product of one driver's technique. But, as I have mentioned before in this book, the *Maid of Astolat* was a very fast young thing on the downhill stretches, and this run was not the first occasion on which she had taken me through Broad Clyst at 88 mph. The second run, with No 779, *Sir Colgrevance*, was distinguished by a most brilliant start out of Salisbury and by a big sustained effort that made 'even-time' soon after Yeovil. At Hewish Summit, Milepost $133\frac{1}{4}$, No 779 was $3\frac{1}{2}$ minutes ahead of the next fastest engine; this advantage was gained chiefly by such grand uphill efforts as 52 mph over Semley, and 42 at Hewish itself. Of course the output of power that produced such an average speed as 58·2 mph over the five miles from Tisbury to Semley – five miles including $1\frac{3}{4}$ at 1 in 270 and $2\frac{1}{4}$ at 1 in 145 – could not have been sustained by an engine of such moderate size as a 'King Arthur' and the downhill stretch to Templecombe was no doubt used for recovering breath. The rate of acceleration from Semley was much swifter with *Maid of Astolat*, which had been driven more easily uphill from Wilton, and between Gillingham and Templecombe the 'Maid' actually gained on *Sir Colgrevance*.

On No 3 run, *King Arthur* himself, with a 450-ton train, did splendidly throughout: not so fast as *Sir Colgrevance* in the early stages, but with good hill-climbing and a very fast finish a clear six minutes was gained on booked time, giving an average speed of 57·3 mph from start-to-stop. Actually, the maximum speed at Broad Clyst did not quite equal that attained by *Maid of Astolat*, but *King Arthur* came over the hump between Sidmouth Junction and Whimple at a rather higher speed. The average speed between Honiton and Exmouth Junction, 15·7 miles, was 78·6 mph against 75·5 by engine No 744. The last of the four runs included some of the finest work of all. No 768, *Sir Balin*, dropped slightly behind *King Arthur* in the early stages, and at Templecombe he was only half a minute ahead of *Maid of Astolat*. But from that point onwards a really phenomenal effort began. Despite the heavier load of 455 tons, against 415, No 768 kept practically level with No 779 as far as Seaton Junction, and then the engine with the heaviest load made the fastest climb of all up Honiton bank. From Seaton Junction the gradient is 1 in 80 continuously to the tunnel entrance, marked by Milepost 152½, and it eases to nothing more than 1 in 132 through the tunnel itself. Yet after the hard running that had preceded the climb the engine was driven uphill to such effect as to pass the 152½ milepost at 26½ mph and to recover through the tunnel to 32. If one takes the time of *Sir Colgrevance* to Chard Junction, that of *Sir Balin* onwards to Honiton, and that of *King Arthur* to Exmouth Junction, the extraordinary aggregate of 83 minutes 15 seconds from Salisbury is attained. This can be improved by a further four seconds by substituting the times of *Maid of Astolat* from Gillingham to Templecombe. The summary time from Salisbury to Exeter thus becomes 85 minutes 17 seconds, an average of 61·8 mph. One could hardly wish for a finer collective tribute to the capacity of the 'King Arthur' class engines, nor to the enterprise and skill of their drivers and firemen.

CHAPTER TWELVE

THE TRANSITION: MAUNSELL TO BULLEID

At the end of the year 1937 Maunsell's health began to show marked signs of deterioration, and for the first time the management had to give some thoughts to his possible successor. The organization set-up in 1923 had continued with scarcely a break. Pearson was still in office at Ashford; Clayton and Holcroft were in their same positions, and although there had been changes in works personnel at Ashford, Brighton and Eastleigh, and also at the carriage works at Lancing, no outstanding personality had begun to arise. The chief mechanical engineer's department was small enough for the Chief to take a keen personal interest in problems of production and in the working details of locomotives, and the policy of the management in gradually extending the electrified system of the Southern Railway tended to minimize the work so far as steam locomotives were concerned. A certain number of experiments had taken place to try and improve the performance of the 'Lord Nelson' class engines, but otherwise locomotive affairs were virtually at a standstill.

In addition to this, Sir Herbert Walker himself was nearing the time of retirement. It was generally believed that his successor would be Major-General Gilbert Szlumper, and there was no reason to imagine that a change in managership of the railway would initiate any appreciable change of policy so far as the extending of the electrified system was concerned. Szlumper had been so closely associated with Walker, and in so cordial and wholehearted a manner, as to suggest complete continuity of policy. The only area where the existing steam locomotives were not entirely on top of the job was in the working of the Continental boat trains. On these duties the day-to-day variations of the 'Lord

Nelsons' could be something of an embarrassment and, as previously mentioned, I have logged an excellent run with a certain engine of the class one day, and had a serious loss of time two days later with the same engine, apparently through poor steaming. But this was a very small fraction of the entire Southern Railway steam locomotive activity, and a little sustained research and experimentation, such as had taken place soon after grouping with the 'N15' class 4-6-0s of the London & South Western Railway, should have found a simple and effective solution.

Nevertheless, the management of the Southern evidently felt it was worth while to cast the net wide for a successor to Maunsell, and the choice fell upon O. V. S. Bulleid who, since the formation of the LNER in 1923, had been assistant to Sir Nigel Gresley. It is well known that Bulleid had played a very big part, albeit in the capacity of an assistant, in the development of steam locomotive power on the LNER, particularly in connexion with the introduction of the super high-speed trains and the spectacular streamlining of the 'Pacific' locomotives. Although his light had to some extent been hidden under the massive bushel of Sir Nigel Gresley's brilliant career, it was well known in railway circles that Bulleid was a very strong character, an individualist and inventor, and a man to whom the conventions meant very little. He succeeded Maunsell in October 1937 and almost immediately applied himself to the problem of improving the performance of the 'Lord Nelsons', these improvements being considered no more than a stop-gap measure pending the introduction of locomotives of considerably greater basic capacity. In view of the heavy trains to be worked and the sharp gradients involved, it is perhaps not surprising that his thoughts first turned towards the 2-8-2 type, which had been very successfully applied on the LNER to the onerous working conditions of the East Coast main line between Edinburgh and Aberdeen.

Bulleid had always been closely associated with the work of Sir Nigel Gresley, and from 1930 onwards much had been done on the LNER towards the improvement of locomotive front-ends. He was frequently in France, on Sir Nigel Gresley's behalf, and was keenly aware of the prowess and development of the Chapelon principles. Bulleid had the task of taking the *Cock o' the North* to the SNCF stationary testing plant at Vitry, and of witnessing some of the difficulties that famous engine got into during the trials. The *Cock o' the North* was probably the first British example of a really modern front-end, with very large steam and exhaust passages and greatly-improved draughting arrangements. In favourable conditions the performance of that engine could be phenomenal, but certain lessons were also learnt both at Vitry and in regular working on the Edinburgh–Aberdeen line. The fruits of this experience were embodied in the ever-famous 'A4' class of 'Pacifics', not so much in the very skil-ful design of aerodynamic screening but in every feature of the steam circuit: and I hardly need to recall that these engines proved to be the fastest steam locomotives ever to be constructed anywhere in the world.

When it came to considering improvement to the 'Lord Nelson' class on the Southern Railway, Bulleid attacked the problem in exactly the same way that Chapelon had done on the Paris–Orleans railway some dozen years earlier. The cylinders were completely redesigned and, instead of the ordinary single blast-pipe, Bulleid chose the Lemaître arrangement, which consisted of a series of jets, in contrast to the double jet of the Kylchap used on the *Cock o' the North* and on some of the 'A4' 'Pacifics'. In passing, it may be mentioned that a double blast-pipe had been tried by Maunsell on one of the 'Lord Nelsons', No 862, *Lord Colling-wood*, but it did not appear to have made any difference to the steaming; in fact, that engine in its modified condition contributed to the rather large collection of indifferent runs I personally experienced with the 'Lord Nelson' class engines on the Southern Railway in the last years of the Maunsell régime.

The theory behind multiple, as distinct from single-jet blast-pipes, is worth emphasizing at this stage, because the multiple-jet blast-pipe was to become a standard feature of

all Bulleid locomotives on the Southern Railway. A locomotive designer has ordinarily to make a compromise
between two opposing factors when it comes to designing a
satisfactory draughting arrangement. One requires to have a
strong draught in the smokebox in order to sustain a high
rate of evaporation in the boiler; and in the past a regret-
tably easy way of doing this was to increase the speed of the
jet from the tip of the blast-pipe to the chimney by keeping
the blast-pipe orifice small. This, in turn, created a relatively
high back pressure in the cylinders and, of course, led to un-
economic working and a high rate of coal consumption. In
certain circumstances, good steaming would be more important than economic working. It is no use having a very
economical locomotive if it will not do the job, and it was
considered better to have an engine that would steam and
get the train to its destination on time, albeit at the cost of
higher coal consumption. In earlier days, if an engine would
not steam freely, it was a well-known trick on the part of
individual drivers to fit a crude little device called a 'dart'
over the blast-pipe cap to sharpen up the blast and improve
the draughting on the fire.

Draughting on the fire is proportional, however, not only
to the speed of the exhaust gases through the smokebox but
to the surface area of the jet passing through; so that if one
settles upon a certain cross-sectional area of the blast-pipe
to give economical working and low back pressure, it is
necessary to find some means by which the surface area of
the cone can be increased without any alteration to the cross-
sectional area. If this can be done the draught on the fire
will be increased. The blast-pipe of the Kylchap arrangement did this, and the multiple jet of the Lemaître achieved
it in another way. Bulleid applied the Lemaître blast-pipe in
addition to a redesign of the cylinders to the 'Lord Nelson'
class, and completely transformed their performance. From
being engines whose range of performance varied from the
very good to the mediocre, they stepped immediately into
the front rank. I always feel it is a great pity that these
engines in their newly rebuilt form, as they were running in

1939, were not compared with their contemporaries on other railways. I feel sure the results would have been highly gratifying to everyone concerned on the Southern Region.

My own experience of the rebuilt engines prior to the outbreak of war in 1939 was confined to a single run from Bournemouth to Waterloo, but it was most impressive in the astonishing difference in the whole character of the running, as compared with what one had grown accustomed to with the 'Lord Nelsons' in their original state. The engine in question, No 862, *Lord Collingwood*, seemed completely revitalized, and where previous engines of this class, with loads of more than 400 tons, had seemingly scraped along with nothing in reserve – that is when they were not losing time – the modernized engine handled her load with ease and showed a positive contempt for the scheduled times. This was a very good run in itself, but when I came to ride on the footplate of engines of this class after the Second World War I was extremely pleased to find that their performance had not deteriorated at all during the emergency, although naturally they were not in the same immaculate external condition as they were when first rebuilt.

Although Bulleid's interest extended to every facet of mechanical engineering work on the railway, he was above all a locomotive man, with an intense interest in every detail of locomotive working and manufacture, and in the first months after he took over from Maunsell he spent a considerable time riding on Southern Railway locomotives and forming his own opinion of them. The rebuilding of the 'Nelsons' was one of the first fruits of this activity of the new Chief. Apparently his impressions of the 'King Arthur' were not particularly favourable, and I shall always remember with amusement an experience in connexion with an earlier book on locomotive working, in which I had a chapter entitled 'Modern 4-6-0 Locomotives of the Southern Railway'. It dealt with the 'King Arthurs' and the 'S15' mixed-traffic 4-6-0, as well as the 'Nelsons'. Mr Bulleid had been kind enough to help me in many ways towards collecting the data for this book and I sent the draft of the chapter to him for

his scrutiny. It came back with an alteration in the title, because he felt that the engines about which I had been writing
could not be considered as *modern*!

On the other hand, he was delighted with the 'Schools'
class, and was full of praise for the ease with which these
relatively small locomotives handled very heavy trains on
the Bournemouth service. He fitted one or two of them with
multiple-jet blast-pipes to improve their performances
further, and at one time he was proposing to streamline one
or two of them with a view to running high-speed services on
the lines of the LNER 'Silver Jubilee'. By way of an experiment, a test was made with engine No 931, *Epsom*, fitted
with multiple-jet blast-pipe, on the winter run of the
'Atlantic Coast Express' between Waterloo and Salisbury
and the resulting performance was certainly a record for the
run up to that time. The full log of this most exciting affair
is shown in the table opposite. Some of the multiple-jet
blast-pipe engines were put on to the Hastings line and
did very good work, and two runs in particular that I made
on the footplate just after the war showed a high standard of
performance. Nevertheless the change at the front-end did
not make so much difference to the 'Schools' as it had done
to the 'Nelsons'. In the former case Bulleid, of course, was
dealing with inherently good engines, whereas the original
'Nelsons' had been, on the whole, disappointing.

In the years leading up to the Second World War Bulleid
had shown that he had little regard for the traditional, either
in the detail of locomotive design, in administration, or in
anything else. He was a natural publicist, and it was characteristic of him to persuade the management of the Southern
Railway to change the locomotive and carriage livery from
a rather sombre olive green to an intensely vivid malachite
green. A Maunsell train with engine and carriages in the old
colours was quite unobtrusive either in the open country, or,
in an area of intense railway activity, among many other
trains; but a Bulleid train with both engine and carriages in
malachite green was a startling apparition that simply com-
pelled attention, and that was just what Bulleid wanted. It

goes almost without saying that he completely changed the organization of the chief mechanical engineer's department. Whereas Maunsell had set great store upon teamwork and had played the part of a fatherly but very shrewd administrator, Bulleid was himself the initiator of all new activity.

SOUTHERN RAILWAY: WATERLOO–SALISBURY

Load: 288 tons tare, 305 tons full
Engine: 'Schools' class 4–4–0 No 931

Distance miles		Sch. min	Actual min sec		Av. Speed mph
0·0	WATERLOO	0	0	00	—
3·9	CLAPHAM JUNCTION	7	7	10	32·6
7·3	Wimbledon	—	10	55	54·4
12·0	Surbiton	—	15	20	63·8
14·4	Esher	—	17	15	75·2
19·1	Weybridge	—	21	15	70·6
21·7	Byfleet	—	23	20	74·8
24·4	WOKING	30	25	30	74·8
28·0	Brookwood	—	28	30	72·0
33·2	Farnborough	—	32	45	73·5
36·5	Fleet	—	35	15	79·2
42·2	Hook	—	39	35	78·9
47·8	BASINGSTOKE	53	43	50	79·1
52·4	Oakley	—	48	00	66·4
55·6	Overton	—	50	45	69·8
61·1	Hurstbourne	—	55	00	77·6
66·4	ANDOVER	—	58	45	84·7
72·8	Grateley	—	64	00	73·2
78·3	Porton	—	71	20	—
—	—	—	74	30	—
83·8	SALISBURY	88	81	50	—

He required intelligent executive assistants, not to advise him or to put forward ideas, but simply to carry out his commands. Maunsell's two personal assistants, James Clayton and Harold Holcroft, stayed on for a time, but with every vestige of their previous power gone.

Bulleid's ideas were worked out by his chief draughtsman, Clifford Cocks. It was a difficult and unsettling time for a staff which had been so long used to Maunsell's ways; but

Bulleid, by sheer force of personality, carried his new department along with him, and he was to achieve some remarkable feats of productivity, not only in locomotive design, but in carriage and wagon production. Shortly after the outbreak of war, Gilbert Szlumper was succeeded as general manager of the Southern Railway by E. J. Missenden, and Bulleid was fortunate in enlisting his sympathy and backing for his entire programme. It is very important that the development of this pleasant relationship at Waterloo should be fully appreciated, because otherwise it is very difficult to appreciate how Bulleid obtained authority for large-scale construction of new steam locomotives after the end of the war, while Maunsell, in his time, had been forced to exist on a shoestring for so many years.

Although Bulleid had a slight figure and a rather shy demeanour he had the heart of a lion. He had served in France in the Railway Operating Division during the First World War, and he let it be known to all around him that he regarded the Second World War not so much a tragedy as a challenge to his ingenuity and resource, and to his department as a whole. Far from being overawed or disheartened by the restrictions placed upon him by war conditions, he actively sought out means of furthering the plans he had for development on the Southern Railway, despite the circumstances imposed by the war. Wartime austerity was made the excuse – if one may express it so – for the production of one of the most extraordinary-looking locomotives that has ever taken the road in Great Britain. But before I come to describe this weird creation reference must be made to the last Maunsell new design for the Southern Railway, the 'Q' class 0–6–0 goods engine of 1938. This was just a simple, straightforward 0–6–0 version of the 'L1' class express passenger 4–4–0.

Replacements were needed for the old 'Beattie' and 'Stirling' goods engines, many of which were still in service on the Southern Railway. They had been maintained because they were the only locomotives on the strength that could be permitted to run over certain lines on account of weight restrictions. Replacements were necessary, and the 'Q' class 0-6-0 was a lightweight, handsome-looking engine with a maximum axle-load of eighteen tons. It was not regarded as a standard, but as a lightweight necessity for branch-line duties. The design was wholly traditional, using a great number of existing patterns and tools, and the engine's economical performance was ensured by the incorporation of long-lap, long-travel valves. Bulleid, however, was quite disgusted that such a nondescript, pedestrian type of engine should have been built in the Year of Grace 1938; and, in referring to them, he was once heard to remark that he arrived on the Southern Railway too late to prevent them being built. What he would have done as an alternative in those pre-war years we do not know, but when the need arose in the early days of the war for new general-purpose engines he himself produced the rather fantastic 'Q1' class.

The austerity of war conditions was then striking the country in full force. Convention in many directions was being thrown to the winds, and in following out a perfectly logical approach to the design of a general-purpose mixed-traffic engine Bulleid so ignored the conventions surrounding locomotive lineaments as to attract some useful publicity, an indication of the extent to which the Southern Railway was 'with it' in conforming to the spirit of the times. In a talk to the locomotive men of the Southern Railway at Feltham in November 1942, Bulleid described in simple language exactly how he had conceived and built up the locomotive that attracted so much attention. The chief civil engineer had stated that he could accept no greater total weight for an 0-6-0 engine than 54 tons, and while the Maunsell 'Q' class would conform to that restriction and was giving reasonably good service Bulleid felt that, to meet the requirements of war traffic, a larger boiler and firebox were desirable. He therefore decided on the size of the boiler first.

An important consideration was to avoid making special tooling, flanging blocks and suchlike, and so he began by taking the largest firebox which could be fitted inside the Southern loading gauge, namely, that of the 'Lord Nelson' class, and this formed the starting point of the design. The 'Nelson' firebox in itself would have been too large for the 0-6-0 engine, but shortened to provide a grate area of 27 sq ft it provided an excellent basis for the new design and made possible the use of existing tools. The wheelbase was to be the same as 'Q' class, which limited the length of the boiler but, again, existing flanging blocks could be used. Preliminary calculations showed that the boiler and firebox would weigh 21¼ tons in working order and this would leave only 32¾ tons for the rest of the locomotive. Bulleid and his drawing office staff managed to keep within the set limits by discarding everything that was not absolutely necessary, and using lighter components wherever possible.

The result was an engine which, by older standards, looked as though it was only half finished. There were no running plates; no splashers over the driving wheels, and a particularly simple and lighter form of casing had been designed for the lagging of the boiler. The cab was constructed from thin sheet material, and castings were dispensed with wherever possible and fabrications used instead. As a result, this engine, which was fundamentally correct and adequate, had a most stark uncompromising appearance, which touched off a veritable howl of protest from those who believed that a locomotive, to be a 'proper' locomotive, must have some pretence of aesthetic appearance. Bulleid was about the last person to pay any form of service to convention, and seems to have rather delighted in the hostile reception accorded to this engine's appearance. It goes without saying that these locomotives gave a good account of themselves in service and were generally liked by the men. A superficial point of difference between them and previous practice in Great Britain was the system of numbering on Continental lines, in which 'C' by itself stood for what has always previously been known as an 0-6-0. This system of numbering was, of course, shared by the 'Pacific' engines of Bulleid's design which are referred to in a later chapter.

From the viewpoint of technical details, the 'Q1's had long-lap, long-travel valves actuated by Stephenson's link

motion; the layout of ports and steam passages was designed
to give the freest possible flow of steam, and the smokeboxes
were fitted with the five-nozzle multiple-jet blast-pipes
which had proved to successful in improving the performance of the 'Lord Nelson' class. As finally designed, the
'Q1' turned the scale at $51\frac{1}{2}$ tons as compared with 49·1 tons
for the 'Q'. The nominal tractive effort was only slightly increased, by the use of a boiler pressure of 230 lb against 200.

TABLE 39

0–6–0 LOCOMOTIVE COMPARISON

Class	'Q'	'Q1'
Cylinders diameter and stroke (in)	19×26	19×26
Wheel diameter (ft in)	$5 - 1$	$5 - 1$
Total length over buffers, engine and tender (ft in)	$53 - 9\frac{1}{2}$	$54 - 10\frac{1}{2}$
Boiler pressure (p.s.i.)	200	230
Heating surfaces:		
Tubes (sq ft)	1,247	1,472
Firebox (sq ft)	122	170
Superheater (sq ft)	185	210
COMBINED TOTAL	1,554	1,852
Grate area (sq ft)	21·9	27·0
Max axle load (tons)	18	18·5
Weight of engine only, working order (tons)	49·5	51·25
Weight of tender in working order (tons)	40·5	38·2

But, apart from this increase in nominal tractive effort, the
enhanced capacity of the 'Q1', as compared to the 'Q' was
more correctly indicated by the relative size of the grate
areas, namely, 21·9 and 27 sq ft. Taken all in all, the 'Q1'
was a clever piece of designing and carried Bulleid's style a
stage further than the 'Pacifics' which had appeared a year
earlier. Whether or not the same result could not have been
obtained within a more pleasing outline is really beside the
question; Bulleid had no time for aesthetics so far as locomotive appearance was concerned, and the 'Q1' was above
all a vivid exposition of this particular side of his nature.
The comparative dimensions of the 'Q' and 'Q1' classes of
engine are shown in Table 39.

CHAPTER THIRTEEN

THE 'MERCHANT NAVY' CLASS

In describing the 'Q1' class 0–6–0 in the previous chapter I have stepped a little out of strict chronological order. But perhaps this is not altogether illogical, because the 'Q1' was essentially a tool of wartime, as well as being produced in wartime; whereas in his 'Pacifics', which preceded the 'Q1' by a full year, Bulleid was looking ahead to post-war conditions, although the engines themselves fulfilled a very useful wartime function. In a paper read to the Institution of Mechanical Engineers in December 1945 Bulleid revealed the very exacting traffic specification that had been laid down. Having regard to the predilection of the Southern operating departments for working trains of moderate coach formation, not to mention the platform lengths at Victoria, Waterloo and elsewhere, it is difficult to imagine the traffic people setting such a target. But the fact remains that Bulleid set out to provide for the haulage of trains of 550–600 tons at start-to-stop average speeds of 70 mph on the Western Section, and at 60 mph between London and Dover on the Continental boat trains. It is more than likely that Bulleid set the target himself.

At first he had some difficulty in getting a design accepted, for weight distribution, by the civil engineer. With the gradients of the old South Eastern & Chatham lines prominently in mind, it was at first proposed to use the 2–8–2 wheel arrangement, inspired no doubt by the success of Sir Nigel Gresley's 'P2' engines on the LNER; but the preliminary calculations came out too heavy and the 4–6–2 type was eventually decided upon, with a maximum weight for the engine of about 95 tons. To produce the power needed for the heavy tasks of haulage just mentioned it was calculated that a locomotive with a nominal tractive effort of 37,500 lb would be needed. One of the first basic dimensions decided upon was the grate area, namely $48\frac{1}{2}$ sq ft, and specially arranged for burning low-grade fuel.

As in the case of the 'Q1' class engine, Bulleid's first consideration was the boiler. Like so many eminent engineers before him, the boiler was to him the centrepiece of the locomotive. Nothing could make up for inadequacy in steaming, and in conjunction with the grate area of $48\frac{1}{2}$ sq ft he designed about the largest boiler that could be accommodated on the frames of his proposed 4–6–2 engine. To facilitate steaming, the firebox was to be equipped with two Nicholson thermic syphons to accelerate the circulation of the water, and the smoke-box was to be equipped with a five-nozzle multiple-jet blast-pipe, as on the 'Lord Nelson' and 'Q1' classes.

After the preliminary design of the boiler had been got out and its weight estimated, it was clear that if the overall weight of about 95 tons was not to be exceeded, stringent economies in weight would have to be effected elsewhere in the locomotive. These economies took some distinctly unusual forms, and a fundamental point of the design centred upon the use of relatively small cylinders and pistons to reduce weight, coupled with a very high boiler pressure in order to obtain the necessary tractive effort. The cylinders on this very large locomotive were no more than 18 ins in diameter by 24-in stroke, while the boiler pressure was fixed at 280 lb per sq in, the highest that had ever been used in a British locomotive up to that time. A pressure of 280 lb per sq in led to a number of interesting problems in boiler design which, in the manner of their solution, led once again to further economies in weight. Experience on the Southern Railway with copper fireboxes on the 'Lord Nelson' class engines had not been too satisfactory, even with a boiler pressure of 220 lb per sq in, and Bulleid decided that the time had come to adopt steel fireboxes, welded throughout.

He sought the advice and help of the North British Locomotive Company, who had already had considerable experience in building steel fireboxes in locomotives for overseas, and the boilers for the first ten locomotives of the new 4–6–2 class were built in Glasgow. Weight was saved by eliminating the double thicknesses of metal that were necessary in a riveted form of firebox construction, and it was felt that a completely even thickness of metal throughout would also help to remove possible sources of overheating. As finally designed, the boiler was of very large diameter, tapering from 5 ft 9¾ ins to 6 ft 3½ ins, while the distance between the tube-plates was only 17 ft – relatively short for so large an engine. The shortness of the barrel, in combination with the large diameter of the ordinary flue-tubes would, in themselves, assist in producing a very free-steaming boiler; but the inclusion of thermic syphons in the firebox and the benefits of the multiple-jet blast-pipe combined to produce a boiler of such vast steam-raising capacity that its limit proved to be beyond anything that could be determined on test. We shall never know what the maximum rate of evaporation of a 'Merchant Navy' boiler was!

In working out the rest of the design Bulleid introduced a number of somewhat revolutionary features which unhappily were not so successful in service as the boiler. With the idea of reducing the day-to-day maintenance work at sheds to a minimum, the whole of the valve motion was completely enclosed, as were the centre connecting-rod and crank axle. The idea was that these parts, running completely enclosed in an oil-bath, would need no attention during the entire span of service of the locomotive from one works overhaul to the next. This feature, which was novel so far as steam locomotives were concerned, brought a number of problems, not the least of which was that of keeping the oil in the oil-bath. Unless the engines were exceptionally well maintained it seemed to get everywhere else: on to the track, into the boiler lagging and, worst of all, on to the wheel treads.

Even so, it was not the oil-bath and what escaped from it that proved the 'Achilles heel' of the Bulleid 'Pacifics', though it was certainly the decision to have it that led to still greater troubles. The space inside was relatively small. No ordinary valve gear could be got in, so Bulleid designed a special gear to meet the circumstances – one set for each of

Upper: London express leaving Brighton: engine 'King Arthur' class 4-6-0 No 803 *Sir Harry de Fiselake*

Lower: A striking broadside shot of a 'Nelson' No 858, *Lord Duncan*, near Bromley South

'Nelsons' at Waterloo in pre-war days. On left engine No 856 *Lord St Vincent*, just under way with the first part of the

Dynamometer car test run with a rebuilt 'Merchant Navy' class 4-6-2 No 35020 *Bibby Line* leaving Basingstoke

Upper: The up 'Devon Belle' near Overton, hauled by 4-6-2 No 21 C18, *British India Line*

Lower: Fourteen-coach 'Devon Belle' climbing Honiton Bank with engine No 21 C8 *Orient Line*

Upper: Dynamometer car test run, on Eastern Region: 4-6-2 No 35017, *Belgian Marine*, preparing to leave Kings Cross for Leeds in 1948

Lower: Controlled Road Test, with LMSR Mobile Test Unit: 4-6-2 No 35005, *Canadian Pacific*, preparing to leave Clapham Junction

Upper: The Interchange Trials of 1948. 4-6-2 No 35019, *French Line CGT*, approaching Reading on Plymouth–Paddington test run

Lower: The down 'Golden Arrow' negotiating the re-aligned junctions at Chislehurst: engine No 34085, *501 Squadron*, (Battle of Britain class

Upper: A 'West Country' 4-6-2 No 34108, *Wincanton*, leaving Honiton Tunnel with a down express

Lower: A rebuilt 'Merchant Navy' 4-6-2 No 35009 *Shaw Savill* leaving the east end of Honiton Tunnel

Upper: A 'West Country' Pacific No 21 C110 *Sidmouth* as originall
built, in malachite green

Lower: A rebuilt 'West Country' No 34052, *Lord Dowding*, (Battle o
Britain series)

the three cylinders. The principal feature of this new valve gear was that it was chain-driven, and that no valve spindles of the conventional kind were used at all. All three sets of valve gear were inside the frames. If connexion had been required to ordinary valve spindles, it would have had to be made at some point through the casing of the oil-bath, thus introducing a further source of leakage.

When new or newly-shopped after general repair this special radial valve gear gave excellent results and contributed to a very free-running engine; but it seemed to lose its adjustment very quickly and the valve timing then became erratic. It was very difficult to keep engines running at a constant cut-off. The steam distribution would appear to vary, and when one of the 'Merchant Navy' class engines was on the stationary testing plant at Rugby it was impossible even in such carefully-controlled conditions, to keep the distribution from wandering about, cut-off wise. Even when the bridle-rod was bolted there was still variation in cut-off. On the majority of engines the steam-operated reversing gear was difficult to set, and certainly difficult if any fine adjustment to cut-off was desired by the driver. In consequence, drivers found some position of the reverser in which the engine ran freely, and then drove almost entirely on the throttle. When one of the 'Merchant Navy' class engines was on test at Rugby two different series of trials were run, on the first of which the engine was worked in the theoretically-correct way, with wide-open regulator and cut-off adjusted to produce the power required, and on the second with a much longer cut-off, and power output varied by means of the regulator. There was actually very little difference in thermal efficiency between these two methods of working, and on the engine in question full-regulator working and short cut-offs tended to produce severe vibration.

In riding on these engines I found that the steam reverser was a rather fiddling thing to adjust, and one felt sympathetic to the driver who found some position of good compromise and left it there. It has often been said that the pointer scale of the reverser is 'the biggest liar on the engine', and in certain of the Bulleid 'Pacifics' on which I rode even this would be an understatement. I shall always remember a trip on one of the 'West Country' class engines, when we were storming up the bank from New Cross towards Elmstead Tunnel in terrific style and I crossed over momentarily to the driver's side to see what the cut-off was. If the pointer was to be believed the engine was in backward gear!

The story of the 'Merchant Navy' class from 1945 onwards until their conversion to a standard form of valve gear was one of constant vicissitudes. At first, a number of attempts were made to demonstrate their very high haulage capacity, and fast trial runs were made over the Bournemouth, West of England and Continental boat train routes. The logs of some runs are tabulated at the end of this chapter, and it will be seen that some extremely good work was done. Also, in the summer of 1947, the new 'Devon Belle' was put on, with a regular load at first of fourteen Pullmans.

From the viewpoint of locomotive output, this train did not entail any sustained hard work between London and Salisbury because the schedule was relatively slow. The curious arrangement was also made of running through Salisbury Station without stopping, and of changing engines at Wilton. Evidently the idea was to encourage the building up of a regular de-luxe clientele from London to West Country resorts, and to avoid any intermediate business between Waterloo and Sidmouth Junction. But because of its great weight, the schedules laid down for the train were relatively slow. Much harder work was required on the well-established 'Bournemouth Belle' and in later years, when the loading of the West of England trains diminished, the 'Bournemouth Belle' normally provided the hardest work set to the 'Merchant Navy' class engines.

But neither in the fast trial runs made just after the war, nor in any subsequent task set, did the requirements approach the specification which Bulleid had been set at the time the engines were first designed. The Southern operating authorities always set great store on accurate timekeeping, and there is no doubt that they favoured schedules which gave a considerable margin in reserve to the locomotives employed. It would have been grandly heroic to try and run a train of fourteen Pullmans non-stop from Waterloo to Salisbury at an average speed of 70 mph, as Bulleid stated he had legislated for when the engines were first designed; but in actual practice, and in fairness to Bulleid, I feel that there were very few engines in the links at Nine Elms, Salisbury, or Exmouth Junction which could have run regularly up to that standard.

The story of 'Merchant Navy' performance over the years was punctuated all too frequently by engines becoming complete failures on the road. There is no doubt that the totally-enclosed valve gear and inside connecting-rod was one of the main causes of trouble. Running men have explained it very vividly to me by saying that, with the centre big-end totally enclosed, one could not smell it when it was getting hot, nor hear it when it was knocking; consequently, the first thing one knew was when the connecting-rod came clean through the bottom of the oil-bath.

Bulleid set great score by having the connecting-rod totally enclosed, and when the engines were rebuilt with conventional valve gear, and there was trouble at first with the middle big-end, he took a certain amount of impish delight in this difficulty. But the fact remains that the middle big-ends *did* fail, oil-bath, or no oil-bath; and they had a way of doing so in the most inconvenient places. Many are the stories told – some of them exaggerated, where they are not definitely apocryphal – but one failure I recall, which caused a gargantuan hold-up of road as well as rail traffic, took place one summer Saturday, when an engine transfixed itself right in the centre of the level-crossing at Brockenhurst. Both road and rail traffic were blocked until a breakdown gang from Eastleigh could cut away the damaged parts and remove the engine. I have already mentioned the leakage of oil and this not only caused slipping and other difficulties, but sometimes led to fires, though, fortunately, none were of a very serious character. At their best, the 'Merchant Navy' class engines

TABLE 40
SOUTHERN RAILWAY:
BOURNEMOUTH–WATERLOO

Load: 12 Pullmans, 491 tons tare, 520 tons full
Engine: 4–6–2 No 35014, *Nederland Line*

Distance miles		Sch. min	Actual min sec	Speeds mph
0·0	BOURNEMOUTH WEST	0	0 00	—
1·2	Gas Works Junction	4½	3 22	
3·4	BOURNEMOUTH	8		
—	CENTRAL		7 35	—
0·0		0	0 00	—
			p.w. slack	15
3·6	Christchurch	—	7 32	52
6·8	Hinton Admiral	—	11 14	53½
				47
9·4	New Milton	—	14 14	56
12·4	Sway	—	17 10	67/61½
15·2	BROCKENHURST	—	19 45	69 (max)
19·8	Beaulieu Road	—	24 02	61½
22·5	Lyndhurst Road	—	26 28	68/65
			—	70½
25·3	Totton	—	29 06	—
28·6	SOUTHAMPTON	34	34 03	—
0·0		0	0 00	—
1·1	Northam Junction	3½	3 15	—
3·5	Swaything	—	6 42	49½
5·7	EASTLEIGH	10	9 15	56
—	*Milepost 71*		—	60
9·0	*Milepost 70¼*	—	13 00	sig stop
			arr	
			13 20	
			dep	
9·5	Shawford	—	16 41	—
12·6	WINCHESTER	—	21 43	51½
14·7	Winchester Junction	—	24 10	56
17·4	Waller's Ash East	—	27 07	54½
21·1	Micheldever	—	31 12	54
23·0	Litchfield Box	—	33 19	53
28·9	Worting Junction	—	39 19	—
31·4	BASINGSTOKE	38	41 30	78
37·0	Hook	—	45 55	72½
39·5	Winchfield	—	47 56	76
42·8	Fleet	—	50 27	82
46·0	Farnborough	—	52 55	77½
48·3	*Milepost 31*	—	54 46	75

TABLE 40—continued

Distance miles		Sch. min.	Actual min sec	Speeds mph
51·2	Brookwood	—	57 06	82
54·9	WOKING	61	60 00	69 (eased)
57·6	Byfleet	—	62 07	78
60·2	Weybridge	—	64 07	71
61·8	Milepost 17½	—	66 00	sig stop
			arr	
			66 43	
			dep	
64·9	Esher	—	72 30	54
			sigs	
67·2	Surbiton	—	75 23	cautious
75·4	CLAPHAM JUNCTION	80	86 50	running
79·3	WATERLOO	87	94 35	—

were as strong and fast as any engine in the country; at their worst, they were a nightmare.

At various times I had the opportunity of riding on the footplate of quite a few of them, on all the principal express routes where they were employed. One journey on the 'Bournemouth Belle', when I was making a round trip from Waterloo to Bournemouth West and back in the same day, provided a remarkable example of how relatively easy it was for a man to master the firing of them. We were enjoying a very comfortable, trouble-free journey down from London, with a first-class Nine Elms crew, when, on passing East-leigh, the coal-watering hose slipped out of the fireman's hand and, before it could be recovered, was splashing scalding water all over the footplate. The driver and I were, luckily, unaffected, but the fireman was badly scalded on one leg and had to be given first-aid treatment immediately we reached Southampton.

A young fireman who was waiting to work a stopping train from Southampton to Bournemouth was immediately switched to our train, and I believe it was the first time he had ever been on a 'Merchant Navy' class engine. Fortunately, the fire was in good shape and, despite the young-ster's inexperience, the driver was able to nurse the engine through to Bournemouth without any loss of time. While we were standing at Bournemouth West awaiting the return working, the driver was able to give him some tuition, and when we started away again it was evident that the young man was well on the way to mastering the art of firing one of these big engines. Even so, he was fully expecting to be relieved at Southampton, but on a summer Saturday reliefs are not quite so readily forthcoming as that. None was available at Southampton, and so this lad had to fire the 'Bournemouth Belle' right through to Waterloo. He did so splendidly, and assisted in no small measure in the making of the fine run shown in Table 40.

On the West of England road I made one trip on a really dreadful engine. It was not long after the end of the war, and the engine seemed well overdue for shopping. She was very weak on the banks; the vibration was indescribable, especially when the driver let her go full tilt down Seaton bank to try and make up some lost time, and we reached a maximum speed of 85 mph at the bottom. Generally, however, I found the 'Merchant Navys' very steady-riding engines, if they were not always smooth. They never glided along like the 'Pacifics' of the Northern lines. One never got that Rolls-Royce feeling that so often came on a Stanier 'Duchess' or a Gresley 'Pacific'. The vibration was nearly always there, and I shall not soon forget an occasion on the outward-bound 'Golden Arrow' when the driver really opened out after Ashford and took a 425-ton train over Westenhanger summit at 72 mph. The vibration in the cab was so terrific that it danced the driver's tea-can off the shelf just above the fire door.

Generally speaking, I never experienced from the footplate those incessant bouts of slipping that were indulged in all too frequently by the 'Merchant Navy' class engines, though on one occasion, when the rails were bad, I did see one slip itself to a standstill backing 'light engine' out of Waterloo. One of the worst cases I had with slipping was on the inward-bound Night Ferry train, when we had a bad rail out of Dover and the engine was slipping incessantly most of the way to Folkestone. Slipping was most alarming when it occurred at high speed, and I had one hair-raising occasion on the up 'Golden Arrow' when the engine suddenly went into a violent slip when travelling at 75 mph. It was not nice! The crack drivers became very expert at checking the slipping of these engines, but there were times when it could not be avoided and there were some very difficult moments in later years when one of them was being tested on the Controlled Road Testing principle, with a dynamometer-car, on the Settle and Carlisle line.

TABLE 41

SOUTHERN RAILWAY:
EXETER CENTRAL–YEOVIL JUNCTION

Load: 325 tons tare, 345 tons full
Engine: 4–6–2 No 21C13, *Blue Funnel*

Distance miles		Actual min sec		Speeds mph
0·0	EXETER CENTRAL	0	00	—
1·1	Exmouth Junction	3	25	—
2·9	Pinhoe	5	51	—
4·8	Broad Clyst	7	30	74
8·5	Whimple	10	50	58
12·2	SIDMOUTH JUNCTION	14	40	—
16·8	Honiton	18	37	—
18·2	*Honiton Tunnel West End*	20	04	62
—				96
23·8	Seaton Junction	24	11	78
—				86
27·0	Axminster	26	35	—
32·1	Chard Junction	30	33	—
37·5	*Hewish Siding*	35	10	67
40·1	Crewkerne	37	15	90
46·7	Sutton Bingham	41	55	—
49·9	YEOVIL JUNCTION	44	14	—

It was slipping, of course, that imposed a limit of performance in the full-dress trials carried out on the Rugby testing plant, and on the Settle and Carlisle line, because it was found that the slips were so violent as to cause damage to the machinery. This could not be risked. The steam locomotive has very often been likened to a human being, in the numerous semi-human attributes and foibles that it displays at various times. The Bulleid 'Pacifics' were certainly unpredictable and, taken all in all, one could sum up their work as 'brilliant but erratic'. All these traits were to be reproduced faithfully in the smaller 'Pacifics' of the West Country class which came out in 1945.

Turning to the runs in detail, there is first of all a very exciting affair in the West of England road, with engine No 21C13, *Blue Funnel* (Table 41). The load was no more than moderate, but the speeds were terrific. The start out of Exeter was normal, but then from Broad Clyst the 13·4 miles up to Honiton Tunnel were covered in 12 minutes 34 seconds, and the tunnel itself entered at 62 mph. Descending to Seaton Junction, 96 mph was attained before being checked by brakes to 78 mph over the curves approaching Seaton Junction. With another very fast climb from Axminster to Hewish, and a maximum of 90 mph below Crewkerne, nearly 11 minutes were cut from the schedule of this particular train between Exeter and Yeovil Junction.

The next log, Table 42, gives details of a special high-speed test run from Victoria to Dover, when the net average speed was slightly over 60 mph start-to-stop with a load of 460 tons. There was not much chance to get going until after Paddock Wood; but then some hard running was made to Westenhanger. This run was perhaps not much more than ordinary top-class performance with the 'Merchant Navy' class engines, and I have certainly beaten the climb to Westenhanger on an ordinary run with the 'Golden Arrow' so far as speed was concerned, though with a lighter load of 425 tons. Nevertheless, this run of 1945 with the engine *Union Castle* was a very fine one.

The run of my own on the 'Bournemouth Belle', when we had a hurriedly-collected fireman, is also tabulated in detail. The engine was worked in typical style, with an unchanged cut-off of 25 per cent throughout once the train was under way from each stop, and all variations in power output were made by adjustments of the regulator. The young fire-

TABLE 42

SOUTHERN RAILWAY:
VICTORIA–DOVER MARINE: TEST RUN

Load: 454 tons tare, 460 tons full
Engine: 4–6–2 No 21C2, *Union Castle*

Distance miles		Sch. min	Actual min sec		Speeds mph
0·0	VICTORIA	0	0	00	—
3·2	Brixton	—	5	40	—
4·0	HERNE HILL	8	6	40	*30
5·7	Sydenham Hill	—	9	11	47
7·2	Penge East	—	11	06	*44
8·7	BECKENHAM JUNCTION	16	12	38	—
10·9	BROMLEY SOUTH	—	14	46	60
12·6	Bickley Junction	—	16	54	*23
14·9	ORPINGTON	26	20	38	38
16·4	Chelsfield	—	22	40	—
17·7	Knockholt	—	24	26	48
			sigs		20
21·7	Dunton Green	—	30	05	—
23·2	SEVENOAKS	36	32	00	45
28·1	Hildenborough	—	37	04	78
30·6	TONBRIDGE	43½	39	23	*32
			p.w.s.		20
35·9	Paddock Wood	49	45	16	—
40·5	Marden	—	48	46	81
43·0	Staplehurst	—	50	44	77
46·3	Headcorn	—	53	01	83
51·5	Pluckley	—	56	43	68
57·2	ASHFORD	68	60	57	85
61·5	Smeeth	—	64	21	80
65·3	Westenhanger	—	67	33	69
66·5	Sandling Junction	77	68	44	*30
			p.w.s.		15
71·0	FOLKESTONE JUNCTION	82	75	16	50
			sig stop		—
78·0	DOVER MARINE	90	84	55	—

Net time: 77½ minutes.   * Service slack.

man had no difficulty in keeping steam pressure at 240–260
lb per sq in, but the regulator was closed to such an extent
that there was rarely half this pressure in the steam-chests.
From the signal stop at Otterbourne, near Shawford, the
readings of steam-chest pressure on the run to Waterloo

were 180 on restarting and maintained to Winchester Junction; 130 to Litchfield, 100 from Worting Junction to Brookwood, and then only 80 lb per sq in afterwards. In other words, the engine was being very lightly steamed. Yet, as the table shows, we were making some fast running with this heavy train, and undelayed could quite comfortably have run up from Southampton in 77 minutes.

The last of these runs (Table 43) shows a piece of superla-

TABLE 43

SOUTHERN RAILWAY:
WILTON–SIDMOUTH JUNCTION

Load: 14 Pullmans, 543 tons tare, 575 tons full
Engine: 4–6–2 No 21C7, *Aberdeen Commonwealth*

Distance miles		Actual min sec		Speeds mph
0·0	WILTON	0	00	—
5·7	Dinton	10	23	56
10·0	Tisbury	15	15	52/56
15·0	Semley	20	54	48
19·1	Gillingham	24	18	86
21·4	*Milepost 107½*	25	59	70
25·9	TEMPLECOMBE	29	16	87
28·3	Milborne Port	31	36	57
32·0	Sherborne	34	29	90/77
36·6	YEOVIL JUNCTION	37	47	80
40·2	*Milepost 126¼*	41	10	56
45·4	Crewkerne	45	44	73
47·0	*Milepost 133*	47	54	40
53·4	Chard Junction	53	54	70/65
58·5	Axminster	58	00	82
61·7	Seaton Junction	60	40	—
66·5	*Milepost 152½*	69	19	22
67·5	*Milepost 153½*	71	49	—
68·7	Honiton	73	31	80
73·3	SIDMOUTH JUNCTION	78	19	

tive performance on the 'Devon Belle' with the full load of fourteen Pullmans. It must be admitted that this particular driver turned a completely blind eye to the speed limit of 75 mph which was then in force throughout this route. I have

o information as to whether there was a late start from
Wilton; but the fact remains that nearly five minutes were cut
om schedule time between Wilton and Sidmouth Junction,
ooked in 83 minutes. On a route like this, with a perfect
switchback of a gradient profile, maximum speeds count
eavily towards the making of a high overall average. In
SWR days, the little Drummond 'T9' 4–4–0s had no
ifficulty in maintaining the 54 mph bookings non-stop
om Salisbury to Exeter, with loads of 250 tons or more,
imply because they were permitted to run very fast down-
ill. It was the same on this run with the 'Devon Belle'.
peeds of 86 mph at Gillingham, 87 near Templecombe and
o through Sherborne, took the train sweeping up the next
ncline with consummate ease.

After Chard Junction, when the train was apparently
etting well ahead of time, things were taken more easily,
nd in climbing Honiton bank the engine started slipping on
he 1 in 80 gradient, and eventually came down to 22 mph
efore entering the tunnel. On another run with the same
ngine made at about the same time, some considerably
arder work was done up the bank. The speed did not fall
elow 27 mph and Sidmouth Junction was reached in the
emarkable time of $74\frac{1}{2}$ minutes from Wilton. Performance
n the 'Devon Belle' was, nevertheless, not always of this
uality, and when I made a trip on the footplate of engine
21C8', *Orient Line*, again with a load of fourteen Pullmans,
e took 81 minutes to pass Milepost $153\frac{1}{2}$, and $88\frac{1}{4}$ minutes
o Sidmouth Junction. With a guest on the footplate – more-
ver a guest with two watches and a large notebook – the
river was much more meticulous in his attentions to the
peed limit. We did not exceed $73\frac{1}{2}$ mph anywhere, and our
phill minimum speeds were 42 at Semley, 40 near Milborne
ort, $42\frac{1}{2}$ at Milepost $126\frac{1}{4}$ and 31 mph at Milepost 133.
xminster was passed in exactly 67 minutes and we, too,
ll to 22 mph in the ascent of Honiton bank.

CHAPTER FOURTEEN

POST-WAR DEVELOPMENT

In the years between the end of the war and the nationalization of the British Railways on January 1st, 1948, the Bulleid 'Pacifics' came into general use all over the Southern Railway system. While the 'Merchant Navy' class were confined to the heaviest express runs between Waterloo and Bournemouth, Waterloo and Exeter, and on the Continental boat expresses, the 'West Country' and the 'Battle of Britain' engines were very widely used on services ranging from the Kent Coast expresses to a multiplicity of duties west of Exeter. They were also used, turn and turn about, with the 'Merchant Navy' class on many heavy main-line expresses.

There is no doubt that the unconventional appearance of these engines captured public imagination to a remarkable degree. After the drab years of endurance and austerity during the war, and the necessity to make do with existing tools, there was, all over the country, a yearning for new things, whether they happened to be locomotives, household goods or even one's own personal wardrobe. Anything with a 'new look' was welcomed, and however much locomotive enthusiasts with a love of the conventional deplored the strange appearance of Bulleid's creations, to the public they were something 'new' and as such they were widely acclaimed.

I shall never forget an incident that occurred one day in the late summer of 1945 when I had travelled down to Exeter to make my first footplate journeys on 'West Country' 'Pacifics' operating between there and Ilfracombe. I had come down from London on a 'Merchant Navy', and at Exeter Central we duly changed engines. The 'Merchant Navy' was still in wartime black; but the 'West Country' which backed on in its place was brand new, positively glittering in the pre-war livery of garish malachite green and yellow, and as this apparition came backing down on to the train one could sense the hush that came over the group of onlookers. When I went forward and climbed up on to the footplate several people, thinking I was a railway official, came forward to bombard me with questions about the new engine. I remember one man in particular who remarked in an awestruck voice: 'Don't they look *powerful*'. How a rather shapeless steel casing could give the impression of power I do not know, and not for nothing were these engines later nicknamed 'Spam Cans'. But for good or ill, Bulleid had accurately interpreted popular sentiment of the day, and in the public view the Southern was the only railway in the country that seemed to be breaking fresh ground.

The 'West Country' 'Pacifics' reproduced faithfully all the strength and all the weakness of their larger contemporaries; but there can be no doubt that the management of the Southern were satisfied with their record. The first order was for seventy of them, and the type was eventually multiplied until there were no fewer than 110 of them at work. At the time of nationalization, all the first batch of 'West Country' engines had been completed, with numbers ranging from 21C101 to 21C170. The remainder were built between April 1948 and January 1951.

An interesting feature of the period between the end of the war and the time of nationalization was the way in which older engines were maintained in good order and were thus able to do satisfactory work in traffic. Through the interest of Mr Bulleid himself, and with the help of the locomotive running superintendents, I was able to make quite a number of footplate journeys on older engines, ranging from the London & South Western 'T9' and 'D15' classes, to the Brighton 'I3' and 'J' tank engines. The latter were working on the Tunbridge Wells services from Victoria to Oxted, and the climbing of the heavy gradients on this route was most impressive.

During this time also, a number of engines were altered to oil firing, and it was the intention to make the sheds at

Fratton and Exmouth Junction entirely oil fired. But, unfortunately, the very large Government-sponsored project for conversion to oil firing had to be abandoned owing to lack of the necessary foreign exchange to purchase the oil. The Southern engines that were converted appeared to work well, though it was rather surprising that, so far as the Southern Railway was concerned, so many relatively small engines were scheduled to be altered. In a project whose aim was to save coal one would have thought that the engines first scheduled for conversion would have been those that used the most coal, namely, the heavy main-line 'Pacifics'; whereas the plan originally provided for conversion of only a very few 'West Country' 'Pacifics' and no 'Merchant Navys' at all.

By the time nationalization occurred, work was well advanced on Bulleid's experimental double-ended tank engines, the first of the ill-starred 'Leader' class. Even at this distance in time, it is still rather difficult to understand what was the real object behind the construction of these locomotives. It was stated that they were intended to have very high availability, and to keep steam on the map in an age when rival forms of railway traction were pressing hard for its elimination. A frank and sympathetic description of the 'Leader' class and its ultimate fate is to be found in Sean Day-Lewis' book, *Bulleid – the last Giant of Steam*. There, of course, the subject is treated with special sympathy, but without attempting to hide or 'whitewash' the serious difficulties experienced with these most unorthodox engines. But, despite the time that has elapsed since the experiment was brought to an end by the central authorities of the nationalized British Railways, I feel it is still too early to give a reasoned appraisal of an experiment which can only be described as fully in keeping with the personality and career of the designer.

Immediately after nationalization in January 1948, Mr R. A. Riddles, the member responsible for mechanical and electrical engineering in the newly-formed Railway Executive, decided to carry out an extensive series of interchange trials between locomotives of the former independent companies, with a view to ascertaining the design features most worthy of consideration in a new range of British standard locomotives. At that time, the country was deep in the throes of post-war austerity, and on more than one occasion Riddles expressed his conviction that the new organization should purchase that form of motive power which yielded the highest tractive effort per pound sterling of capital cost – in other words, steam. It was Riddles' view that steam should carry on until such time as capital would be available for main-line electrification. His views coincided precisely with the policy that had been adopted by the Southern Railway in pre-nationalization days, and it was through Mr Bulleid's energy and enthusiasm that the Southern had embarked upon a considerable programme of steam-locomotive construction after the Second World War. The object of that programme had been to handle the traffic over non-electrified routes with steam power, of the most advanced design which could then be provided, at a very much lower capital cost than that of diesel locomotives.

Riddles virtually threw the great bulk of modern motive power of British Railways into a vast forum for competitive examination, as it were. The test routes for the interchange trials were to extend from London to Plymouth, from London to Leeds, and to Carlisle; from Perth to Inverness; over both competitive routes from London through the Midlands to Manchester; and for freight-train workings from Bristol to Eastleigh. Bulleid 'Pacifics' were the only engines chosen to represent the Southern, and in any case they were the only engines, apart from the mixed-traffic 'Q1' o–6–os, that Bulleid himself considered were at all modern. Both 'Merchant Navy' and 'West Country' classes were pitted against the flower of the Northern lines and, of course, against the Great Western. It was a magnificent opportunity for the Southern enginemen to show that their queerly-shaped air-smoothed engines were capable of very hard work on the road; and there is no doubt that the drivers and firemen selected went out on their unaccustomed task with tremendous zest, and an avowed intention of 'licking the pants off everybody'. All the Southern men concerned came from the Nine Elms shed, and all received the most enthusiastic briefing from their shed superintendent, that delightful character and lifelong enthusiast, the late J. Pelham-Maitland.

Quite apart from working over roads that were entirely strange to them, the Southern men had to learn some unaccustomed tasks in the working of their engines. The lengths of the non-stop runs were, in certain cases, greater than the water capacity of the tenders, and so the engines had to be equipped with tenders from the regions over which they were working. An unfamiliar tender can be a handicap to a fireman, just as much as a driver can be put out in having an unfamiliar engine. Furthermore, one of the test trains worked on the Western Region involved detaching a slip coach. This would not have been so bad if it had been a case of a straight slip at full speed; but the train concerned was the 8.30 AM from Plymouth to Paddington which slipped at Reading. In detaching the slip coach it is, of course, essential to have the brakes fully released so that the vacuum cylinders on the slip portion are fully exhausted and the slip guard has, to use a colloquialism, 'plenty of vacuum' with which to control the running of the coach after it has been detached from the main train. Approaching Reading from the 'Berks and Hants' line, the train is slowed down to observe speed restrictions at Southcote Junction and Oxford Road Junction, and the driver of an express approaching Reading from this direction has, therefore, to complete all his brake applications well before the station so that he can fully release the brakes and charge the vacuum system on the slipped portion while the train is rolling freely. All these unfamiliar tasks the Southern men very quickly mastered and then proceeded to do some really splendid work on the foreign lines.

Strange though it may seem, the farther away they got from their own lines the harder they seemed to go. Some of the least interesting work in the trials was done by the

'Merchant Navy' class engines that worked between Paddington and Plymouth, while some of the most exciting was done by the 'West Country' 'Pacific' that went to Inverness. It was typical of the spirit of enterprise shown by the Nine Elms crew that went to Scotland that they worked their way over the entire route. The driver and fireman who, in the first weeks of the exchange, took the 'Merchant Navy' from Euston to Carlisle during the competitive trials over the London Midland main line were also chosen for the Highland tests. They worked there and back as pilots to ordinary trains. When he got back, it was the proud boast of Fireman Hooker, now a top-link driver, that he was the only man who had ever shovelled his way over the entire distance from London to Inverness. It is almost certain that this unique distinction will remain his for all time!

When the test results came to be examined, the 'Merchant Navy' class engines surprised everyone by their relatively moderate coal consumption. Almost from the day of their inception on the Southern Railway they were regarded as heavy coal burners; but the results of the tests showed that their overall consumption in pounds of coal per drawbar horsepower hour was not greatly in excess of the other class '8' engines engaged in the heavy express passenger trials. The actual figures are shown below.

1948 INTERCHANGE TRIALS
Coal Consumption Records of Express Passenger Engines

Comparative figures of		all coal all work
Region	Engine Class	Coal per DHP hr in lb
Western	'King'	3·57
Eastern	'A4' 'Pacific'	3·06
LM	'Duchess'	3·12
LM	'Royal Scot'	3·38
Southern	'Merchant Navy'	3·60

But it was the 'West Countrys' that fairly stole the show. Wherever these small Bulleid 'Pacifics' went, their drivers and firemen set about things with a vigour that made nonsense of the existing timetables. Of course, this exuberant behaviour rather confused the issue and undoubtedly contributed to the high coal-consumption figures they returned; but everyone who had anything to do with them was tremendously impressed by the capacity of these engines for very hard and fast work, and some of their performances on the Western Region lines between Bristol and Exeter, for example; on the Great Central; and above all on the Highland, are still talked about today. It is remarkable that some of the highest figures of drawbar horsepower recorded behind any locomotive in any part of the trials should have been registered, not by the class '8' express passenger engines but by the Bulleid 'West Country' 'Pacifics'. The following tables, Nos 44 and 45, give a few examples of their outstanding performance. At the same time, their coal consumption was definitely high, even in relation to the very high outputs of power that were recorded with them.

On pages 184-191 logs, set out in Tables 46 to 53, of some of the more outstanding runs with these engines in many parts of the country are tabulated, while Tables 44 and 45 give the corresponding technical particulars of the runs concerned. These latter details have been extracted from the official report of the interchange trials published by the British Railways Board. The logs are compiled from the notes taken during the tests by myself and a number of friends, and include some published by Mr Cecil J. Allen in his book *The Locomotive Exchanges*, published by Ian Allan Ltd.

These logs and the accompanying technical data provide a comprehensive picture of the work of the Bulleid 'Pacifics', both 'Merchant Navy' and 'West Country' classes, because it covers their work not only on their own lines, but over all the test routes operated by both express passenger and mixed-traffic locomotives. Because of the complete similarity in performance characteristics of the 'Merchant Navy' and 'West Country' class engines, the record is perhaps the most

TABLE 44
BULLEID 'PACIFIC' TEST PERFORMANCES

Engine No Class Route	35017 'MN' Leeds–Kings X	35017 'MN' Carlisle–Euston	35019 'MN' Plymouth–Paddington	34006 'WC' Plymouth–Bristol	34005 'WC' St Pancras–Manchester	34006 'WC' Marylebone–Manchester	34004 'WC' Perth–Inverness	
Average speed mph	47·9	43·8	47·6	47·3	45·1	41·3	34·45	40·71
Coal per mile lb	44·14	50·22	47·83	62·22	46·04	52·47	66·12	63·48
Coal per DHP hr lb	3·63	3·86	3·71	4·9	3·74	4·07	4·80	4·70
Water gals per mile	36·7	41·4	42·5	41·9	40·7	40·5	46·8	42·3
Lb water per lb coal	8·32	8·24	8·88	6·74	8·83	7·71	7·08	6·66
Average drawbar horsepower (under power)	708	795	779	814	753	803	734	825
Date of trip	28/5/48	14/5/48	28/4/48	21/7/48	22/6/48	8/6/48	13/7/48	14/7/48

TABLE 45
BULLEID 'PACIFIC' POWER-OUTPUT RECORDS

Engine	Location	Region	Gradient 1 in	Speed mph	Recorded DHP	Equivalent DHP
'MN'	Wellington bank	WR	174	48·0	1,178	1,423
'MN'	Hele	WR	523	54·0	1,210	1,410
'MN'	Great Ponton	ER	200	45·5	1,411	1,659
'MN'	Climbing Shap	LMR	130	49·8	1,697	1,929
'MN'	Shap Incline	LMR	75	41·5	1,530	1,835
'WC'	Stoke Canon	WR	L	54·5	1,532	1,631
'WC'	Cullompton	WR	155	63·0	1,469	1,565
'WC'	Annesley	ER	132	46·0	1,574	1,962
'WC'	Whetstone	ER	176	67·8	1,667	2,010
'WC'	Millers Dale	LMR	124 (av)	39·4	1,040	1,370
'WC'	Edendon	ScR	70	36·3	1,100	1,506
'WC'	Drumuachdar	ScR	80	46·2	1,555	1,912
'WC'	Drumuachdar	ScR	80	47·0	1,515	1,950

TABLE 46
WESTERN REGION: TAUNTON–PADDINGTON

Load: to Reading: 492 tons tare, 525 tons full
Load: to Paddington: 455 tons tare, 485 tons full
Engine: 'MN' class 4–6–2 No 35019, *French Line*

Distance miles		Sch. min	Actual min sec		Speeds mph
0·0	TAUNTON	0	0	00	—
2·5	*Creech Junction*	4	4	53	51
8·0	Athelney	—	10	54	64½
11·9	*Curry Rivel Junction*	—	14	41	66
17·2	Somerton	—	20	01	54/65
20·5	Charlton Mackrell	—	23	15	60
25·4	Alford	—	27	52	70½
27·5	CASTLE CARY	31	29	41	64½
31·0	Bruton	—	33	18	51
34·5	*Brewham*	—	38	00	35
36·3	Witham	—	40	04	61
40·2	*Blatchbridge Junction*	46	43	47	71½
42·4	*Clink Road Junction*	48½	45	37	64½
45·7	*Fairwood Junction*	52½	49	02	66/*42
47·1	WESTBURY	55	51	30	
1·0	*Heywood Road Junction*	—	3	15	—
4·2	Edington	—	7	53	51
8·7	Lavington	—	12	40	60
14·5	Patney	19½	19	23	49
20·3	Pewsey	—	25	16	65
25·5	SAVERNAKE	33	30	26	55½
29·2	Bedwyn	37	34	16	54
34·1	Hungerford	—	39	25	64
			sigs		*24
37·1	Kintbury	—	43	05	
42·5	NEWBURY	50½	50	02	65
48·8	Midgham	—	60	41	70½
57·7	*Southcote Junction*	—	63	58	*53
59·6	READING (slip)	{pass	pass		*40
		{71	66	30	*36
			p.w.r.		
64·6	Twyford	77	72	52	—
71·4	MAIDENHEAD	84	80	30	66
77·1	SLOUGH	90	85	33	71½/66
82·4	West Drayton	—	90	10	68
86·5	SOUTHALL	100	93	49	69
89·9	Ealing Broadway	—	96	45	71½
92·3	*Old Oak Common W. Junction*	—	99	10	—
95·6	PADDINGTON	113	105	10	—

* Speed restrictions.

TABLE 47

LM REGION: PENRITH–PRESTON

Load: 503 tons tare, 525 tons full
Engine: 'MN' class 4–6–2 No 35017, *Belgian Marine*

Distance miles		Sch. min	Actual min sec		Speeds mph
0·0	PENRITH	0	0	00	—
3·2	*Eden Valley Junction*	—	6	14	46
4·2	Clifton	—	7	34	42
5·2	*Milepost 46*	—	9	01	41
6·2	*Milepost 45*	—	10	29	41
7·2	*Milepost 44*	—	11	57	41
8·2	*Milepost 43*	—	13	25	41
9·2	*Milepost 42*	—	14	52	42
10·2	*Milepost 41*	—	16	16	43½
11·2	*Milepost 40*	—	17	37	46
11·5	Shap	—	17	56	—
12·2	*Milepost 39*	—	18	50	51
13·2	*Milepost 38*	—	20	08	46½
13·5	*Shap Summit*	27	20	31	—
19·0	Tebay	33	25	53	71½/*61
23·3	Low Gill	—	29	43	70½/61
25·0	Grayrigg	—	31	28	64½/60
28·6	*Hay Fell*	—	34	44	71½/*64
32·1	OXENHOLME	45	37	48	70/75
37·6	Milnthorpe	—	42	32	71½
40·4	Burton	—	45	00	61/69
44·9	CARNFORTH	57	49	10	*65
48·1	Hest Bank	—	52	05	66/57½
51·2	LANCASTER	63	55	17	—
			p.w.r.		*22
52·3	*Lancaster No 1*	—	56	43	—
56·9	Bay Horse	—	62	43	56½
62·7	Garstang	75	68	30	64½
67·4	Barton	—	73	00	65/61
			p.w.r.		*22
70·9	*Oxheys*	83	77	02	—
72·2	PRESTON	†86	†80	03	*28

* Speed restrictions.   † Passing time.

TABLE 48
EASTERN REGION: GRANTHAM–KING'S CROSS
Load: 500 tons tare, 535 tons full
Engine: 'MN' class 4–6–2 No 35017, *Belgian Marine*

Distance miles		Sch. min	Actual min sec	Speeds mph
0·0	GRANTHAM	0	0 00	—
3·5	Great Ponton	—	7 07	44
4·2	*High Dyke*	—	8 03	47½
5·4	*Stoke*	—	9 37	46
8·4	Corby Glen	—	12 37	70½
13·3	Little Bytham	—	16 53	70½
16·9	Essendine	—	19 57	eased
20·7	Tallington	—	23 24	eased
23·6	*Helpston*	—	26 50	eased
26·0	*Werrington Junction*	—	29 22	57½
29·1	PETERBOROUGH NORTH	36	34 13	*21
30·5	*Fletton Junction*	—	36 52	41
32·9	Yaxley	—	39 53	56½
36·1	Holme	—	43 00	66
38·1	*Connington South*	—	44 55	61
42·0	Abbots Ripton	—	49 07	51
43·5	*Milepost* 62	—	51 00	47½
46·6	HUNTINGDON	55	54 01	71½
49·5	Offord	—	56 36	67
53·8	St Neots	—	60 46	54
58·0	Tempsford	—	64 55	68
61·4	Sandy	—	68 07	60
64·4	Biggleswade	—	71 12	53
68·5	Arlesey	—	75 43	61
72·2	*Cadwell*	—	79 29	57½
73·6	HITCHIN	83	81 02	53
76·9	Stevenage	—	85 08	47
—			—	57½
80·5	Knebworth	91	89 06	54
85·2	Welwyn Garden City	—	93 48	70½
87·8	HATFIELD	99	96 18	*50
92·8	Potters Bar	105	102 05	53½
96·3	New Barnet	—	105 32	66
100·5	Wood Green	—	109 23	*60
103·0	FINSBURY PARK	—	112 47	*5
—			sigs	
105·5	KING'S CROSS	122	120 20	—
105·5	Net times (minutes)	122	120 20	—

Net times: 117 minutes.   * Speed restrictions.

TABLE 49

WESTERN REGION: EXETER–BRISTOL

Load: 449 tons tare, 475 tons full
Engine: 'West Country' 4–6–2 No 34006, *Bude*

Distance miles		Sch. min	Actual min sec		Speeds mph
0·0	EXETER	0	0	00	—
1·3	*Cowley Bridge Junction*	—	3	29	50
3·4	Stoke Canon	—	6	10	55
7·2	Silverton	—	10	05	60
8·4	Hele	—	11	17	66
12·6	Cullompton	—	15	00	68/60
14·9	Tiverton Junction	—	17	09	66½
16·7	Sampford Peverell	—	18	45	64½
19·2	Burlescombe	—	21	21	53
19·9	*Whiteball*	—	22	19	—
			p.w.r.		*30
23·7	Wellington	—	27	07	76
28·8	Norton Fitzwarren	—	31	27	—
30·8	TAUNTON	38	34	53	—
0·0		0	0	00	—
2·4	*Creech Junction*	4	4	20	55
5·8	Durston	—	7	32	70½
11·6	BRIDGWATER	—	12	23	72
14·1	Dunball	—	14	28	73
17·9	HIGHBRIDGE	20	17	37	72
20·6	Brent Knoll	—	20	00	66½
25·1	*Uphill Junction*	28	24	06	64
28·0	*Worle Junction*	31	26	42	70
32·8	YATTON	—	30	46	74
36·7	Nailsea	—	33	56	75
38·9	Flax Bourton	—	35	49	70
41·6	Long Ashton	—	37	59	75
43·8	Bedminster	—	sig stop		—
44·8	BRISTOL (Temple Meads)	53	47	59	—

* Speed restriction.

TABLE 50
EASTERN REGION: MARYLEBONE–LEICESTER

Load: 360 tons tare, 380 tons full
Engine: 'West Country' 4–6–2 No 34006, *Bude*

Distance miles		Sch. min	Actual min sec	Speeds mph
0·0	MARYLEBONE	0	0 00	—
3·0	Kilburn		6 44	37/36
5·1	*Neasden South Junction*	11	9 13	66
			p.w.r.	*18
6·4	Wembley Park		11 02	—
			p.w.r.	*5
9·2	HARROW	17	17 38	—
			p.w.r.	eased
2·2	Pinner	—	4 42	50
			sig stop	
4·5	Northwood		11 05	—
			p.w.r.	*30
8·0	RICKMANSWORTH	14	16 57	*27
10·2	Chorley Wood	—	21 09	33
12·4	Chalfont	22	24 36	41
14·4	Amersham	—	27 25	45
19·6	Great Missenden	30	32 24	71½/60
24·1	Wendover		36 33	74
			p.w.r.	*35
28·7	AYLESBURY	40	42 45	—
6·2	Quainton Road	—	7 57	69/76½
8·9	*Grendon Underwood Junction*	11	10 18	*67
10·9	Calvert	—	12 04	65/71½
16·6	Finmere	—	17 18	59/75
21·4	Brackley	—	21 42	68
24·6	Helmdon	—	24 46	64/69
28·2	Culworth	—	28 01	65
29·4	*Culworth Junction*	32	29 07	69
31·2	WOODFORD	35	31 24	—
2·4	Charwelton	—	4 49	53½
6·1	*Staverton Road*	—	8 17	—
9·4	Braunston		11 06	76½
			p.w.r.	*30
14·1	RUGBY	17	18 15	—
3·6	*Shawell*	—	5 03	60/61
6·8	Lutterworth	—	8 04	71½/61
10·7	Ashby Magna	—	11 22	75
15·2	Whetstone	—	15 13	eased
18·9	*Leicester Goods Junction, S.*	—	18 30	*62
19·9	LEICESTER	23	20 07	—

* Speed restrictions.

TABLE 51

LM REGION: LEICESTER–MANCHESTER

Load: 310 tons tare, 325 tons full
Engine: 'West Country' 4–6–2 No 34005, *Barnstaple*

Distance miles		Sch. min	Actual min sec		Speeds mph
0·0	LEICESTER	0	0	00	—
4·7	Syston	—	6	13	62½
9·8	Barrow-on-Soar	—	11	01	70
12·5	LOUGHBOROUGH	16	13	58	—
2·8	Hathern	4½	4	37	56
4·8	Kegworth	—	6	29	72
7·7	*Trent Junction*	—	9	12	*50
8·8	Sawley Junction	11	10	29	48
10·8	Draycott	—	12	39	61
14·8	*Spondon Junction*	—	16	47	*48
16·9	DERBY	23	20	32	—
3·2	*Little Eaton Junction*	—	6	10	39
7·8	Belper	—	11	20	63½
10·4	AMBERGATE	15	14	48	*22
13·4	*High Peak Junction*	—	19	21	49
16·1	Matlock Bath	—	22	34	46
17·2	MATLOCK	24	24	30	—
2·2	Darley Dale	—	4	13	54
			p.w.r.		
4·5	Rowsley	7	7	35	*17/32½
6·4	*Haddon*	—	11	40	30/37½
7·8	Bakewell	—	14	04	36½
8·8	Hassop	—	15	38	39½
10·8	*Headstone Tunnel South End*	—	18	29	42½
11·6	Monsal Dale	—	19	24	53
13·0	*Milepost 158*	—	21	12	42
14·3	MILLERS DALE	23	23	09	—
1·3	*Millers Dale Junction*	—	3	37	29½
2·9	*Tunstead*	—	6	43	32
4·6	Peak Forest	10	9	47	32½
			—		64½
8·3	Chapel-le-Frith	—	13	59	*55
			p.w.r.		*18
10·2	CHINLEY	20	18	07	—
2·7	*New Mills South Junction*	4	4	04	66½/*53
11·8	CHEADLE HEATH	13	13	01	72
16·2	*Chorlton Junction*	18	17	02	*33
18·2	*Throstle Nest E. Junction*	22	20	18	*24
19·7	MANCHESTER CENTRAL	25	24	45	—

* Speed restrictions.

TABLE 52
SCOTTISH REGION: PERTH–AVIEMORE
Load: 361 tons tare, 380 tons full
Engine: 'West Country' 4–6–2 No 34004, *Yeovil*

Distance miles		Sch. min	Actual min sec	Speeds mph
0·0	PERTH	0	0 00	—
1·6	*Almond Valley Junction*	4	3 48	—
4·1	Luncarty	—	6 48	48
7·1	Stanley Junction	12	10 28	42½
8·5	*Milepost 8½*	—	12 49	34½
10·2	Murthly	18	15 13	*33
12·7	*Kingswood*	23	19 56	28
			sig stop	
15·5	DUNKELD	28	27 57	
20·2	Dalguise	35	35 12	*33
			p.w.r.	*20
23·6	BALLINLUIG	41	42 14	—
4·7	PITLOCHRY	8	9 48	—
1·4	*Milepost 29¾*	—	4 55	25½
3·7	Killiecrankie	7	8 31	*25
6·9	BLAIR ATHOLL	13	13 56	—
1·8	*Milepost 37*	—	3 29	46
4·4	Struan	9	7 20	—
3·9	*Dalanvaoch*	—	7 09	42½/34½/39
11·3	Dalnaspidal	31	19 23	—
2·1	*Druimuachdar*			
—	(*Milepost 53*)	—	4 58	28
			p.w.r.	*20
7·6	Dalwhinnie	11	13 57	—
4·2	*Inchlea*	7	6 39	49/*36
7·5	*Etteridge*	11	12 16	*33
10·2	Newtonmore	15	16 17	—
2·8	Kingussie	5	5 41	—
6·0	Kincraig	9	9 23	—
5·8	AVIEMORE	10	10 56	—

Banked in rear from Blair Atholl to Dalnaspidal by ex-'Caledonian'
4–4–0 No 14501.
* Speed restrictions.

comprehensive of any relating to the interchange trials of
1948. It is true that locomotives of LMS and LNER design
worked over all the same test routes; but in their cases the
design of the express passenger and the mixed-traffic loco-

TABLE 53
SCOTTISH REGION: AVIEMORE–PERTH
Load: 356 tons tare, 375 tons full
Engine: 'West Country' 4–6–2 No 34004, *Yeovil*

Distance miles		Sch. min	Actual min sec		Average mph
0·0	AVIEMORE	0	0	00	—
5·8	Kincraig	8	9	10	42/65
11·8	Kingussie	16	16	01	—
2·8	Newtonmore	5	5	09	—
2·7	*Etteridge*	6	5	43	—
6·0	*Inchlea*	11	10	20	50/52
10·2	Dalwhinnie	18	15	55	—
0·5	*Milepost 58*	—	2	20	—
5·5	*Druimuachdar (Milepost 53)*	—	10	28	47½/44
7·5	Dalnaspidal	15	12	43	*41
10·5	*Edendon*	—	16	23	eased
15·0	*Dalanroch*	—	21	04	—
18·7	Struan	29	24	56	—
23·3	BLAIR ATHOLL	35	30	19	—
3·2	Killiecrankie	5	5	03	45
6·9	PITLOCHRY	10	10	01	—
4·8	Ballinluig	7	5	59	64/*41
				p.w.r.	*26
8·0	Dalguise	12	11	39	39
12·8	DUNKELD	18	17	23	54/*50
15·5	*Kingswood*	23	21	05	39
18·0	Murthly	26	23	43	*47
19·2	*Milepost 9*	—	25	21	46
21·2	Stanley Junction	30	27	57	*26
24·2	Luncarty	—	31	26	70
26·7	*Almond Valley Junction*	37	33	36	—
28·3	PERTH	41	36	17	—

* Speed restrictions.

motive differed considerably, although coming from the same design school. For example, there was a very considerable difference both in size and features of design between the Gresley 'A4' 'Pacifics' and the Thompson 'B1' 4–6–0 of the LNER. Some of the finest work of all was done by the 'West Country' 'Pacifics' on the Western Region line between Bristol and Exeter, on the Great Central line, and on the Highland; while the 'Merchant Navy' did some very fine work in climbing over Shap.

But although their capacity for high power output was very clearly demonstrated during these trials, the general principles on which the Bulleid 'Pacifics' were based were not accepted by the designers of the nationalized British Railways except in one detail, namely, the pitching of the main frames of the locomotive at such a width apart that they came centrally on the horn blocks. This feature was adopted in the 'Britannia' and 'Clan' class 'Pacifics' of British standard design.

Bulleid found himself out of sympathy with the new régime, and he retired in the autumn of 1949 to become consulting engineer to the Irish National Railways. At that time, the ill-fated 'Leader' class engines were on trial and giving a great deal of trouble; but Bulleid's resignation really marked the end of the individual achievements of steam-locomotive men on the Southern. Nevertheless, many years were to pass before the full story of Southern steam came to an end, and it was a curious twist of irony that the one region on British Railways whose motive-power practice had swung furthest away from steam in past years, and was set on its further elimination, should have been the very last to operate express passenger services of a first-class quality still entirely worked by steam. One feels that here the wise policy of Sir Herbert Walker and his successors was being worked out to its logical conclusion, namely, that steam should carry on until the time came for full electrification.

There were some experiments with diesel traction, and three excellent diesel-electric locomotives were built by the English Electric Company for service on the Southern. But under the motive-power policy of British Railways after nationalization these locomotives were moved elsewhere, and the Bournemouth and the West of England expresses of the Southern continued to be worked entirely by steam. Only in Scotland, on the former Caledonian main line between Glasgow and Aberdeen, has steam haulage of regular express passenger trains continued so long, and then only to a partial extent. The story of steam on the Southern Region, after the resignation of Bulleid, is thus very largely confined to the Bournemouth and West of England trains, although there was much fine work done in Kent on the seaside trains and on the Continental boat expresses until the whole of that area was electrified in 1960.

CHAPTER FIFTEEN

THE FINAL PHASE

There is no doubt that the Bulleid 'Pacifics', for all their great qualities and despite their capacity for producing vast outputs of power, were a perennial headache to the operating departments and to the chief mechanical engineer of the Southern Region. I have already referred to the failures which took place owing to the peculiarity of the valve gear and to the fire hazards that were inherent in the liberal permeation of all parts of the locomotive and the boiler cladding with oil. The engines were also notorious fire-throwers, and during the summer months, when there happened to be any fine dry spells of weather, British Railways had some considerable bills to pay in compensation for crop fires along the lineside. In fact, the fitting of a Giesl oblong ejector to engine No 34064 of the 'West Country' class was tried as much with the idea of reducing fire-throwing as of obtaining improved draughting. It was felt that the cost of fitting Giesl ejectors would be more than conpensated for by the avoidance of heavy bills for damage from fire.

But it was, above all, the unorthodox front-end that was the major cause of trouble, particularly as the standards of maintenance at running sheds tended to deteriorate as British Railways' policy for the elimination of steam was rapidly developed. On the Southern, as briefly mentioned in the previous chapter, no major plan for dieselization was prepared. Steam was to carry on until such time as the main lines could be electrified; and although the dieselization programme was gathering momentum in other parts of the country, sufficient steam locomotives of first-line power capacity were not being displaced to enable a major transfer of power to be made to the Southern. The Bulleid 'Pacifics' had to carry on; and investigations were made to discover what savings were likely if a certain number of the engines were rebuilt with orthodox front-ends. The object was to save maintenance costs; to reduce coal consumption; to increase availability by eliminating the cause of most of the major failures in traffic, and to reduce fire-throwing.

The results of the investigations were favourable, and authority was given for the conversion of a number of locomotives of both 'Merchant Navy' and 'West Country' classes to a straightforward front-end layout using three sets of Walschaerts valve gear arranged in the orthodox manner. At the same time the air-smoothing was removed from the boilers and normal cladding arrangements substituted. Of course, the highly-distinctive appearance of both classes of engine completely disappeared, though the rebuilt engines, in a much more orthodox way, were nevertheless highly impressive and distinctive machines, with their Boxpok wheels and their distinctive cabs and tenders. In their rebuilt form they did some excellent work, but they never seemed to rise to the same heights of brilliance that the original engines attained, although their general level of perform-ances and standards of reliability were much higher.

Prior to any rebuilding it must be added that a decision had been taken to reduce the boiler pressure from 280 to 250 lb per sq in, and this naturally had a lowering effect on their performance and capabilities. I know from my own experience on the footplate, and from the reports of many friends, that the full 280 lb per sq in of the original engines was very rarely utilized for achieving a high ratio of expan-sion. Much more frequently the engines were driven with long cut-offs and regulator openings that rarely produced steam-chest pressures much above 200 lb per sq in. But the total heat in the steam produced by the boiler was there, and even if it went through the process of wire-drawing in passing through the relatively narrow opening of the regulator, the steam passages and the components of the steam-flow circuit throughout were so well designed, and permitted so free a flow of steam, that the thermodynamic loss due to wire-drawing was minimized.

One of the most interesting runs I had with one of the

rebuilt engines was when a 'Merchant Navy', No 35020,
Bibby Line, was being put through a series of full-dress trials
with the dynamometer-car between Basingstoke and Exeter.
The tests were being carried out by my old friends of the
chief mechanical engineer's department of the Western
Region at Swindon, and I was privileged to ride in the
dynamometer-car on a day when tests were being carried

TABLE 54
SOUTHERN REGION: EXETER–SALISBURY
'ATLANTIC COAST EXPRESS'

Load: 363 tons tare, 385 tons full
Engine: Rebuilt 'Merchant Navy' class 4–6–2 No 35020, *Bibby Line*

Distance miles		Sch. min	Actual min sec		Speeds mph	DBHP
0·0	EXETER	0	0	00	—	—
4·8	Broad Clyst		8	04	66	—
			p.w.s.		18	—
10·5	*Milepost* 161		17	28	40	1,050
12·2	SIDMOUTH JUNCTION	18	20	05	—	
1·8	*Milepost* 157½		—		50	—
4·6	Honiton		7	37	38/41	1,100
5·8	*Milepost* 153½		9	20	40	1,100
11·5	SEATON JUNCTION		14	57	80*	—
14·8	Axminster		17	38	77†	1,100
19·9	Chard Junction		21	59	66	900
25·8	*Milepost* 133½		27	36	58	1,150
27·9	Crewkerne		29	31	82	100
33·1	*Milepost* 126¼		33	32	69	800
36·7	YEOVIL JUNCTION	39	36	25	78	—
41·3	Sherborne		40	02	74	1,000
43·9	*Milepost* 115½		42	20	56	1,350
47·4	TEMPLECOMBE		45	45	78	150
51·9	*Milepost* 107½		49	28	60	1,000
54·2	Gillingham		51	28	74	—
—			p.w.s.		40	—
58·3	Semley		56	57	46	1,350
63·3	Tisbury		61	33	72	400
67·6	Dinton		65	06	82	850
73·3	Wilton		69	42	—	—
75·8	SALISBURY	79	74	13	—	—

* Maximum before Seaton Junction.
† Maximum after Seaton Junction.

TABLE 55
SOUTHERN REGION: SALISBURY–WATERLOO
'ATLANTIC COAST EXPRESS'

Load: 428 tons tare, 465 tons full
Engine: Rebuilt 'Merchant Navy' class 4–6–2 No 35020, *Bibby Line*

Distance miles		Sch. min	Actual min sec	DBHP
0·0	SALISBURY	0	0 00	—
1·1	*Tunnel Junction*	3	3 18	—
5·5	Porton		9 16	1,120
11·0	Grateley		15 39	1,200
17·4	ANDOVER JUNCTION	22	20 37	200
22·7	Hurstbourne		25 40	—
			sigs	
24·6	Whitchurch		28 09	850
31·4	Oakley		36 37	1,100
33·5	*Worting Junction*	36	38 23	1,000
			sig stop	
36·0	BASINGSTOKE		43 27	900
41·6	Hook		49 02	900
50·6	Farnborough		56 00	900
52·8	*Milepost 31*		57 41	900
59·4	WOKING	58	62 44	350
64·7	Weybridge		66 47	700
71·8	Surbiton		72 29	nil
79·9	CLAPHAM JUNCTION	78	80 49	—
83·8	WATERLOO	85	87 52	—
	Net time min		81½	
	Speeds:			
	Min, Porton bank		44½	
	Max, Andover		81	
	Average, Hook–Surbiton		77·3	
	Max, Woking (or near)		80	
	Departure from Salisbury (min)		time	
	Arrival in Waterloo (min)		2¾ late	

out on an ordinary service run of the up 'Atlantic Coast
Express'. Full details are given in the accompanying Tables
54 and 55. The work was efficiently done, but there were no
really high spots in the performance as a strict timekeeping
journey was required.

It was on that journey particularly that I was impressed by the attention given by the Southern Railway operating authorities to regulation of the loading of their principal express passenger trains. The 'Atlantic Coast Express' was then sharply timed through from Exeter to Waterloo, and the normal loading was one of twelve coaches as far as Salisbury and thirteen from there eastwards. All opportunities for a trial at high power output were eliminated by the instructions of the operating authorities, who insisted that the additional weight of the dynamometer-car in the train should be compensated for by carrying one less coach throughout. Fortunately, these tests were carried out in the early summer, before the main holiday traffic to the West of England had commenced to build up, and so there was no resultant overcrowding of the train.

The accompanying logs give details of the times and speeds achieved and also the value of the drawbar horsepower as noted direct from the instruments in the dynamometer-car. For all the harder work, the steam pressures were in the region of 210 to 215 lb per sq in, while the boiler pressure was mostly around 235. The Swindon dynamometer-car then in use, which was the old GWR Churchward car extensively modernized, had a very comprehensive collection of instruments, and from one of the dials, as just mentioned, the drawbar horsepower could be read directly. This figure was, of course, the actual drawbar horsepower; whereas for comparison with data secured on the stationary testing plant the figures required to be corrected for gradient by adding the power needed to lift the weight of the engine and tender against gravity at that speed. As shown in the log, the highest figure recorded between Exeter and Salisbury was 1,350, both on the Sherborne bank and approaching Semley. In the latter case the equivalent drawbar horsepower was 1,750.

From the integrator in the dynamometer-car, which at any moment shows the total amount of work done since the commencement of the test, the average drawbar horsepower for the whole journey can be readily calculated. In making the actual time of $74\frac{1}{4}$ minutes start-to-stop over the $75\cdot8$ miles from Sidmouth Junction to Salisbury, the average drawbar horsepower was 715.

The second log, Table 55, shows the continuation of the run forward from Salisbury to Waterloo. In some ways this was disappointing, in that after the train had been stopped by signal at Winklebury, between Worting and Basingstoke, no particular effort was made to regain the lost time. In view of the very fast running often performed by the 'Merchant Navy' class engines east of Basingstoke, this was rather disappointing, because it would have been very interesting to observe from the dynamometer-car the actual power output required for such efforts. As it was, the average speed between Hook and Surbiton was no more than $77\cdot3$ mph with a maximum of 80. The average drawbar horsepower between Salisbury and Waterloo on this run works out at no more than 610. It was quite a good run, with a net gain of $3\frac{1}{2}$ minutes on schedule; but it was not anything to tax the capacity of the locomotive in any way.

One cannot leave the work of the Bulleid 'Pacifics', rebuilt or otherwise, without some reference to their regular use on the Somerset and Dorset line between Bournemouth and Bath. Only the 'West Country' class were permitted to run over this exceedingly difficult route; but by the use of locomotives of such high nominal tractive power, and of exceptionally high steam-raising capacity, it was hoped to reduce the large amount of double-heading necessary between Evercreech Junction and Bath during the summer holiday season. When traffic over this route was at its zenith, in the years between 1950 and 1960, the number of 'specials' on summer Saturdays, and their large formation, created a problem for the locomotive authorities. Almost every train in both directions needed double-heading, except the 'all stations' locals and I have known engines such as the standard LMS 0–6–0 shunting tanks pressed into service as pilots.

With the Stanier class '5' 4–6–0s of the LMS which were the largest engines normally used on passenger trains prior to the introduction of the Bulleid 'Pacifics', the maximum load that could be taken unassisted between Evercreech Junction and Bath was eight coaches. Most of the holiday trains were loaded to just above those figures, many being ten-coach trains; and it could be well appreciated that if locomotives were available that could take ten-coach trains without assistance, the general motive-power position on summer Saturdays would be greatly relieved. Unfortunately, the liability of the Bulleid 'Pacifics' to slip completely counteracted any advantages that might have been derived from their high nominal tractive effort, and great steaming capacity, and it was found that they could not be relied on with more than eight coaches. While their availability added to the stock of engines on hand, it did not relieve the double-heading position, and I have no record of runs of any particular merit made with them over the severely-graded section of line between Bath and Evercreech Junction.

And so, with a mention of the working of these engines over the Somerset and Dorset Joint Line, we come to the end of the story of Southern steam, and perhaps I may conclude with a few lasting impressions. During the Maunsell era, all locomotives were maintained in first-class mechanical condition, and externally the majority were immaculate. Cleaning of engines was still a serious business of the Southern even into the first years of the Second World War, and I was greatly touched by the story of certain survivors from Dunkirk who, when landed at Dover, were still sufficiently conscious of what was going on around them to notice the clean and shining Southern Railway locomotives that hauled the evacuation trains.

In the post-war years, Bulleid's enterprise and the novelty of his new locomotives undoubtedly sent a strong surge of pride through the locomotive department of the Southern Railway. This was felt not only on the main lines but in secondary services as well, and my impressions of footplate journeys in the years 1947 and 1948 on secondary trains are uniformly of the excellent mechanical condition of the engines concerned. Even after the modernization plan for

British Railways was announced, and further large-scale schemes of electrification on the Southern were authorized, there was still a high standard of maintenance in the rapidly-declining steam stock. It is only in the last few years that serious deterioration has set in.

All in all, the Southern Railway, from its formation in January 1923 to the virtual end of its status as a steam railway at the end of 1965, has a notable record of achievement. And, in their respective spheres, the names of Maunsell and Bulleid will always be greatly honoured among locomotive men.

APPENDIX 1

SOUTHERN STEAM LOCOMOTIVES

Type	Class	Cylinders			Coupled Wheel Dia. ft in	Heating surfaces in sq ft				Grate Area sq ft	Boiler Pressure lb/sq in	Nom: TE at 85% Boiler Pressure lb	Total weight in Working Order Tons	
		No	Dia. in	Stroke in		Tubes	Firebox	Super-heater	Combined Total				Engine	Tender
ex. LSWR														
4-6-0	'H15'	2	21	28	6 0	1716	162	337	2215	30	180	26,200	79·95	57·65
4-6-0	'T14'	4	15	26	6 7	1280	158	295	1733	31·5	175	22,030	76·5	60·4
4-6-0	'D15'	2	20	26	6 7	1139·5	144·5	252	1536	27	180	20,100	61·65	39·6
0-4-4	'M7'	2	18½	26	5 7	1067	124	—	1191	20·36	175	19,750	60·15	—
4-6-2T	'H16'	2	21	28	5 7	1267	139	252	1658	27	180	23,200	96·4	—
4-8-0T	'G16'	2	22	28	5 1	1267	139	252	1658	27	180	34,000	95·1	—
ex. LBSC														
4-6-0*	'N15/X'	2	21	28	6 9	1664·5	152·1	383	2199·6	26·68	180	23,300	73·1	57·65
4-4-2	'H2'	2	21	26	6 7½	1895	134·5	460	2491·5	30·95	170	24,520	68·25	39·25
2-6-0	'K'	2	21	26	5 6	1155	139	279	1573	24·8	170	26,600	63·75	41·5
4-6-2T	'J1'	2	21	26	6 7½	1462	124	357	1943	25·16	170	20,800	89	—
4-4-2T	'I3'	2	21	26	6 7½	1126	120	254	1500	23·75	180	22,100	76	—
ex. SECR														
4-4-0	'D1'	2	19	26	6 8	1149·9	127·1	228	1505	24	180	17,950	52·2	39
2-6-0	'N'	3	19	28	5 6	1390·6	135	285	1810·6	25	200	26,040	61·2	42·4
2-6-0	'N1'	3	16	28	5 6	1390·6	135	285	1810·6	25	200	27,700	64·25	42·4

* Rebuilt from 4-6-4 tank engines.

SOUTHERN STEAM LOCOMOTIVES

Type	Class	Cylinders			Coupled Wheel Dia. ft in	Heating surfaces in sq ft				Grate Area sq ft	Boiler Pressure lb/sq in	Nom: TE at 85% Boiler Pressure lb	Total weight in Working Order Tons	
		No	Dia. in	Stroke in		Tubes	Firebox	Super-heater	Combined Total				Engine	Tender
Southern														
4-6-0	'Nelson'	4	16¼	26	6 7	1795	194	376	2365	33	220	33,500	83·5	57·95
4-6-0	'Arthur'	2	20½	28	6 7	1716	162	337	2215	30	200	25,320	80·95	57·65
2-6-0	'U1'	3	16	28	6 0	1390·6	135	285	1810·6	25	200	25,387	65·3	42·4
2-6-0	'U'	3	19	28	6 0	1390·6	135	285	1810·6	25	200	23,866	62·3	42·4
4-4-0	'Schools'	3	16½	26	6 8	1604	162	283	2049	28·3	220	25,130	67·1	42·4
4-4-0	'L1'	2	19½	26	6 8	1252·5	134·5	235	1642	22·5	180	18,910	57·8	40·5
4-4-0	'S15'	2	20½	28	5 7	1716	162	337	2215	28	200	29,860	79·25	56·4
0-6-0	'Q'	2	19	26	5 1	1125	122	185	1432	21·9	200	26,157	49·5	40·5
0-6-0	'Q1'	2	19	26	5 1	1302	170	218	1690	27	230	30,000	51·25	38·0
2-6-4T	'W'	3	16½	28	5 6	1390·6	135	285	1810·6	25	200	29,452	90·7	—
0-8-0T	'Z'	3	16	28	4 8	1173	106	—	1279	18·64	180	29,376	71·6	—
4-6-2	'Merchant Navy'	3	18	24	6 2	2175·9	275	822	3272·9	48·5	280	37,500	94·75	49·35
4-6-2	'West Country'	3	16¾	24	6 2	1869	253	545	2667	38·25	280	31,000	86	42·6

APPENDIX 2

Engine names (other than Maunsell types given in the text)

LBSC 'Atlantics':

Non-superheated:

2037	Selsey Bill
2038	Portland Bill
2039	Hartland Point
2040	St Catherine's Point
2041	Peveril Point
2421	South Foreland

Superheated:

2422	North Foreland
2423	The Needles
2424	Beachey Head
2425	Trevose Head
2426	St Albans Head

'Remembrance' class (LBSC 4–6–4T rebuilt as 4–6–0):

2327	Trevithick
2328	Hackworth
2329	Stephenson
2330	Cudworth

2331	Beattie
2332	Stroudley
2333	Remembrance

'Merchant Navy' class 4–6–2:

35001	Channel Packet
35002	Union Castle
35003	Royal Mail
35004	Cunard White Star
35005	Canadian Pacific
35006	Peninsular & Oriental SN Co
35007	Aberdeen Commonwealth
35008	Orient Line
35009	Shaw Savill
35010	Blue Star
35011	General Steam Navigation
35012	United States Lines

35013	Blue Funnel
35014	Nederland Line
35015	Rotterdam Lloyd
35016	Elders Fyffes
35017	Belgian Marine
35018	British India Line
35019	French Line CGT
35020	Bibby Line
35021	New Zealand Line
35022	Holland–America Line
35023	Holland–Afrika Line
35024	East Asiatic Company

35025	Brocklebank Line	35028	Clan Line
35026	Lamport & Holt Line	35029	Ellerman Lines
35027	Port Line	35030	Elder Dempster Lines

'West Country' and 'Battle of Britain' class:

34001	Exeter	34032	Camelford
34002	Salisbury	34033	Chard
34003	Plymouth	34034	Honiton
34004	Yeovil	34035	Shaftesbury
34005	Barnstaple	34036	Westward Ho
34006	Bude	34037	Clovelly
34007	Wadebridge	34038	Lynton
34008	Padstow	34039	Boscastle
34009	Lyme Regis	34040	Crewkerne
34010	Sidmouth	34041	Wilton
34011	Tavistock	34042	Dorchester
34012	Launceston	34043	Combe Martin
34013	Okehampton	34044	Woolacombe
34014	Budleigh Salterton	34045	Ottery St Mary
34015	Exmouth	34046	Braunton
34016	Bodmin	34047	Callington
34017	Ilfracombe	34048	Crediton
34018	Axminster	34049	Anti-Aircraft Command
34019	Bideford		
34020	Seaton	34050	Royal Observer Corps
34021	Dartmoor		
34022	Exmoor	34051	Winston Churchill
34023	Blackmore Vale	34052	Lord Dowding
34024	Tamar Valley	34053	Sir Keith Park
34025	Whimple	34054	Lord Beaverbrook
34026	Yes Tor	34055	Fighter Pilot
34027	Taw Valley	34056	Croydon
34028	Eddystone	34057	Biggin Hill
34029	Lundy	34058	Sir Frederick Pile
34030	Watersmeet	34059	Sir Archibald Sinclair
34031	Torrington		

34060	*25 Squadron*	34087	*145 Squadron*
34061	*73 Squadron*	34088	*213 Squadron*
34062	*17 Squadron*	34089	*602 Squadron*
34063	*229 Squadron*	34090	*Sir Eustace*
34064	*Fighter Command*		*Missenden,*
34065	*Hurricane*		*Southern Railway*
34066	*Spitfire*	34091	*Weymouth*
34067	*Tangmere*	34092	*City of Wells*
34068	*Kenley*	34093	*Saunton*
34069	*Hawkinge*	34094	*Mortehoe*
34070	*Manston*	34095	*Brentor*
34071	*601 Squadron*	34096	*Trevone*
34072	*257 Squadron*	34097	*Holsworthy*
34073	*249 Squadron*	34098	*Templecombe*
34074	*46 Squadron*	34099	*Lynmouth*
34075	*264 Squadron*	34100	*Appledore*
34076	*41 Squadron*	34101	*Hartland*
34077	*603 Squadron*	34102	*Lapford*
34078	*222 Squadron*	34103	*Calstock*
34079	*141 Squadron*	34104	*Bere Alston*
34080	*74 Squadron*	34105	*Swanage*
34081	*92 Squadron*	34106	*Lydford*
34082	*615 Squadron*	34107	*Blandford Forum*
34083	*605 Squadron*	34108	*Wincanton*
34084	*253 Squadron*	34109	*Sir Trafford*
34085	*501 Squadron*		*Leigh-Mallory*
34086	*219 Squadron*	34110	*66 Squadron*

INDEX

David & Charles Series and Railway Enthusiasts' Series

Regional History and David & Charles Series

These and other PAN Books are obtainable from all booksellers and newsagents. If you have any difficulty please send purchase price plus 5p postage to P.O. Box 11, Falmouth, Cornwall.

While every effort is made to keep prices low, it is sometimes necessary to increase prices at short notice. PAN Books reserve the right to show new retail prices on covers which may differ from those previously advertised in the text or elsewhere.